Hobbes

'In short, this is a fine and authoritative study by an acknowledged master of his subject. No serious student of Hobbes or early modern philosophy should ignore this book.'
Paul Kelly, London School of Economics, UK

'This is an excellent book, well suited to the aims of the *Routledge Philosophers* series. It is clearly and accessibly written, comprehensive, up to date on current scholarship, well organized, and often humorous. I think undergraduates will find the book both readable and enjoyable. Teachers will find it very helpful.'
S. A. Lloyd, University of Southern California, USA

Routledge Philosophers

Edited by Brian Leiter
University of Texas, Austin

Routledge Philosophers is a major series of introductions to the great Western philosophers. Each book places a major philosopher or thinker in historical context, explains and assesses their key arguments, and considers their legacy. Additional features include a chronology of major dates and events, chapter summaries, annotated suggestions for further reading and a glossary of technical terms.

An ideal starting point for those new to philosophy, they are also essential reading for those interested in the subject at any level.

Leibniz	Nicholas Jolley
Locke	E. J. Lowe
Hegel	Frederick Beiser
Rousseau	Nicholas Dent
Schopenhauer	Julian Young
Freud	Jonathan Lear

Forthcoming:

Spinoza	Michael Della Rocca
Hume	Don Garrett
Kant	Paul Guyer
Fichte and Schelling	Sebastian Gardner
Husserl	David Woodruff Smith
Rawls	Samuel Freeman

A. P. Martinich

Hobbes

Routledge
Taylor & Francis Group

NEW YORK AND LONDON

First published 2005
by Routledge
270 Madison Ave, New York, NY 10016

Simultaneously published in the UK
by Routledge
2 Park Square, Milton Park, Abingdon, Oxon OX14 4RN

Routledge is an imprint of the Taylor & Francis Group

© 2005 A. P. Martinich

Typeset in Joanna MT and DIN by
RefineCatch Ltd, Bungay, Suffolk
Printed and bound in Great Britain by
TJ International Ltd, Padstow, Cornwall

Library of Congress Cataloging in Publication Data
Martinich, Aloysius.
 Hobbes / by A.P. Martinich.
  p. cm—(Routledge philosophers)
 Includes bibliographical references.
  1. Hobbes, Thomas, 1588–1679. I. Title. II. Series.
B1247.M38 2005
192—dc22   2004024124

British Library Cataloguing in Publication Data
A catalogue record for this book is available from the British Library

ISBN 0-415-28327-2 (hbk)
ISBN 0-415-28328-0 (pbk)

To
Zhou Jianshe, Zhang Yunqiu, Zou Lihzi, and Yincun Dai

Figures

After my book, Hobbes: A Biography (1999) appeared, I intended never to write another one on Hobbes. I thought it completed my mature work on Hobbes, which started with The Two Gods of Leviathan (1992), and continued with A Hobbes Dictionary (1996) and Thomas Hobbes (1997). My biography won the Robert W. Hamilton Book Award for 2000, and I thought I had said everything I wanted to say about Hobbes at book length. I changed my mind when Brian Leiter invited me to contribute to his distinguished series, Routledge Philosophers. I realized I had more to say and could say certain things better. If it hadn't been for Brian, I never would have written this book. My first thanks, then, go to him.

I also want to thank Mark Engleston and Neil Sinhababu for reading various parts of it, and Sharon Lloyd and Leslie Martinich for reading and commenting on all of it.

This book is intended for undergraduate students and non-specialists in the philosophy of Thomas Hobbes, whether they are professional scholars or educated nonscholars. This fact explains why some of my arguments are more explicit than they would be if I had Hobbesian scholars in mind. Except in the last chapter, my primary goal is to explain Hobbes's philosophy, and sometimes to argue with him. For philosophers, such argumentation is a sign of respect.

Acknowledgements

Excerpts from *Leviathan* by Thomas Hobbes, edited by A. P. Martinich, published by Broadview Press, 2002. Reprinted by kind permission of the publisher.

Method of Citations: References to De cive, De corpore, The Elements of Law, Natural and Politic, and Leviathan are by chapter and section or chapter and paragraph. When references are given by page number, the edition used can be found in the bibliography.

AW	Anti-White
B	Behemoth
BB	An Answer to Bishop Bramhall's Book, 'The Catching of the Leviathan'
DC	De cive
DCo	De corpore
DH	De homine
DPS	Dialogue Between a Philosopher and a Student of the Common Laws
DP	Dialogus physicus
EL	The Elements of Law, Natural and Politic
EW	English Works
L	Leviathan
LL	Latin Leviathan
LN	Of Liberty and Necessity
L R&C	Leviathan, "Review and Conclusion"
OL	Opera Latina
QLNC	Questions Concerning Liberty, Necessity, and Chance

Chronology

One

Life

THE RETURN OF THE NATIVE

In the winter of 1652, at the age of sixty-three, Thomas Hobbes was crossing the English Channel from France to England. He probably thought that he was returning in triumph after a self-imposed exile of ten years. *Leviathan*, his *magnum opus*, had been published in England the preceding spring. A year before that *De corpore politico* (1650) was published. A third version of his political philosophy, *Philosophical Rudiments Concerning Government and Society*, had the date 1651. It was a translation from the Latin of *De cive*, which had first appeared in a small private edition in Paris in 1642, and then was published in 1647 in an expanded version.

In all three versions of his political philosophy, Hobbes argued for what is known as "absolute sovereignty." This could have two different meanings, and Hobbes seemed to support both. The weaker form was that the sovereign did not share political power with any other entity. In this sense, it contrasted with mixed governments. The stronger form was that the sovereign or government had all the political power and had authority over every aspect of life. In this sense, the doctrine of absolute sovereignty was easily contrasted with the theory of limited sovereignty held by contemporary democratic theorists. According to limited sovereignty, either the government does not have authority over every aspect of life or the political power is split between two or more agencies, and usually both. Even in constitutional monarchies, the power of the monarch and the scope of its authority are limited. In the

United States the constitutional doctrine of privacy is a result of the government's limited power, and the separation of powers into legislative, executive and judicial is a result of the limited scope of any one part of government.

Hobbes certainly acted as if his return to England were triumphant. He settled in London, where the political and intellectual action was, rather than north in Derbyshire, where he had been employed for decades, earlier in his life. In London, he attended social gatherings with many distinguished people.

However, Hobbes also had to deal with some situations that he didn't like. King Charles I, whom Hobbes had favored before and during the English Civil War, had been executed in 1649. And although Hobbes had presented the exiled King Charles II a magnificent copy of *Leviathan*, handwritten on vellum, he made his peace with Charles's enemies, the newly created Commonwealth of England. Many royalists were deeply disturbed by Parliament's requirement that all adult male citizens sign the Engagement, a loyalty oath, because they thought that they were obligated to the monarchy by prior oaths. For these men, the fact that the current monarch was in exile did not diminish their obligation. Hobbes, however, had a way around these scruples. For him, a "government" that is unable to protect its citizens is not a government. More precisely, an entity that is unable to protect people is not the sovereign of those people. Since the only entity that was able to protect people in England was the Commonwealth, the Commonwealth was the only sovereign. Hobbes had written about this in other places but he addressed it directly in "A Review and Conclusion" of *Leviathan*. Although he thought the execution of Charles I had been unfortunate and preferred monarchy over any other form of government, his political philosophy was not tied to monarchy. Aristocracy and democracy were equally legitimate forms of government according to him.

His prominence as a political theorist in the early 1650s was somewhat strange since a large part, possibly the largest part, of his life during the 1630s and 1640s had been dedicated to mathematics and natural science. He had been a member of the scientific circle of William Cavendish, the future duke of Newcastle, in the 1630s. In Paris in 1635, he met Marin Mersenne, who was the leader of a scientific circle in Paris, not to mention other French philosophers and scientists. In the spring of 1636 he met with Galileo in Florence. In 1637, he received a copy of Descartes's *Discourse on the Method* from Sir Kenelm Digby, a well-connected patron of science.

When Hobbes was preparing to leave England in late 1640, he corresponded with Mersenne, possibly to arrange to meet with him in Paris. In 1644, he contributed an article on ballistics to Mersenne's *Ballistica*. During the 1640s, Hobbes's major project was the first part of his envisioned tripartite work in philosophy, *Elementa philosophiae* [*The Elements of Philosophy*]. The first part was named *De corpore*, but Hobbes did not complete it during the 1640s or even during the first half of the 1650s. In a letter of June 1646, Hobbes wrote:

> Part of the reason why I am taking so long over the first section of my Elements is partly laziness, but mostly the fact that I find it difficult to explain my meanings to my own satisfaction. For I am seeking to achieve in metaphysics and physics what I hope I have achieved in moral philosophy, so that there may be no room left for any critic to write against me.
>
> (Hobbes 1994: 133)

Most scholars think that it was not laziness but the difficulty Hobbes was having with the proofs that delayed its completion.

Shortly after it appeared in 1655 (in translation, 1656), *De corpore* began to cause Hobbes trouble that continued for the next twenty years. The source of the trouble was his materialism, which most critics thought was inconsistent with Christianity. Also controversial was his alleged proof of squaring a circle, that is, the proof that there was a way to construct a square equal in area to a given circle using only a straightedge and compass. In a series of books and pamphlets during the 1650s, 1660s, and into the 1670s, Hobbes and John Wallis, Savilian Professor of Geometry at Oxford, debated various versions of Hobbes's proofs, all of which were recognized by competent, emotionally uninvolved mathematicians as defective. Although Wallis was more than competent as a mathematician and recognized the faults in Hobbes's proofs, he was emotionally involved; and this caused him to insert into the debate issues of religion and politics that were irrelevant to the mathematical issues. Hobbes won the irrelevant battles, I think, but lost the mathematical war. By 1670, Hobbes's reputation as a mathematician and scientist was irreparably damaged.

EARLY LIFE

When Hobbes was born prematurely on April 15, 1588, just outside of Malmesbury, Wiltshire, no one could have predicted the eventual eminence he would attain. In his autobiography, Hobbes said that he was born a twin with fear. Some scholars doubt that he was born prematurely since the attempted invasion of the Spanish Armada did not occur until July. That is a very comfortable judgment to make from the heights of 300 years. A pregnant woman with little protection against an invasion might well have carried fear along with her child.

Hobbes's father, Thomas, was an ignorant and alcoholic clergyman. When he fled Malmesbury in the direction of London after a brawl with another clergyman he disappeared from history. This happened about the time Hobbes was leaving for Magdalen Hall, Oxford. His education was paid for by his uncle Francis, a successful glover.

Hobbes was precocious. He began school at the age of four and knew Latin, Greek, and arithmetic before setting off for Oxford. He was somewhat younger than the other boys at Magdalen Hall when he arrived, but he did well although he denigrates the Aristotelianism that was being taught and brags about the time he spent catching birds and visiting bookshops to pore over maps. He graduated in

February 1608 and, upon the recommendation of the Principal, he was hired by William Cavendish to tutor his son William, the future earl of Devonshire. In fact, Hobbes was at least as much a companion as a tutor. They went on a Grand Tour of the Continent in 1614, Hobbes's first trip abroad. They visited Paris, Venice, and Rome, among other places, and traveled at least as far south as Naples. Back in England in 1615, Hobbes translated the correspondence of Fulgentio Micanzio to William from Italian into English until 1628. Micanzio was the secretary of Paulo Sarpi, the state theologian for Venice. He reported on battles of the Thirty Years War in the vicinity of Italy and indirectly tried to get William to move James I to support the Venetian cause. One path to James was through Francis Bacon, and Micanzio came to correspond with Bacon too. John Aubrey, Hobbes's first biographer, said that Hobbes was Bacon's secretary for some time and translated some of his essays into Latin. This probably occurred in the middle of the 1620s. Not much more is known about Hobbes's life between 1615 and 1620.

Between 1620 and 1630, Hobbes carried out various tasks for William. He was a shareholder in the Virginia Company, one of the earliest companies intended to colonize America, and attended its meetings between 1622 and 1624. But he also secured loans to help sustain William's spendthrift life. William died in 1628, just two years after becoming the 2nd earl of Devonshire.

Hobbes dedicated his translation of Thucydides' History of the Peloponnesian War (1629) to William. In a rare personal note, Hobbes, late in life, said that his years with William were the happiest of his life and that he continued to dream about them. Hobbes probably considered his translation of Thucydides' work a political action in part. Presenting a translation of the history by Thucydides, whose disdain for democracy was well known, could easily be seen as support for Charles I, who was having trouble with the supporters of Parliament during the second half of the 1620s. In his address "To the Readers," Hobbes said "the principal and proper work of history . . . [is] to instruct and enable men, by the knowledge of actions past, to bear themselves prudently in the present and providently towards the future" (Hobbes 1629: xxi). The 1620s are usually considered the humanistic phase in Hobbes's life. This judgment is justified by the time he spent translating the letters of Micanzio, his translation from the Greek of Thucydides' history, and his introduction to the translation, "On the Life and History of Thucydides," which is "constructed according to the precepts laid down in classical handbooks of rhetoric for the presentation of persuasive arguments" (Skinner 2002: 5).

William's widow Christian probably had blamed Hobbes to some extent for the dire condition of the estate when William died. Hobbes was let go but then promptly hired by a neighbor Gervaise Clifton to take his son on a Grand Tour during 1629–30, which was Hobbes's second trip to the Continent. During this trip Hobbes probably came upon the proof of the Pythagorean theorem in Euclid's geometry. At first he doubted the proof: "By G_, this is impossible," he reportedly said. But he checked the proofs of its premises, and then the premises of those proofs until eventually he became convinced. "This," says John Aubrey, "made him in love with geometry" (Aubrey 1680: 332). Some scholars, notably Leo Strauss, downplay the importance of science and geometry for Hobbes. They claim he remained a humanist in a scientist's clothing. I think that natural science, and especially geometry, inspired Hobbes to present his philosophy rigorously. If he failed to do that, it was not for lack of trying. This is not to deny that Hobbes made a conscious effort in Leviathan to make his argument persuasive to less rigorous thinkers. What Hobbes especially liked about geometry was the method of laying down definitions and then drawing logical consequences from them. Properly executed, the result is a tower of interlocking propositions, built upon a foundation of incontestable definitions, incontestable because they are true by stipulation. The influence of geometrical method on Hobbes's general philosophy is clearest in De corpore (1655).

Once back in England, Hobbes was rehired by Christian

Cavendish. In 1634, he took William, the 3rd earl of Devonshire, on a Grand Tour of France and Italy. Hobbes, now well into his forties, lacked the inclination to keep a tight rein on the rambunctious teenager and occupied himself intellectually on the principles of physics. Hobbes spent a great deal of his time with Marin Mersenne's circle. He was particularly intrigued by the mechanics of sensation. The key to understanding sensation was that if all physical things were at rest or if everything moved at the same speed and in the same direction, then there would be no way to distinguish one thing from another and hence no sensation (AW 323). Consequently, he held that the cause of all things was the difference between motions. In *De corpore*, he filled out this idea: "Sense, therefore, in the sentient can be nothing else but motion in some of the internal parts of the sentient, and the parts so moved are parts of the organs of sense" (DCo 25.2). His idea that our qualitative experiences of color, smell, taste, and sound are not accurate representations of the way things are in themselves was first asserted by Galileo, whom he probably met in Florence during the spring of 1636. Hobbes returned to England in the fall of that year.

SCIENCE AND INTERNATIONAL RELATIONS

Not much of Hobbes's life during the 1630s is known. An interesting tidbit is that he probably played a part in Ben Jonson's entertainment for Charles I in 1633 (Martinich 1998a: 370–1). More importantly, Hobbes associated with the circle of mathematicians and scientists assembled by William Cavendish, later the duke of Newcastle, a cousin of the "Devonshire" Cavendishes. His association with Newcastle began several years earlier when Hobbes and Newcastle were part of a party exploring the neighboring Peak District and out of which came a Latin poem written by Hobbes, *De mirabilibus pecci*. The purpose of the trip was to discover "the causes of things" (OL 5: 327; see also Martinich 1998b).

In 1634, Hobbes visited Malmesbury for, so far as we know, the last time. During this visit, he met a bright eight-year-old pupil of his old teacher, Robert Latimer. This was a propitious meeting because the pupil was John Aubrey, who came to know Hobbes well and provided us with a vivid, fact-filled, though not always accurate, account of much of Hobbes's life. There's no reason to doubt that Hobbes had a daughter, whom he referred to as the joy of his youth. He never married because a person in his position, an intellectual and dependent on wealthy patrons, could not conveniently have a family.

In addition to his association with the members of Mersenne's circle and Newcastle's circle, Hobbes probably visited Great Tew, near Oxford, after he returned to England in October 1636. The circle of Great Tew included several men destined for distinction, such as Lucius Cary, William Chillingworth, Henry Hammond, Edward Hyde, and Edmund Waller. The major subjects of discussion there included the early history of Christianity and the relation between reason and revelation.

Science and religion, two of the three major topics of interest to the people that Hobbes interacted with during the 1630s, were also two of the three major topics of Hobbes's writings from 1640 onward. The third was political theory. In *The Elements of Law, Natural and Politic*, which circulated in manuscript in the spring of 1640, Hobbes first presented his political theory and the part of science about human beings. Part I of the manuscript, "*Humane Nature*," gave a naturalistic and materialist account of sensation, imagination, rationality, and the emotions. It also contained the twin foundations of his political theory, the idea that human beings in the state of nature are equal and at war with each other and the idea that they can escape this condition if they lay down their rights to all things, as dictated by the laws of nature. Part II, "*De corpore politico*," talked about the kinds of governments – monarchy, aristocracy, and democracy – the supremacy of the sovereign, the causes of rebellion (a touchy subject in 1640) and the duties of the sovereign power. As the Long Parliament was about to begin in late 1640, Hobbes thought that England was no longer safe for him, in large part because of the views he expressed in *The Elements of Law*, and that a civil war was likely. Thus he left England, "the first of those who fled," as he later said of himself. Fighting broke out in 1642 and ended with the execution of Charles I in 1649.

In Paris, where Hobbes spent the decade of the 1640s, he was a valued member of Mersenne's circle. He contributed one of the first sets of objections to Descartes's *Meditations*, published in 1641. Hobbes is a wholly unsympathetic commentator. I want to consider Hobbes's relationship with Descartes, emotional and philosophical, at some length, because of the light it throws on his personality.

Hobbes criticizes Descartes's apparent inference from "I am thinking" to "I am thought" (Descartes 1641: 122). It is no better, says Hobbes, than the argument that "I am walking" entails "I am a walk." Hobbes thinks that the inference from "I am thinking," to "I exist," is not the result of some intuition or direct awareness of oneself, but from the fact that humans are unable "to conceive of an act without its subject." Descartes, in other words, was not distinguishing between a subject and its properties. Hobbes then says, "It seems to follow from this that a thinking thing is something corporeal;" and Descartes sharply retorts that Hobbes's assertion is "quite without any reason, and in violation of all usage and all logic" (Descartes 1641: 124). Fifteen years later, Hobbes diagnoses Descartes's mistake as the result of inferring from the fact that "it is possible to consider thinking without considering body" that something can be a thinking thing without a body (DCo 3.5).

Hobbes thinks that another part of Descartes's problem arises from a false theory of what reasoning is. Hobbes suggests what he would later assert, namely, that "reasoning is simply the joining together and linking of names." Further, since names are arbitrary labels that humans attach to things, the inferences of reasoning say nothing about things but about the labels applied to them (Hobbes 1641: 125).

> Now, what shall we say if it turns out that reasoning is simply the joining together and linking of names or labels by means of the word 'is'? It would follow that the inferences in our reasoning tell us nothing at all about the nature of things, but merely tell us about the labels applied to them; that is, all we can infer is whether or not we are combining the names of things in accordance with the arbitrary conventions which we have laid down in respect of their meaning.
>
> (Hobbes 1641: 125–6)

Descartes replies that there is no need to focus exclusively on the origin of names. When people reason, they don't link names but the "things that are signified by the names" (Descartes 1641: 126). Frenchmen and Germans reason about the same things even though they use different words.

One of the most important differences between Hobbes and Descartes concerned human knowledge of God. Hobbes, who thought that all ideas ultimately derive from sensation, thought that humans had virtually no knowledge of God, because he is never the object of a sensation. Hobbes seems to think that humans have two kinds of images or ideas. One kind we might call "resembling" ideas. They are ideas that purport to represent or picture some material object; and these are the ideas that are properly so called. It makes sense to ask whether one's image of a tree or even a chimera is "the likeness" of some object. It does not make sense to ask of the other kind of ideas, "nonresembling" ones. When a person thinks of an angel, his or her thought may be accompanied by the image of a flame or of "a beautiful child with wings," but the person does not think that these images are supposed to present a likeness of an angel. The same goes for whatever image might accompany a thought about God: "[We] have no idea or image corresponding to the sacred name of God." In short, "there is no idea of God in us" (Hobbes 1641: 127). The thought underlying Hobbes's claim about angels and God does not apply only to them. He also thinks that people have no idea of substance; it is something the existence of which people arrive at by reasoning (Hobbes 1641: 130). A more important example of an object for which there is no corresponding image involves a blind man. He has no image resembling fire, even though he "recognizes that there is something which makes him hot." The blind man's belief that fire exists is the result of an inference from his experience and not a direct result of any experience.

Hobbes uses this example of a blind man's belief that fire exists as an analogy for knowledge that God exists. Hobbes's proof for the existence of God is a casual rendition of a cosmological argument: humans recognize that

> there must be some cause of his images or ideas, and that this cause must have a prior cause, and so on; he is finally led to the supposition of some eternal cause which never began to exist and hence cannot have a cause prior to itself, and he concludes that something eternal must necessarily exist.
>
> (Hobbes 1641: 127)

And this thing he calls God.

Hobbes would use a similar argument a decade later in *Leviathan*:

> Curiosity or love of the knowledge of causes draws a man from consideration of the effect to seek the cause, and again, the cause of that cause, till of necessity he must come to this thought at last that there is some cause whereof there is no former cause but is eternal; which is it men call God . . . though they cannot have any idea of him in their mind answerable to his nature.
>
> (L 11.25)

Hobbes compares human knowledge of God to that of a person "born blind, hearing men talk of warming themselves by the fire and being brought to warm himself" (L 11.25). The blind person thereby comes to believe that fire exists without having a resembling idea of it. Hobbes's proofs for the existence of God are short and rather perfunctory. Since there were precious few atheists in the middle of seventeenth-century England, deploying an elaborate argument for the existence of God would have been pointless.

Hobbes and Descartes also disagree about the meaning of "infinite." Hobbes's notion is negative. He says, "to be infinite . . . is [to be] impossible for me to conceive or imagine any supposed limits or extremities without being able to imagine further limits beyond them." What follows from this is "that what arises in connection with the term 'infinite' is not the idea of the infinity of God but the idea of my own boundaries or limits" (Hobbes 1641: 131). In contrast, Descartes has a positive idea of infinity. Although God does not resemble any exterior material object, we can have an idea of the ways in which he is infinite by extrapolating from certain ideas. From the idea of human understanding, which is finite, we project to an idea of God's understanding, which is infinite.

Descartes is nonplussed at Hobbes's inability to do what philosophers for almost two millennia have been able to do: to conceive of an immaterial object. From this point on, Hobbes's objections become more dismissive, and Descartes's replies testier. In one, three sentences long, Descartes says, "I see nothing here that needs answering." In his next objection Hobbes says, "If we do not have an idea of God (and it is not proved that we do)" and Descartes counters, "If we do have an idea of God – and it is manifest that we do" (Hobbes 1641: 127, Descartes 1641: 127).

In retrospect, the failure of Hobbes and Descartes to engage each other is not surprising. Hobbes was an inveterate monist and materialist. Descartes an inveterate dualist and rationalist. Each thought too well of himself and seems to have believed that philosophical distinction was a zero-sum game.

By 1640, Hobbes had worked out his views about optics, views that would eventually be published as part of De homine in 1658. He spent a large part of the 1640s working on De corpore, which was to be the first part of Elementa philosophiae. He was up to Chapter 13 by May 1645 and probably Chapter 25 by August 1648. But he was unable to put it into a form that suited him. In a letter of June

1646, he wrote that he was trying to put his scientific views in a form that would leave "no room for any critic to write against me" and then later that it was not "the effort of finding out the truth but that of explaining and demonstrating it which is holding up publication" (quoted from Skinner 2002: 11). Such explanations and demonstrations were slow in coming. There is some reason to believe that he was dithering. He wrote a very large manuscript, usually called "Anti-White," which, in addition to being a critique of Thomas White's book, De mundo (1642), vetted many of the views that would eventually go into De corpore. Also, in 1647, he accepted the job of tutoring the future king of England, Charles II, in mathematics. However, he still had time for his own studies (Skinner 2002: 17) and may have been composing the parts of Leviathan about Robert Bellarmine (Schuhmann 2004). Some expected De corpore to be finished around the beginning of 1647. But after that date, his friends saw that it would not be completed for at least another year. In June 1649, Hobbes himself was optimistically predicting that he would finish it before the end of the summer. As things went, its publication was still many years in the future. De corpore was published in 1655, with an English translation the following year. As we shall see, Hobbes's writer's block, if that term is appropriate, did not extend to political philosophy or to other aspects of his philosophy. In 1645, he wrote a draft of his optics in English, half of which was published in Latin in 1658 as part of De homine.

In 1645, Newcastle, who, like Hobbes, was in voluntary exile in Paris, invited Hobbes and John Bramhall to debate the issue of free will. Bramhall held the conventional scholastic view that human beings have free will, which is a necessary condition for attributions of praise and blame and distribution of rewards and punishments. Hobbes thought that the concept of free will was internally contradictory. What is free is the human being who acts; the will is the last desire the person has before acting. People can be compelled but not desires. Praise and rewards are given to people who act in a certain desired way, while blame and punishment are given to people who break a law.

Newcastle enjoyed the debate, which, so far as we know, was not acrimonious, and asked Hobbes and Bramhall to write down their views for his perusal. In 1654, Hobbes's essay, *Of Liberty and Necessity*, was published without his knowledge by an acquaintance, who contributed an offensive preface. Thinking that the publication was Hobbes's idea, Bramhall published his own contribution, *A Defence of True Liberty* (1655). Not one to run from a fight – not from an intellectual fight anyway – Hobbes replied with *The Questions Concerning Liberty, Necessity, and Chance* in 1656, which included his text, Bramhall's text, and then his replies to Bramhall's text. Then Bramhall replied the next year with *Castigations of Mr Hobbes* (with *The Catching of Leviathan* as an appendix). Hobbes wrote *An Answer to . . . 'The Catching of Leviathan'* around 1668, but it was not published until 1682. (Due to various confusions, many sources give different dates from those in this paragraph.)

In the summer of 1647, Hobbes was seriously ill, serious enough for him to confess his sins to one Anglican cleric and to receive the Eucharist from another. About this time, his hands began to shake in a way now associated with Parkinson's disease. The shaking progressed until some years later when he could hardly write his name legibly.

Notwithstanding his concentration on science, the book Hobbes published in the 1640s was about political philosophy, *De cive*, which to a large extent was a reworking of much of *The Elements of Law, Natural and Politic*. Because the titles of several of Hobbes's major works and their relations to each other are complicated, I give here a list of his major philosophical works between 1640 and 1670.

The Elements of Law, Natural and Politic, circulated in manuscript in 1640; published in two parts as:

Humane Nature (1650)
De corpore politico (1650)

Elementa philosophiae [The Elements of Philosophy], published in three sections:

Section 1: *De corpore* (1655), translated and published in English as *The Elements of Philosophy, the First Section, Concerning Body* in 1656.
Section 2: *De homine* (1658) [not translated into English until the twentieth century].
Section 3: *De cive* (1642, 1647), translated and published in 1651 as *Philosophical Rudiments Concerning Government and Society*.

Leviathan (1651), translated into Latin in a slightly different form and published in 1668.

POLITICAL VIEWS

Given the success of *De cive*, it is not completely clear why Hobbes wrote *Leviathan*. Part of the reason was personal. Some of the Roman Catholic clergy in France were unhappy with Hobbes. Also Mersenne died in September 1648, and Gassendi left Paris. These factors gave him a motive to return to England. And there were others. Charles I had been executed in 1649 by a remnant of the Long Parliament. Although the execution had been illegal – Parliament had no authority to sit in judgment of the king – a new government was formed, called "the Commonwealth," which abolished the monarchy and the House of Lords.

What Hobbes allegedly said to Edward Hyde, the earl of Clarendon, should not be discounted: "The truth is, I have a mind to go home." This does not mean that he misrepresented his positions or even changed some simply to be more acceptable to the antimonarchical leaders of England. But it does mean that he could emphasize some aspects of his views that he might otherwise have underplayed. And Hobbes does speak directly to the circumstances of England after the Civil War in the famous "Review and Conclusions," the last chapter of *Leviathan*. The Commonwealth, conscious of its tenuous legitimacy, required all adult males to sign the Engagement, an oath expressing their support for the new government.

Royalists believed themselves to be committed by a prior oath to the monarchy, and there was a titular monarch, Charles II, in exile.

> And because I find by divers English books lately printed, that the Civill warres have not yet sufficiently taught men, in what point of time it is, that a Subject becomes obliged to the Conquerour; nor what is Conquest; nor how it comes about, that it obliges men to obey his Laws: Therefore for farther satisfaction of men therein, I say, the point of time, wherein a man becomes subject to a Conqueror, is that point, wherein having liberty to submit to him, he consenteth, either by expresse words, or by other sufficient sign, to be his Subject.
>
> (L R&C 6)

In effect, Hobbes was telling Englishmen who were faithful to the king during the Civil War what they could do in good conscience. A royalist could take the Engagement because a citizen's obligation to a sovereign ceases when the sovereign can no longer protect him. And the exiled Charles II could not protect people in England. The fact that the Commonwealth was generated by an illegal act does not change the fact that it was now the legitimate government of England because many English subjects had joined it and it had the power to protect them.

Moreover, Hobbes spins a self-serving argument into one that makes taking the Engagement to be of greater potential help to the king in exile than resisting the government of the Commonwealth would be:

> Besides, if a man consider that they who submit, assist the Enemy but with part of their estates, whereas they that refuse, assist him with the whole, there is no reason to call their Submission, or Composition an Assistance; but rather a Detriment to the Enemy.
>
> (L R&C 6)

Hobbes may also intend to give an explicit defense for the actions of his former student, the 3rd earl of Devonshire, who had returned to England and made peace with the new government.

Some critics have accused Hobbes of compromising his royalist sympathies merely to smooth his return to England. I think Hobbes merely saw that his theory had a result that had the advantage of being convenient for him and his fellow citizens. Nonetheless, most of *Leviathan* has no direct relevance to the specific issue of the legitimacy of the English government in 1651, and much of it was offensive to its leaders.

Although I have focused on the relation of *Leviathan* to the political circumstances of 1651, its importance as a work of philosophy is due to other features. *Leviathan* sketches a materialist metaphysics and an egoistic psychology, from which a justification for the civil state is generated. *Leviathan* talks about the nature and necessity of government, the obligations that subjects have to it, the relation of Church to State, and a philosophy of the Christian religion. Much of the rest of this book will be devoted to explaining Hobbes's views on these matters.

The 1650s were probably the single best decade of Hobbes's life. He was safe and famous in England. He associated with some of the best people in London, like John Selden, William Harvey, and Charles Scarborough, and attended social gatherings where he would teach his philosophy to anyone who was interested. But woe betide the man who contradicted him: "He was impatient of contradiction. . . . if anyone objected against his dictates, he would leave the company in a passion, saying, his business was to teach, not dispute" (Pope 1697: 118). This attitude was also expressed in *De cive*: "[F]or I do not indulge in controversy, I simply reason" (Tuck 1988a: 19–20).

Even the beginning of the Restoration looked promising to Hobbes. Although he had been out of favor at the court of Charles II when he decided to return to England, Charles II liked him, and this is reflected in a story told by John Aubrey:

> It happened about two or three days after His Majesty's happy
> return that, as he was passing in his coach through the Strand,
> Mr. Hobbes was standing at Little Salisbury House gate . . . The
> king espied him, put off his hat very kindly to him and asked him
> how he did. About a week after, he had oral conference with his
> majesty at Mr. S. Cowper's house, where, as he sat for his picture,
> he was diverted by Mr. Hobbes's pleasant discourse. Here His
> Majesty's favours were redintegrated to him and order was given
> that he should have free access to his majesty, who was always
> much delighted in his wit and smart repartees.
>
> (Aubrey 1680: 340)

Nonetheless, the 1660s were not a particularly happy time for Hobbes because he was embroiled in disputations with some of the most important churchmen, scientists and mathematicians of that era. The disputes began in the 1650s and continued until the early 1670s. His run-in with John Bramhall in the mid 1650s over the issue of free will has already been discussed.

RELIGIOUS, MATHEMATICAL, AND SCIENTIFIC DISPUTES

The most unpleasant of the other disputes was with the mathematician John Wallis, the Savilian Professor of Geometry at Oxford. The central topic was supposedly the validity of Hobbes's proof that he had squared the circle. But the topics ranged far from this one, and included what each had done for each side during the Civil War and what their religious beliefs were. Wallis started the debate in 1655 by publishing a refutation of Hobbes's proof that a square could be constructed equal in area to a given circle. Hobbes responded in "Six Lessons to the Professors of the Mathematics," which he appended to the 1656 English translation of *De corpore*. Wallis then published *Due Correction for Mr Hobbes, or School Discipline, For Not Saying His Lessons Right* (1656). Hobbes again took the offensive by publishing a work with the subtitle, *Marks of the Absurd Geometry, Rural Language, Scottish Church Politics and Barbarisms of John Wallis Professor of*

Geometry and Doctor of Divinity (1657). Mathematics, religion, politics, and even grammar were now all mixed up in the debate. The exchange of polemical writings continued through the 1660s and into the 1670s, and included, notably, his *Mr. Hobbes Considered in his Loyalty, Religion, Reputation, and Manners* (1662).

One of the more important mathematical aspects of the debate was Hobbes's championing the primacy of geometry over arithmetic. In ancient Greece, geometry and arithmetic were simply two branches of mathematics. Some modern mathematicians, notably Descartes and Wallis, claimed that arithmetic was logically prior to geometry. Wallis said that a 2-foot line added to a 2-foot line made a 4-foot line (a geometrical example) because two plus two equals four and not vice versa. Isaac Barrow argued the other side. If arithmetic were logically prior to geometry, then two apples added to a 2-foot line would be four of something. But that is absurd. Barrow, then, maintains that two plus two equals four when the matter underlying each number is two. He says, "a Mathematical Number has no existence proper to itself, and really distinct from the magnitude it denominates, but is only a kind of note or sign of magnitude considered after a certain manner" (quoted from Jesseph 1996: 323 n. 21). Hobbes's view is, I think, even more sophisticated. One reason that Hobbes thought geometry was superior to algebra was that numbers are generated from the division of bodies into parts.

Hobbes also debated Robert Boyle, a prominent member of the Royal Society, over whether Boyle's experiments provided good evidence that vacuums existed. Boyle is credited with having created a vacuum with a device that basically consisted of a glass globe, a connector with a stopcock, and a cylinder into which fit a wooden piston. To put the experiment a bit simply, air was removed from the globe by pulling the piston back and then opening the stopcock. This allowed air from the globe to enter the cylinder. The cock was then closed and the piston pushed back up the cylinder. (The air in the cylinder escaped through a brass valve that could be opened and closed just beneath the stopcock.) The process was then repeated – the piston being pulled back, etc. – until all the air had been emptied. In *Dialogus physicus* (1661) Hobbes criticized the experiment by pointing out that air possibly leaked into the globe at the point where the stopcock joined the apparatus and that possibly when the gross air in the globe was extracted, it was replaced by subtle air that could enter the globe by passing through the glass itself. These were interesting possibilities, even though they were not true in fact. Boyle defended himself in *An Examen of Mr. T. Hobbes his Dialogue Physicus de Natura Aeris* (1662).

Part of what irritated Hobbes about Wallis and Boyle in the 1660s was that they were members of the Royal Society, and he was not. Various explanations have been offered for Hobbes's exclusion. One is that he was hard to get along with. This comes out in a letter written by Robert Hooke to Boyle:

> I found him [Hobbes] to lard and settle every observation with a round oath, to undervalue all other men's opinions and judgments, to defend to the utmost what he asserted though never so absurd, to have a high conceit of his own abilities and performances though never so absurd and pitiful.
>
> (Hooke 1663)

Although he could be genial, he could also be cantankerous when someone challenged his view. But this was not the only and possibly not the chief objection to him.

Another reason that may have played a part in the minds of some members of the Royal Society was Hobbes's belief that science did not need extensive experimentation. This belief ran directly contrary to the professed purpose of the society to promote knowledge by experimentation. Robert Hooke wrote that the society "will not own any hypothesis, system or doctrine of the principles of natural philosophy . . . whose recourse must be had to original cause . . . nor dogmatically define nor fix axioms of scientifical things" (quoted in Martinich 1999: 297). In contrast, Hobbes thought axioms were the first principles of science, from which other propositions were deduced. He thought that nature provided experiments enough in tides, eclipses, falling objects, and similar things, and that the Royal Society would make more progress if they threw away their machines and paraphernalia and continued deducing theorems from his *De corpore* (DP 379). But, this alone would not have kept Hobbes out of the society since some other members of the society had doubts about "the value of the Society's experimental work" (Skinner 2002: 335).

The worst mark against Hobbes was a combination of two things. The first, ironically, is that his views were too much like those of other prominent members. Joseph Glanvill, like Hobbes, held that nature operates "by corporeal instruments" and that "the divine nature is infinite and our conceptions very shallow and finite" and that people "do not know the essence and ways of acting of the most ordinary and obvious things of nature and therefore must not expect thoroughly to understand the deeper things of God." Seth Ward agreed with Hobbes's view that the sovereign ought to have power over all matters of religion; and Thomas Sprat agreed that religion should be "like the temporal laws of all countries" (Malcolm 1988: 64). The second factor that probably caused Hobbes to be excluded was the fact that he was religiously controversial and believed by some to be an atheist. Many people were suspicious of science and thought that it led to atheism. Consequently members of the society would have been reluctant to appear to endorse someone with Hobbes's reputation.

In 1657, "one Robinson, a Scotchman, . . . a very busy person, and swelling in his own opinion, . . . presented Hobbes's *Leviathan* to the Committee [set up by Parliament], as a most poisonous piece of atheism" (Burton 1828: 348–9). But nothing came of it. In October 1666 a bill was introduced into the House of Commons to determine whether Hobbes should be prosecuted for atheism or heresy. Again nothing came of it. No charges were brought against Hobbes, who prudently burned some of his papers in order to protect himself. Some think that this is evidence that he was an atheist or heretic. I hope they never sit on juries. An innocent person might very well possess items that might tend to incriminate him of some crime if they were introduced into evidence during a trial. This tendency does not mean that the evidence is a reliable guide to the truth, and a prudent person would take appropriate steps to prevent them from being used against him. During the McCarthy era in the early 1950s, many innocent Americans were harassed by a congressional committee and governmental agencies simply because of their friendships and memberships, and not because they had committed any crimes.

Directly or indirectly, the antagonism of some churchmen and other bigots motivated Hobbes to write about the nature of heresy and the appropriate sanctions against it in the late 1660s. One of these writings was *Historical Narration Concerning Heresy, and the Punishment Thereof*, which was finished by July 1668 (Hobbes 1994: 699). Also published in the same year was a Latin translation of *Leviathan*, which appeared with a number of his other Latin works in *Opera philosophica*. The Latin *Leviathan* was somewhat shorter than the English version and less acerbic. It included an appendix, devoted in part to heresy, which contained most of what was in *Historical Narration*.

In the late 1660s or possibly 1670, Hobbes wrote *Behemoth*, his history of the English Civil War. He used the events around the Civil War to press his political views that religion should be controlled by the sovereign and that the power and authority of the sovereign ought to be absolute. When these conditions are not satisfied, civil war is the result. Although he asked Charles II to let it be published, Charles refused. It was published in 1679, the year Hobbes died.

By the mid 1670s, Hobbes was getting tired of it all. In 1675, Hobbes left London for good and spent his last years at Chatsworth and Hardwick Hall. But he was not idle. He translated both the *Odyssey* and *Iliad* of Homer. Those translations have often been criticized for their inaccuracies and leadenness. Notwithstanding these criticisms, I think Hobbes's translations are extremely readable and closer in spirit to Homer's epics than some well-regarded translations (see Martinich 1999: 338–43).

Hobbes died on December 4, 1679 after a long illness and was buried in the church near Hardwick Hall in Derbyshire. His friend James Wheldon said that Hobbes died "rather from want of fuel . . . and mere weakness and decay than by the power of his disease, which was thought to be only an effect of his age and weakness." Although he had taught that death was the greatest evil, in a variant ending of his verse autobiography, he wrote, "And Death, standing close to me, says, 'Do not be afraid'."

FURTHER READING

Aubrey, J. (1680) Brief Lives, Vol. I, Andrew Clark (ed.) (1898) Oxford: Clarendon Press. The most amusing, though not always accurate, biography.

Malcolm, N. (2002) Aspects of Hobbes, Oxford: Clarendon Press. Chapter 1 is a reliable, short biography.

Martinich, A. P. (1999) Hobbes: A Biography, Cambridge: Cambridge University Press. A full-length biography that integrates Hobbes's philosophy with his life and the political context.

Two

Metaphysics and Mind

Hobbes was an uncompromising materialist, mechanist, and determinist. As a materialist, he believed that the only thing that existed was matter. As a mechanist, he believed that all causes operated by one object coming into contact with another object. As a determinist, he believed that every event has a moving cause that determines the effect. Each of these points will be discussed in more detail below, from p. 24 to p. 35.

Concerning the mind, his views flow smoothly from the doctrines just enumerated. He reduced all mental phenomena, including the mind, to bodies moving inside the head and the heart. He was not the least bit disturbed by the apparent discrepancy between the purely quantitative nature of material reality and the qualitative nature of conscious experience. He was convinced that there could be nothing other than bodies in motion and saw no need to try to explain how such things could give rise to consciousness. His views on mind will be discussed further below, from p. 33 to p. 53.

MATERIALISM

For Hobbes, a body is "everything that occupies space, or which can be measured as to length, breadth and depth" (AW 311; see also 320). A body occupies space but is not space. He is not an atomist because theoretically matter can be divided infinitely or without end. Matter comes in very small quantities that are in fact not divided.

Hobbes defines motion as "the continual relinquishing of one place, and acquiring of another" (DCo 8.10; see also 15.1). The matter that makes up the universe has to be in motion, because nothing can move itself, and all changes of motion are caused by other motions. Nothing at rest can initiate motion either in itself or in another. The primary reason depends on his principle of causation and motion: if a body is at rest, then it cannot cause itself to move because only things in motion cause motion. In part, Hobbes held that nothing at rest can initiate motion because he accepted the principle of inertia, formulated by Galileo: a body at rest remains at rest and a body in motion remains in motion unless acted upon by another body (L 2.1; DCo 15.1, 15.7). In *Leviathan*, Hobbes explained the propensity of people to think that motion naturally ran down, as the result of projection. Since people get tired from moving and eventually stop, it might seem that any object in motion would eventually get tired (L 2.1). But this is to anthropomorphize nature.

Hobbes's insistence that everything in motion is moved by something else that is in motion is based upon his insistence that nothing is a self-moved mover, which he proves by *reductio ad absurdum*. The supposition of the *reductio* is this: some body S moves itself at some time t_n in virtue of its having some property P. Now the argument: either S had P at the immediately prior time t_{n-1} or it did not. Let's consider each alternative. If S did have P at t_{n-1}, then S moved itself at that time and not at the later time t_n. Hobbes affirms this consequence because for him a cause acts as soon as it is present. People sometimes hold that striking a match causes the match to burn and also hold that sometimes a striking of a match does not cause the match to burn. Hobbes thinks that this kind of thinking is confused. Only individual events are causes, and every cause is effective: it has an effect (AW 316). So only the striking of the match that results in fire is a cause of fire. It follows from Hobbes's view that if S had P at t_{n-1} and did not cause itself to move at t_{n-1}, then P would not be the thing in virtue of which S causes itself to move; and this contradicts the supposition of the *reductio*.

That leaves the other alternative, namely, that S did not have P at t_{n-1}. In this case, S would have to cause at t_n the cause of P (because P does not exist at t_{n-1}, according to this alternative). But the cause of P is S itself. So S would have to make itself to exist at t_n. But this is just to say that S creates itself, and that is impossible. Here's how Hobbes explains it: "From this [that S causes S] it follows that body has created body, i.e. that it has created itself, which is neither conceivable nor consonant with faith. Hence it remains that, as was to be proved, a body cannot produce its own act" (AW 318).

Since Hobbes's nifty, scholastic-like argument is not easy to understand, a brief restatement may help make it intelligible. The key premise in Hobbes's proof is the disjunctive proposition, "Either S had P beforehand or it did not." The problem Hobbes sees with asserting the first disjunct, that S had P, is simple enough. If S had P earlier, then the action would have occurred earlier (because the action occurs as soon as the cause is present). But that contradicts the supposition. The problem with the second disjunct is that if P is not present at t_n, then S has to cause to exist the thing that makes P present. But, what causes P to exist is S. Thus, S would have to cause itself to exist. This is impossible. Therefore, there are no self-movers.

It might be urged that if there are no self-movers, then God is not a self-mover, and if God is not a self-mover, then something must cause God to exist. And this is heretical. Two responses are appropriate here. The first is that in the argument above, Hobbes is restricting the universe of discourse to finite objects. So nothing is being proved about God. However, one might raise the question specifically about God. Is God a self-mover or not? According to Hobbes's principles, God is not a self-mover, because every cause is a moving cause. In Leviathan, Hobbes proves the existence of God on the principle that for each cause there must be an earlier cause, and hence there is a first cause, which, he announces in traditional fashion, is God. So Hobbes is caught in a contradiction: every cause is in motion and God, the first cause, does not move. The fact that he never resolved this problem nor seemed to be bothered by it, has led many scholars to conclude that he must not have believed in God. For myself, this conclusion is not justified. There were many contradictions in Hobbes's work that did not seem to bother him (Martinich 2004). Also, Hobbes, with the Calvinists, is content to say that God is incomprehensible to the human mind.

Why does Hobbes go through such subtle metaphysical reasoning to prove that there are no self-movers? There are two reasons. One is that Hobbes in fact accepted the scholastic principle, "Everything that is moved is moved by another" (AW 447). So it made sense for him to figure out the consequences of that principle. The other reason is that Hobbes was trying to refute a scholastically trained philosopher, Thomas White, who himself accepted it. So in order to get White to see that he was mistaken, Hobbes used the vocabulary and kind of argument that should have convinced White.

Hobbes may also have had a deeper motive for using the motion principle. He may have wanted to show the scholastic philosophers that they did not know what they were talking about. They had a true principle, "Everything that is moved is moved by another," but they did not know what its consequences were: there are no unmoved movers.

The scholastics would have objected that Hobbes was misinterpreting their maxim. It should be understood as saying that everything that is in motion is moved by another. This leaves open the possibility that there is a kind of cause that moves other things without itself moving. Hobbes would have said that this scholastic claim is unintelligible. Nothing happens without motion. Although no cause moves itself, every cause itself moves. Apparent cases of self-moving causes, such as a sedentary (nonmoving) person getting up from his couch to get a beer, can be explained in terms of small and imperceptible motions inside the person that move him. Modern science provides the sequential details of how chemicals in the stomach, bloodstream, brain, and muscles move Jane Doe to the refrigerator.

Hobbes criticizes White on other matters. White claimed that the existence of the universe is caused by something external to it. Hobbes pointed out that strictly the universe is "the aggregate of all things" (AW 318). From this it follows that nothing can be outside of the universe, for whatever would be "outside" the universe would be a thing and hence part of the aggregate: "[T]here can be no beginning of motion, but from an external and moved body" (DCo 30.2). Later philosophers used the fact that it makes no sense to talk about something external to the universe and the fact that everything that people know about causes pertains only to things and events inside the universe to conclude that it makes no literal sense to talk about a God, external to the universe, as causing it.

One final general point might be made about the broader implications of Hobbes's use of the motion principle. For ancient Greek philosophers and medieval and modern scholastics, rest or stability was superior to change; not moving was superior to moving. They believed that the best kind of being is one that would always have everything that was good for it to have. Since every change is either the gaining or losing of some property, every change would either be the losing or gaining of some perfection; and in either case, the object that moved would not be perfect. Bodies seemed to these philosophers to be inherently imperfect. To be a body was to be material and to be material was to be able to be something other than what it was. In contrast with this view, the modern view, which Hobbes helped to propagate, does not understand the universe in moral terms; there is no good or bad inherent in motion or its absence. But if one is better than the other, motion seems better than rest. Certainly, motion is no less natural than absence of motion.

CONATUS

Just as there are smallest parts of matter, there are also smallest parts of motion: "Moreover, it is clear that every part of a movement is motion and that the principle of anything at all is its primary parts"

(AW 148). Hobbes calls these smallest motions "*conatus*" in his Latin works; and it is usually translated as "endeavors." "Endeavor" suggests that an effort is being put forward. This seems to be language that applies particularly to animals, not to inanimate objects. However, Hobbes applies *conatus* to inanimate objects as much as to animate ones. To a large extent, his purpose for doing so is to get people to think that the principles for animate objects are the same as those for inanimate ones, and vice versa. This purpose is illustrated in the Introduction of *Leviathan*, where Hobbes says that animals are machines and machines are alive:

> For seeing life is but a motion of limbs, the beginning whereof is in some principal part within, why may we not say that all *automata* (engines that move themselves by springs and wheels as doth a watch) have an artificial life? For what is the *heart*, but a *spring*, and the *nerves*, but so many *strings*; and the *joints*, but so many *wheels*, giving motion to the whole body, such as was intended by the Artificer?
>
> (L Introduction 1)

Hobbes defines *conatus* in various ways. One is that *conatus* is a motion that is too small to be measured (DCo 10.2). This makes *conatus* a relative concept. Something is or is not a motion depending upon how finely one can measure motions. If a person is using a ruler on which the smallest unit is an inch, then a body that "moves" only one half of an inch does not move according to this measure. We use this fact in daily life although we do not always pay attention to it. We would say that the water in a glass on a sturdy table is motionless and so it appears. But if we apply our knowledge of physics to the water, we know that it is moving relative to the fine standard that scientists use.

Another definition is that *conatus* is motion through the length of a point. This definition will at first appear absurd or, at best, metaphorical, because according to the standard understanding of a point, a point has no dimensions at all and hence no length.

However, Hobbes's definition of "endeavor" is sensible because he uses a nonstandard definition of a point. As I said at the beginning of this chapter, Hobbes was an uncompromising materialist. Every body, every thing, is a bit of matter and hence has dimensions (DCo 10.2). Hence, a point is a body, of which the length, breadth and depth is ignored (DCo 15.2; EW 7: 201). A line then is a body, of which the breadth and depth are ignored. A plane is a body, of which the depth is ignored.

Normally, *conatus* are motions so small as to be imperceptible. Hobbes knows that there must be such motions because any object that travels over a large distance has to travel over the intermediate smaller distances that make up the whole. There is no limit to how many times a space can be divided. Hence, there are motions that are imperceptibly small. "For let a space be never so little, that which is moved over a greater space, whereof that little one is a part, must first be moved over that" (L 6.1).

Hobbes uses *conatus* to define other concepts of natural science. Resistance is the *conatus* of one body against another body that is in motion. Pressure is the *conatus* of one body against another (DCo 15.2). Hobbes also uses *conatus* or "endeavor" as an important concept in his philosophy of the mental, which will be discussed below.

MECHANISM

Hobbes believed that the only kind of causation occurred through contact of one moving body with another (DCo 15.1, 9.7, 25.2; DP, Epistle Dedicatory). For scientists, action at a distance was mysterious and typically unacceptable. Newton was perplexed by the fact that gravity seemed to be a case of action at a distance. It was a problem for Hobbes too, but he proffered an explanation. Objects that fall to the earth seem to be pulled from a distance. Hobbes's explanation is not crystal clear, but it goes something like this: When an object, say, a rock, is thrown into the air, it leaves a space where it had been on the earth. This space, which needs to be filled, is filled by the air around it. This causes the air above that space to move downward in order to fill the spaces left by the air that filled the original space of the rock. Some of this air is above the ascending rock. This downward-flowing air causes the rock to slow, and eventually it reverses the motion of the rock, which then falls to earth; hence, the action of gravity (DCo 30.5). I don't think that Hobbes considered the fact that when the rock is returning to earth, the reverse process of space-filling occurs. In the process of the air beneath the rock flowing to fill the space above the rock, air beneath the rock is moving upwards and exerting a force on the rock. However, because there is relatively little air beneath the rock, its action cannot prevent the rock from falling to earth.

DETERMINISM

Determinism is the view that every event has a cause. For Hobbes it is analytic, true by definition, that a cause determines its effect and that hence every event is determined by its cause. One might hold that Hobbes's view does not describe the ordinary view of causation, as it applies to human action; and since it does not, his view does not have the sting that it is thought to have, namely, that people are not responsible for their actions. For example, one might hold that, by the ordinary concept of causation, a person P's threat, uttered at time t caused person Q to run away at t_1, but that it is also the case that P's threat at t might have caused Q to stand Q's ground at t_1. Since Q has free will, Q is able to choose which way Q will react to P's threat.

Hobbes would object to this supposed counterexample, because it does not contain a complete description of Q's action. One cause can have only one possible, determinate effect, not two incompatible ones. If Q can either run away or stand Q's ground in the face of P's threat, then P's threat is not the complete cause of Q's reaction. People often mistake some salient event that is a necessary condition for an effect for the complete cause of that effect. For example, people sometimes say that the striking of a match caused the match to burn, but the striking was not the entire cause. The surrounding oxygen and the absence of water were also part of the cause. So, if P's threat can result in two different effects, P's threat is not the complete cause. Something else must be operating in order to yield the behavior. For example, P's threat, uttered at time t, caused person Q to have the desire (fear), and this desire caused Q to run away. If P's threat, uttered at time t, caused Q to have the desire to be brave, then this desire caused Q to stand Q's ground. The different desires of fear and bravery explain the difference of the results. Of course this is not a complete story because some explanation would have to be given for why P's threat in one case caused fear and in the other case bravery.

We have said that Hobbes thinks that a cause can have only one possible effect. It is the result of his worldview, according to which every event without exception is governed by general physical laws that determine only one outcome for each event. But what forces upon us the idea that one cause can have only one possible effect? Nothing, I think. One consideration that allows one to give up the inevitability of a determinate effect is the fact that quantum theory is able to explain physical events and it does not have deterministic laws, but statistical ones. Another consideration is that people acquire the concept of a cause through experience of specific actions and events, which do not include deterministic necessity. People learn that a knife cuts bread and striking a match causes a fire even though sometimes a knife does not cut or a match does not ignite wood. These facts do not interfere with acquiring the concept of a cause; in other words, someone might argue that the concept of a cause is the concept of making something happen or bringing something into existence; necessity, then would not be part of the ordinary concept of a cause. However, it is for Hobbes, and we should assume that it is true in order to understand his views on his own terms.

MIND

Hobbes's earliest published treatment of mental phenomena was his set of replies to Descartes's *Meditations*, which was discussed in Chapter 1. His first major work, in which he wrote down his mature thoughts about mental phenomena, was *The Elements of Law, Natural and Politic*, written about 1640, but not published until 1650. The same basic position is later expressed in *Leviathan* and *De homine*.

Although Hobbes divides "the two principal parts of man" into "faculties of the body" and "faculties of the mind," the mind itself is not a properly existing object for Hobbes (EL 1.5). Conceived of as an immaterial object, the mind is a theoretical entity based upon a false metaphysics. The thing that thinks and has emotions is the complex body of a brute animal or human being. It is normal to say that human beings understand various things, or have understanding. In the general sense in which this is true, brute animals also understand things and have understanding. At one point Hobbes says understanding is imagination "raised . . . by words or other voluntary signs" (L 2.10). In another sense, only human beings have understanding. This is the sense in which a person thinks the thoughts that are raised in him by the words concatenated into affirmations (L 4.22 and DH 10.1). Animals initiate and respond to voluntary signs, chirps, and barks, but they do not have language. They can respond to some sounds that are the same as human beings. Carol's dog knows what is coming if you say, "Do you want to take a walk?" and knows what to do if you say, "Come here, Bailey." But dogs and other animals with understanding do not hear human words as human words. They do not have a communication system that has elements out of which one composes an infinite number of sentences, mostly complex ones. Only human beings have language.

SENSATION

The cause of sensation is an external body that presses on a sense organ. These motions of the external body on the sense organ cause other motions in the nerves, and these motions end up in the brain or heart, where a small "resistance or counterpressure" is caused and, because its direction is outward, it causes the animal to think that there are external objects. This resistance is a motion so small that it is an "endeavor" (*conatus*), as mentioned above (L 1.4; see also DCo 15.2, 25.2).

Hobbes's account is both unjustified and naïve. It is unjustified because he did not have sufficient physiological information to indicate that motions in the brain or heart cause a counterpressure that raises the belief that there are bodies external to the human body. It is naïve because he gives no reason why a motion moving away from a person's heart or brain would cause a person to believe that there are external objects. Why wouldn't such a motion cause the person to think that he is asleep or climbing a mountain? It is no good to say that such a motion must somehow be appropriate to or resemble its cause, because, as Hobbes tells the story of sensation, one cannot compare one's qualitative experiences with the motions that cause them.

The properties of the objects that cause various kinds of sensations are nothing like the effects that they cause in the person that senses them. While a person who tastes an orange smells something orangey and has the sensations of juiciness and a pulpy mass, the orange itself does not have these qualities. The orange itself is nothing but a great number of moving bits of matter that cause the characteristic sensation of eating an orange. The objects of sense are nothing "but so many several motions of the matter, by which it [the matter] presseth our organs diversely" (L 1.4). This pressing on our organs causes in us "divers motions (for motion produceth nothing but motion)." Immediately after this sentence, comes this one: "But their appearance to us is fancy" (L 1.4). To most people, there is an enormous gap between tiny bits of the brain and heart moving hither and yon and qualitative experiences of the world. The sight of my blackboard, the scent of my orange, and the sound of the elevator have a "feel" that is not like the feel of bodies moving or not moving. Hobbes thinks that the motions and their appearing to us are identical (and that is the standard view today), but he sees no need for explaining how each could be identical with the other. Perhaps there is no answer, and certainly in the seventeenth century scientists did not know enough to give an answer. What is amazing is how sanguine Hobbes is in simply averring that one is the other, with one exception. In De corpore, he says that "the most admirable" of all phenomena – he means "strange" or "astonishing" – are the "phenomena or appearances" that animals have within themselves (DCo 25.1).

Hobbes's method of explaining qualia in terms of quantity is that of the new modern science of Copernicus and Galileo, and he explicitly rejects the traditional Aristotelian science, which he had been taught at Oxford (L 1.5).

IMAGINATION

Just as sensation is the initial motion in the head or heart, imagination is the motion that continues "after the object is removed or the eye shut" (L 2.2; DCo 25.7). Since there is a slight time lag between when the object begins a motion that causes the motion in the head or heart, the sensation occurs even when the object is removed or the eye is shut, if we want to be precise. But let's ignore this minor complication. For what is important to Hobbes at this point is a certain unity to his science: "Sensation is a motion in a sense organ of an animal, which motion is caused by an external object. . . . Imagination is decaying sense. . . . Therefore, imagination is a decaying motion in a sense organ of an animal, which motion is caused by an external object" (L 1.2). This is the beginning of Hobbes's project of showing how all mental states and events are reducible to the motions of objects. The next step is to give a similar analysis to memory. Hobbes says memory is identical with imagination. Hence, "[m]emory is a decaying motion in a sense organ of an animal, which motion is caused by an external object" (L 2.3). But what about the supposed difference between imagination and memory? According to Hobbes, the difference is linguistic. There are various ways to explain what Hobbes means. One is to distinguish, within the meaning of a word, between its focal and nonfocal meaning. In the word "imagination" the focus is on the fact that it is caused by sensation, so its meaning can be represented in this way:

"Imagination" means decaying **sense**.

In contrast, in the word "memory," the focus is on the decay, so its meaning can be represented in this way:

"Memory" is **decaying** sense.

Experience is "memory of many things" (L 2.4). So we could analyze "experience" like this:

Experience is the **decaying** motions, of many things, in a sense organ of an animal, which motions were caused by external objects.

This definition does not seem to work well. To say that someone has a lot of experience is not to stress that he or she has a lot of decaying motion. The problem stems, I believe, from Hobbes's mistaken identification of memory with imagination. Something weaker is true. Every instance of remembering something is identical with some instance of imagination. But this does not show that "memory" and "experience" mean the same thing. The idea of memory includes the idea that it is the veridical trace of some actual sensation. In contrast, although all imaginings could be traced back ultimately to some sensation, imaginings that are not memories are set free from the requirement that they match the event that caused them. A person can imagine a unicorn but cannot remember one.

Let's pick up with Hobbes's view about the relation between

imagination and dreams. Most imaginations occur while people are awake. But many of them occur to people who are asleep; these are called dreams. In kind, they are no different from waking imaginations; they are motions in the brain or heart. Although Descartes had drawn momentous inferences from the impossibility of finding a criterion that distinguishes dreams from waking experience, Hobbes is sanguine about the fact that there is no such criterion. (Dreams have a dreamlike quality; waking life does not. But this is not a criterion, not a test of wakefulness. In order to conduct a test of anything authoritatively, one has to be awake.) To say that there is no criterion for dreaming is not to say that there are no signs of dreaming. Hobbes reports that his dream fancies lack coherence and that he recognizes their absurdity when he is awake, and "is well satisfied that, being awake, I know I dream not, though when I dream, I think myself awake" (L 2.5; also EL 3.3–10; DCo 25.9).

MENTAL DISCOURSE

When thoughts follow one after another, the result, according to Hobbes is "mental discourse." He says that when a person thinks about something, "his next thought after is not altogether so casual as it seems to be . . . [because] we have no transition from one imagination to another whereof we never had the like before in our senses" (L 3.1). This is inadequate. Having thoughts following one another is a necessary but not sufficient condition for mental discourse. There's a difference between this chain of thoughts: man, animal, walks; and this one: a man is an animal and walks. The difference is not just the greater number of words in the latter. Even if we added "A," "is," "an," and so on, to the first string, the result would not form a thought or a bit of mental discourse, because the (mental) words of a simple sequence do not cohere, do not stick together the way the words of a mental discourse do. Words in discourse have special relationships to each other. The function of the subject of a thought is to denote something that is to be categorized or talked about, and the predicate denotes something that is a property that forms the supposedly appropriate category or says something about the thing denoted by the subject. In other places, Hobbes is sensitive to the fact that mental discourse involves words in special relationships (DCo 3.2).

Hobbes's ordering of mental discourse to follow sensation (and related concepts) fits the normal scholastic view about knowledge. Sensations of individual objects are the atoms of thinking; when these are put together the result is a thought. Most philosophers today would give priority to thoughts, and hold that an individual sensation is identifiable by the contribution it makes to the thought. Hobbes's view is at least plausible. When thoughts that follow one another are not directed by a specific desire, they are ordered by previous experience, but because experience varies from person to person, the sequence cannot be predicted. When thoughts are controlled by some desire, they are regulated (L 3.4). This raises the question, "What is a desire?"

DESIRE, APPETITE, AVERSION

Action begins with something being imagined, because all action depends on a preceding "thought of *whither, which way,* and *what*" (L 6.1). When these imaginings, which are imperceptibly small motions (endeavors), are toward the object that causes them, they are appetites; and when these imaginings are away from the object that causes them, they are aversions. The class of appetites and aversions are desires, although the word "desire" sometimes is used to denote appetites only. ("Desire" is like "animal," which comprises beasts and humans, but sometimes is used to denote only beasts, and like "baby," which sometimes denotes all newly born animals, but sometimes is used to denote only human ones.)

Hobbes's analysis of desire is mistaken. Take a paradigmatic case of a desire, say, hunger. A person's desire for food may be caused by some specific existing food, but it need not be. Usually a person's hunger is caused, not by a specific instance of food, but by a need for food. In today's chemistry, hunger is caused by some chemical.

When the chemical is at a certain level in the body, a message is sent to the brain and the person feels hungry, but food did not cause the hunger. Even though Hobbes could not have known much about the physiology of hunger, he should have recognized that not all hunger is caused by food.

Or consider love and hate. Love, he says, is almost the same thing as appetite, and hate is almost the same thing as aversion. The differences are in connotation, somewhat like the difference between "imagination" and "memory." The word "love" signifies movement toward an object and connotes (or focuses on the fact) that the object is present, while "appetite" connotes (or focuses on the fact) that the object is not present. The word "hate" signifies movement away from an object and connotes (or focuses on the fact) that the object is not present while "aversion" connotes (or focuses on the fact) that the object is absent. If Hobbes were merely stipulating how he will use these words, he would be immunized against objection. But he seems to be reporting what he thinks the difference is in the ordinary meanings or denotations of the words. Understood in this way, there are at least two serious objections to them. First, anyone who has ever pined for a lover or has hated someone who is inaccessible knows that the presence or absence of the object is irrelevant to the emotion. Second, a person can be deeply in love or have a deep hatred for someone without those emotions causing any movement toward or away from the object. They would cause a movement toward or away from the object if the object were relatively close or accessible (and if one of those emotions dominated over all others). What seems to be correct is that love and hate cause a tendency in a person either to go toward or away from the relevant object. (The proper analysis of a tendency is quite complex, and I don't think that I can give one.)

A more serious problem with Hobbes's analyses of love and hate is the same as one of the problems with his analysis of hunger, namely, they do not fit his mechanism. When the object of feeling or emotion is absent, there cannot be causation by contact. His analysis of the attraction that a loved one exerts on the lover is like the attraction of what Aristotle called a final cause, something that puts an object in motion because it is desired. And Hobbes had rejected the existence of a final cause because he conceived of all causation as mechanistic.

One might object that Hobbes in fact did not reject final causes. His definition of a commonwealth has a final cause built right into it: a commonwealth is a group of men who agree to have one person represent them "to the end to live peaceably amongst themselves and be protected against other men" (L 18.1). I think that Hobbes has the resources to answer this point about the definition of a commonwealth, and those resources can also be applied to the point about hunger, love, and hatred. The answer begins with an admission that the explicit definition that Hobbes gave of a commonwealth is unacceptable, precisely because it includes a final cause. We can now give the heart of the answer. A commonwealth can be defined as a group of men who, for fear of death, agree to have themselves represented by one person who is willing and able to protect them. In this definition the teleological element has disappeared. It is replaced by a fear that is present. I suppose that one might still object that *a fear of death* contains death in its analysis, and death is not present to the person who has the fear (both because the person is alive and because death is not a thing).

I think that Hobbes can concede that death is not a thing and not present, without any problem. The property expressed by "x fears death" can be analyzed in terms of motions that are in the person. This analysis would fit Hobbes's explicit materialist and mechanistic program; however, it would, of course, not be Hobbes's solution in the sense that he is saying or implying it in the very analyses he actually uses. This raises a general point about Hobbes's philosophy. What he says he will do he often does not do. What his theory says should be done is often something that is not done by him. This is clearly true about his scientific definitions. He says that a scientific definition ought to state the process by which an object is generated: a circle is generated by fixing one leg of a compass and moving the other leg, which is at a fixed distance from the first one, until a plane figure is made. But it is arguable that none of the definitions of the psychological predicates or properties that we have been discussing has stated the way those predicates or properties are generated.

Interestingly, as regards a commonwealth, although Hobbes begins with a definition that includes a final cause, his actual discussion of a commonwealth does present a description of how the commonwealth is generated: people in the state of nature covenant to transfer all or some of their rights to a sovereign. (A more extended discussion of the origin of a commonwealth will be given in Chapter 4.)

In understanding and evaluating Hobbes's other psychological states, let's waive the objections just discussed.

Hobbes's most controversial definitions are those for "good" and "evil." He defines good as "the object of any man's appetite or desire," and evil as the object of a person's hate (L 6.7). Since different people desire different objects, what is good and what is evil is variable and subjective. This consequence infuriated his contemporaries. But Hobbes is merely describing what he thinks goodness and evil come to, given the way people think and talk about them, not expressing satisfaction that this is what the words mean. And he is not happy about the fact that goodness is variable and subjective. It is a cause of dissension and conflict, as we shall see in later chapters, where he will try to eliminate the variability of goodness by getting everyone in a commonwealth to desire whatever the sovereign desires.

Although he does not say this, I think Hobbes may be hinting that although people use the word "good" as an absolute predicate, "Doing x is good," it is actually a relative predicate, "Doing x is good to me" or "I desire doing x." Pointless and interminable disputes over whether something is "good" or not could be forestalled if potential disputants realized that they simply have different desires.

Hobbes's belief that every good is something desired by a person has a consequence for his view about pleasure. He holds that when a desired object is obtained, it causes a certain motion inside the animal, which appears to the person as "*delight* and *pleasure*" (L 6.10; DCo 25.12). His view should not be confused with the fact that some pleasurable feelings are caused by rubbing or vibrating some part of the body. Pleasure is not a companion of a certain motion; the motion is the pleasure, just as other motions are ideas of things.

Again, Hobbes is sanguine about bodies in motion being qualitative experiences. He holds an even stronger view in *The Elements of Law, Natural and Politic*. After identifying delight with a motion, he says that delight helps or promotes "vital" motion (EL 7.1; see also DCo 25.12). But this is a mistake. Some drugs that cause delight diminish one's vital motion.

In *De homine*, Hobbes says that all desire is delight (DH 11.1). This may seem false if one thinks about pining for a lover. However, pining is a complex emotion. Its pain comes from the desire not being satisfied, but the desire itself is enjoyable. If pining did not have an element of pleasure, people would always try to extinguish it, but they don't.

Hobbes thinks that all other emotions and mental states and events can be defined using seven concepts, all of which reduce to motions inside a body caused by external bodies: appetite, desire, love, aversion, hate, joy ("*pleasures of the mind*" caused by considering consequences of things), and grief (pain caused by considering the consequences of things) (L 6.13). Various emotions consist of one of the basic psychological states combined with the likelihood of obtaining the object; for example, hope is an appetite for something combined with the opinion that it will be obtained. Some emotions consist of one of the basic psychological states combined with a love or hate of that object; for example, fear is an aversion for an object that is hated. Some emotions are a combination of the basic emotions; for example, pusillanimity is a desire for things that do little to help us achieve our goals, combined with a fear of things that do little to hinder us from achieving our goals (L 6.13, 6.14, and 6.25; and DCo 25.12).

Here is a sampling of Hobbes's definitions, with some critical comments (L 6.14 ff.).

> "x has hope" = df "x desires something y and believes that x will get y" ("there exists an object y and x believes that x will get y").
> "x has despair" = df "x desires something y and believes that x will not get y"

There are at least two major problems with the definition of hope and, *mutatis mutandis*, despair. First, people often hope for things that do not exist, such as world peace. Second, people often hope for things they believe they will not get, but may. Third, Hobbes nowhere gives a definition of "belief" ("opinion"). He may have had a sense of how difficult it is to define belief and did not want to raise the issue explicitly. Many twentieth-century philosophers have tried to analyze beliefs in terms of dispositions to behavior, but have not been able to make them work, sometimes because the idea of a disposition is too vague or too complex and sometimes because some beliefs do not seem to involve any distinctive disposition to behavior. Some philosophers define believing as "holding a sentence true." Even if the ideas of sentence and truth are clear enough, the idea of holding is not.

> "x has fear" = df "x believes something y will hurt x."
> "x has courage" = df "x believes something y will hurt x and x believes that x can avoid being hurt by y by resisting."

Hobbes's definition of "fear" is close enough, and the one for "courage" is plausible, but perhaps not correct. Cowards sometimes resist something they think will hurt them. Suppose a small child is trying to stab a cowardly adult with a pin. The adult may strike the child rather than suffer the sting, as a person of some courage would. I suppose that Hobbes could counterclaim that the adult's cowardice caused the adult to have enough courage to resist the child. But this strikes me as another instance of saying whatever is necessary to save the position, no matter how false it is.

> "x is benevolent" = df "x desires that the desires of someone else be satisfied."

This definition seems fine to me. It is consistent with the desire that another person's desires be satisfied only as a means to contributing to one's own happiness. It is also consistent with the proposition that in fact no one is actually benevolent, as Hobbes sometimes suggests. So his definition of benevolence cannot be used to throw light on his views about egoism.

THE IMPORTANCE OF DESIRES

For many of the ancient Greeks and for all the European medieval philosophers, having desires was not something good, and was often considered intrinsically bad. To have a desire was to be deficient in the thing that one wanted. A want is a lack, and a lack is an imperfection. The goal for the ancient and medieval philosophers just mentioned was to strive with all their might to achieve a state in which there were no desires, no passions at all. This state was variously called the finis ultimus and the summum bonum. They engaged in a passionate search for passionless knowledge.[1] Hobbes's view was explicitly, passionately the opposite.

> For there is no such *finis ultimus* (utmost aim) nor *summum bonum* (greatest good) as is spoken of in the books of the old moral philosophers. Nor can a man any more live whose desires are at an end than he whose senses and imaginations are at a stand.
>
> (L 11.1)

Happiness, then, is not an unchanging state, but "a continual progress of the desire from one object to another" (L 11.1). This is a nice characterization of the lives of acquisitive consumers in a late capitalist society.

One consequence of the chain of practically unending desires is that all the while a person is trying to satisfy his current desire, he is trying to satisfy the parallel desire of guaranteeing that he will always have the means to satisfy all the future ones. The only way to do this is to strive for more power: it is "a perpetual and restless desire of power after power that ceaseth only in death" (L 11.2). Because the desires cease only with death, the description of human beings as constantly seeking more power is almost as chilling as his description of the lives of people in the state of nature as solitary, poor, nasty, brutish, and short. Of course, they are connected. People who want more and more power will inevitably come into conflict with each other, and will need to be opposed by people who do not seek more power than they need, and the knowledge of everyone that everyone else may want unlimited power gives everyone more reason to fear everyone else.

Fortunately, the description that everyone seeks ever-more power is true only of madmen like Hitler and Stalin, many politicians, and corporate executives, not ordinary human beings.[2] The latter do not put as much effort into acquiring maximum power as they could. Most Americans do not want their jobs to get too much in the way of their satisfying their desires for an SUV, a digital television, a cell phone, and whatever else has come to the showrooms, shelves, and catalogs since I wrote these words. This is to say that Hobbes has exaggerated the desire for power, and he should have known it. Most people are too desirous of immediate gratification to work continuously to increase their power. It is impossible for a person to maximize two disparate things at once. Hobbes himself seems to recognize this a short time later when he says that one of the reasons that people abandon their search for ever-greater power and are disposed "to obey a common power" is their desire "of ease and sensual delight" (L 11.4). One kind of delight is knowledge, and the desire for it is another reason most people give up the unrestricted search for power (L 11.5). Another reason is the fear of "death and wounds," a point that is crucial to his political philosophy.

Hobbes thinks that the "perpetual and restless desire of power after power" is "a general inclination of all mankind" (L 11.2), and its cause is not usually megalomania but a reasonable fear that one cannot be safe unless one is always acquiring more power. That is, underlying the quest for power is fear, just as it will be when Hobbes discusses one of the causes of the war of all against all in the state of nature (see L 12). However, in addition to the fear of one's life or one's desire for safety, the striving for ever-greater power is sometimes caused by "a new desire . . . of fame" or "admiration or being flattered" by others for some kind of excellence (L 11.2; cf. 11.6). Again this is similar to what Hobbes will say about a cause of war in the state of nature in Chapter 13 of *Leviathan*.

The general topic of Chapter 11 of *Leviathan*, which we have been discussing in this section, is "the qualities of mankind that concern their living together in peace and unity" (L 11.1). From the discussion thus far, little seems to contribute to peace and unity other than, conspicuously, the desires people have for "ease and sensual delight," "leisure," and "praise" (L 11.4, 11.5, 11.6). Later he adds fear of oppression to the qualities that dispose a person to "seek aid by society" (L 11.9). Most desires seem to contribute to animosity and conflict, to war and disunity. In Chapter 11, Hobbes is close to being at his most cynical. Receiving a gift from a person whom we think is inferior to ourselves and not being able to reciprocate causes "secret hatred" because "benefits oblige; and obligation is thralldom; and unrequitable obligation, perpetual thralldom" (L 11.7). It is the gift that keeps on tormenting. Conversely, to injure a person who is unable to exact revenge causes the perpetrator "to hate the sufferer," because he knows that the victim will either seek revenge or will forgive the perpetrator, "both which are hateful" (L 11.8).

Implicit in this discussion of the "Manners" of human beings in Chapter 11 of *Leviathan* is the idea that human beings make life miserable for themselves. This becomes an explicit theme in Chapter 13, "Of the Natural Condition of Mankind as concerning their

Felicity and Misery," which constitutes the first topic we will discuss in the next chapter.[3]

FREE WILL

The issue of free will is important to both metaphysics and ethics; it is important both for knowing what the physical world is like and for knowing what conditions are necessary for responsibility. Hobbes is one of the great contributors to the debate on free will. He always held that human actions are free, but always opposed the theory that they were made free by free will. His rejection of the theory of free will appeared in the early 1640s when he wrote *Anti-White*. There he defines liberty as "the absence of impediments to motion" (AW 446; see also LN 273–4). He says, "For as long as its motion in a given direction is not hindered, for so long, and with reference to the same direction, is something said to be free" (ibid.). Liberty in this sense applies as much to rivers with an unimpeded flow of water as it does to human beings (DCo 25.13). Bramhall calls this a "childish liberty" and a "brutish liberty" (QLNC 39).

Hobbes defended a position known as compatibilism, that is, that free action is compatible with necessity. In *Leviathan*, he presented his view succinctly by defining "deliberation" and then "will" (L 6.49 and 6.53; see also LN 273):

> "x deliberates about whether to do action A" = df "x alternates between having an appetite for doing A and an aversion to doing A, caused by alternatively hoping that doing A will have good consequences and fearing that doing A will have bad consequences."
>
> "x is will" = df "x is the last desire (appetite or aversion) in deliberating."

People knowingly deliberate only about future events, because only they seem to us to depend on our actions. Hobbes also holds that if a person does not know that an event E is past, he may deliberate about E. I think it is more precise to say that such a person thinks he is deliberating about E but in fact is not. This is similar to saying that a person who firmly believes that p and has very good evidence to believe that p only thinks he knows that p if it is false that p. Hobbes's definition of deliberation is deflating in the sense that beasts deliberate as much as humans do, because they, like humans, have desires that alternate.

Two things about Hobbes's definition of "will" should be noticed. First, Hobbes himself defines will as "the last appetite," not as I do above, as "the last desire (appetite or aversion)." I changed Hobbes's wording because appetites are only motions toward something, and an instance of will can also be an aversion, that is, the cause of an animal moving away from something. Second, Hobbes's definition does not make explicit an important part of a willing, namely, that it is part of the cause of an action (LN 274). A willing is the last desire in deliberating, because it is the desire that causes the action. A person who deliberates between eating and not eating a cupcake and then eats it is caused to eat it by the desire to eat it (and other things). If the person were finally to decide not to eat the cupcake, then the desire that caused the action would be the desire not to eat the cupcake. It is also possible for the deliberation to end without an eating of the cupcake or a decision not to. Those desires terminate and some other desire arises. In this case, the last act of deliberation is not a willing. So, Hobbes's definition would be expressed even better like this:

"x is will" = df "in deliberating x is the last desire (appetite or aversion) and is part of the cause of an action."

Contrary to the scholastic doctrine, a will is not a faculty or permanent power in a human being that initiates an action. Wills are, as Hobbes said, desires, and desires are endeavors, the "small beginnings of motion within the body of man, before they appear in walking, speaking, and striking, and other visible actions" (L 6.1). These are the basics of Hobbes's view.

Hobbes's extended discussion of free will occurs in his two works directed against John Bramhall. Recall that Hobbes and Bramhall debated the issue of free will in 1645 but their views were first published in the 1650s. Bramhall defended the existence of free will and its necessity for the justification of assigning praise and blame. Hobbes denied that the concept was intelligible. (See Chapter 1, "Life.")

Bramhall begins his presentation of his position with what he thinks is a knockdown argument:

(1) Either I am free to write this discourse for liberty, or I am not free.
(2) If I am free, then I win the debate and am not blameworthy.
(3) If I am not free, then I should not be blamed for losing the debate.
   Therefore,
(4) Either I win the debate, or I should not be blamed for losing the debate.

But the argument is not cogent. Hobbes rejects premise (2) and Bramhall does not give him a good reason to accept it. Bramhall's being free is not sufficient to establish that he won the debate, for Hobbes also holds that people are sometimes free and act freely. What Bramhall needed to prove is that he had free will. The existence of free will, not freedom, is the issue. So Bramhall's argument commits the fallacy of *ignoratio elenchi* (LN 238–9). In other words, the freedom of human action does not prove that humans have free will. According to Hobbes, the correct account of freedom is given in terms of the cause of the action. If a desire caused the action, then the action is free, but if the action was caused by some violent motion outside of the person, say, a strong wind that blows a person across a street, then the action is not free, but compelled.

So, Bramhall's first major mistake concerns the relation between the concept of a free action and that of free will. Bramhall's second major mistake concerns the relation between free will and responsibility. Bramhall thinks that a necessary condition for being responsible for an action, for deserving praise or blame, is that a person's action be caused by free will. Hobbes summarizes Bramhall's argument like this:

> If there be a necessity of all events, then it will follow that praise and reprehension and reward and punishment are all vain and unjust; and that if God should openly forbid and secretly necessitate the same action, punishing men for what they could not avoid, there would be no belief among them of heaven or hell.
>
> (LN 248)

Bramhall quotes numerous examples of praise and blame from the Bible as evidence for his view. Hobbes points out that these quotations are irrelevant because they do not support Bramhall's position any more than they undermine Hobbes's. What is relevant to assigning praise or blame to an action is whether it is in accord with a moral or civil law or whether it violates a moral or civil law, respectively. Since the quotations from the Bible are about actions that followed or violated a law, they agree with Hobbes's position much as they do with Bramhall's. Hobbes's discussion of one of these examples should suffice:

> The words [of Scripture, quoted by Bramhall] are, "If a wife make a vow, it is left to her husband's choice either to establish or make it void." For it proves no more but that the husband is a free and voluntary agent, but not that his choice therein is not necessitated or not determined to what he shall choose by precedent necessary causes.
>
> (LN 241)

Hobbes treats the actions of God differently. His actions are free but they cannot be unjust because they are subject to no law. He quotes the epistle to the Romans 9:11–14.

> *When they*, meaning Esau and Jacob, *were yet unborn, and had done neither good nor evil, that the purpose of God according to*

*election, not by works, but by him that calls, might remain firm, it
was said unto her* (viz. Rebecca) *that the elder shall serve the
younger, . . . What then shall we say? Is there injustice with God?
God forbid.*

(LN 248)

Hobbes points out that St. Paul continues in this way:

*Who art though, O man, that interrogatest God? Shall the work say
to the workman, why has thou made me thus? Hath not the potter
power over the clay, of the same stuff to make one vessel to honour,
and another to dishonour?*

(LN 248)

That is to say,

the *power* of God alone without other help is sufficient *justification*
of any action he does. That which men make amongst themselves
here by pacts and covenants and call by the name of justice, and
according whereunto men are counted and termed rightly *just* or
unjust, is not that by which God Almighty's actions are to be
measured or called just, no more than his counsels are to be
measured by human wisdom. That which he does, is made just
by his doing it; just, I say, in him, though not always just in us.

(LN 249)

Hobbes expressed this position in several other places: "Power irresistible justifies all actions, really and properly, in whomsoever it be found" (LN
250; see also QLNC 162). Although this is a hard doctrine, it is
supported by Calvinists, armed with biblical texts, for example, one
in the book of Job, where God "justified his afflicting of Job, by
telling him of his power" (LN 249; see also Job 40:9).

The issue of freedom and responsibility is not essentially a
theological problem. Bramhall is afraid that if every action is neces-
sitated by prior events, then laws that prohibit behavior are unjust,
that it is useless to deliberate, that admonitions to children are vain,
and that reward and punishment are pointless (LN 252). Hobbes

disagrees. Concerning laws, Hobbes says that they are meant to prevent "*noxious*" actions: "Men are not therefore put to death, or punished, for that their theft proceedeth from *election*; but because it was *noxious* and contrary to men's preservation" (LN 254). And the point of punishment is not retribution but deterrence: "The intention of the *law* is not to grieve the *delinquent*, for that which is past, and not to be undone; but to make him and others *just*, that else would not be so, and respecteth not the evil act *past*, but the *good to come*" (LN 253).

Concerning deliberation and admonitions, the answer is similar. They are part of the causal chains that result in a person's acting one way or another. If one did not deliberate or admonish, the results would be very different. The person who pays no attention when he crosses a road because he thinks his death is fated, thinks that what will happen will happen no matter what. But this is a mistake. It does not happen no matter what; it happens because of what he does or does not do as regards paying attention to the traffic (LN 254–5). Hobbes is a determinist, not a fatalist.

Hobbes does concede that his doctrine, though true, may have disastrous consequences because most people are governed by the desire for money or sensual pleasures and will misunderstand its consequences. So Hobbes would not have written down his thoughts if Newcastle had not requested it, and he hopes that Newcastle will keep the thoughts private (LN 257).

The compatibility of freedom and necessity is also related to the concept of foreknowledge. For Hobbes, because God is the cause of the world and knows what he causes, he knows everything that will ever happen even before it happens. However, this knowledge does not compel anyone to do anything, for knowledge does not cause things to happen: "[K]nowledge depends on the existence of things known, and not they on it" (LN 246). Hobbes's treatment of this problem ignores a more serious problem. It is not that God knows what will happen that is so troubling but that he knows and wills everything that happens. He is the cause of all things, according to orthodox Christianity and Hobbes's own professed beliefs. But if God wills everything that happens, and nothing a person can do can change this, then a person does not seem to be free.

CONCLUSION

Hobbes's main project in metaphysics and the philosophy of mind was to show how all phenomena consist of nothing more than material bodies in motion. He seems to believe that only bodies are real because he thinks that the only way that anything changes is through a change in the movement of some body. The most difficult cases for a materialist to explain are mental phenomena such as thinking, imagining, loving and fearing. So Hobbes analyzes these and related phenomena in terms of endeavors, small movements of bodies toward and away from other bodies. Hobbes's analyses are actually closer to conceptual analyses than they are to physical analyses, but his project is a thoroughly modern one.

The most significant mental phenomenon for human beings is free will, or, as Hobbes would prefer, freedom. For him, all motions, including human actions, are caused by antecedent motions. This makes every motion or action necessary. People are free when the immediate cause of their action is a desire. So for Hobbes, freedom and necessity are compatible. The concept of free will is incoherent because each willing is a desire that is caused, and only bodies can be free.

FURTHER READING

Peters, R. (1967) *Hobbes* 2nd edn, Harmondsworth: Penguin. Chapters 2–4 and 6 are a good introduction to Hobbes's views about metaphysics and mind.

Sorell, T. (1986) *Hobbes*, London: Routledge. An excellent treatment of Hobbes's metaphysics, although one may disagree with parts of it.

Three

Moral Philosophy

MORAL AND POLITICAL PHILOSOPHY

Hobbes's moral philosophy is designed to be the foundation for his political philosophy, to be an account of satisfying human relationships or human excellence for its own sake. Hobbes has no conception of society independent of a political entity that keeps people from brutalizing and killing each other. In this regard, Hobbes's view is very different from that of John Locke, for whom life in society mediates a solitary human life and life within a civil state. We shall see below that no one could live a "moral" life very long unless he joined with others to form a government. So let's say something about the nature of Hobbes's political philosophy before focusing on his moral theory.

Hobbes's political theory belongs to the general category of social-contract theory. In essence, a social-contract theory is one that maintains that governments come into existence through the contract or agreement of certain parties. Usually the contract is understood to be between the sovereign and his subjects. In the seventeenth century, many English people thought that the English Civil War was justified because the monarch Charles I had broken his contract with the people. Consequently, he was no longer a legitimate king and could justifiably be overthrown. Hobbes disagreed on both points. He thought that a contract not to overthrow the sovereign was made between the subjects themselves. And because the monarch had not been a party to the social contract, he could not have broken it.

Hobbes's political philosophy is detailed and exciting, but it is also hard to interpret because of numerous verbal contradictions; it may also be off-putting because of some opinions that are outrageous by current standards. Many of the verbal contradictions, though probably not all, can be justifiably eliminated by using standard interpretive techniques. Some of his statements can be construed as hyperbole or some other figure of speech, and some can be construed more narrowly than the actual wording suggests by appealing to the context.

Concerning morality, Hobbes says that his moral philosophy consists of "the true doctrine of the laws of nature," that is, the means to peace, to which the virtues of "*justice, gratitude, modesty, equity, mercy*" are crucial (L 15.40; DC 3.32). Nonetheless, some scholars say that he has no moral philosophy because he deduces the laws of nature from egoistic premises. I don't think they have a good case. It's plausible that his egoism is not ethical egoism. Even if it is, his so-called "egoism" is a rule egoism, which prescribes that each person should follow a set of rules that overall would produce the best result for him, such as, make peace, keep your covenants, and don't be cruel. There is even an important, if obscurely argued, passage in which Hobbes claims it is always against reason to act unjustly. It seems senseless to define ethics in a way that excludes a prescriptive system of universal laws that are designed to contribute to human happiness and to make a strong case for justice. But if someone wants to insist that Hobbes does not have a genuine ethics, he can have the word "ethics," and we shall discuss Hobbes's "ethics*." (Hereafter, I will suppress the asterisk.)

There is a different problem with Hobbes's moral philosophy or ethics[1] that relates to his politics. In his diagram of the sciences in *Leviathan*, moral philosophy is grouped with physics, music, poetry, and logic as part of "Natural Philosophy," which seems to be the same as descriptive philosophy, in contrast with "POLITICS, and CIVIL PHILOSOPHY," which is prescriptive philosophy. Hobbes seems to want moral philosophy to have one foot in descriptive philosophy and one foot in prescriptive philosophy in order to bridge the two parts of philosophy. However, since moral philosophy is firmly in the descriptive side, the maneuver does not seem to work any more than Descartes's maneuver to have the pineal gland bridge the gap between mind and matter. The pineal gland is just as material as any other piece of matter. Someone might defend Hobbes by observing that since moral philosophy is the science of just and unjust, it does have one foot in normative philosophy. Further, Hobbes's position that the science of just and unjust is a consequence of "the accidents of bodies natural" is an insightful feature of his philosophy (L 9.3). Justice arises from the physical act of transferring part of one's right to all things. There is no object in the world that is justice or a correlate for the word "justice." Hobbes's antirealism is functioning here.

One objection to this idea of the origin of justice is that transfers of right always generate obligations, and obligations should not belong in the realm of descriptive natural philosophy. A defender of Hobbes might reply that, contrary to the objection, the distinction between natural and civil philosophy is not grounded on the difference between what is descriptive and prescriptive but on what belongs to civil philosophy and what does not. Almost all of the philosophy that does not depend upon the existence of a civil government is descriptive and nonnormative, but not all of it. Moral philosophy belongs to natural philosophy solely by virtue of the fact that conceptually it does not depend on the concept of a government. It differs from the rest of natural philosophy insofar as it is normative. And it is able to bridge the gap between natural and civil philosophy because on the one hand it is part of natural philosophy and on the other hand it has the property that civil philosophy has, normativity.

No doubt the person with the objection can raise an objection to the reply just given;[2] and the debate would probably not end there. Rather than continue the debate or opt for one side or the other, I think we should see the debate as clarifying, albeit not resolving, some difficult aspects of Hobbes's moral philosophy and proceed to a more direct discussion of it by looking at how moral philosophy evolves from his analysis of good and evil and from his idea of the state of nature. Having done that, we will be able to show in the following chapter how his political philosophy evolves from his moral philosophy.

GOOD AND EVIL

Seen from one perspective, Hobbes's discussion of morality in *Leviathan* begins with his description of the state of nature in Chapter 13. Seen from another perspective, it begins in Chapter 6 with his definitions of good and evil. We will soon see that these definitions were offensive to people in three or four respects: they were relational, relativistic, naturalistic, and egoistic. Good, Hobbes seems to say, is "the object of any man's appetite" and evil is "the object of his hate." When he says that nothing is "simply and absolutely" good or evil, he means that they are relations (L 6.7; see also DH 11.4). To bring their relational nature out, let's put his definition in a form of a definition of a predicate expression:

> "x is good" = df "something has an appetite for x" ("there exists an object y such that y has an appetite for x")

and

> "x is evil" = df "something has an aversion for x" ("there exists an object y such that y has an aversion for x")

Let's focus on the definition of "good" since the problems with "evil" will be obvious. Hobbes's relational understanding of good went against the traditional view that goodness was either a thing – God is goodness – or an intrinsic property of things, like being red or being a dog. Whether something was good or not was part of the thing itself – honesty is good and truth-telling is good – it did not depend on something else that it was related to.

But Hobbes's relational understanding of goodness was not its most offensive feature. After all, no one would have objected if he had related what is good to something about God: what is good is what God wants us to do or is what God makes. And few would have been upset if he had said that what is good is what all people (ought to) strive for. This would have been "relationality" without relativism in the bad sense. What offended Hobbes's contemporaries was the variability of goodness. This is relativism in the bad sense. Today, relativism about most things is not objectionable: different strokes for different folks. But in the seventeenth century, everyone was supposed to agree about what was good in morality, politics, and religion.

There is another aspect of Hobbes's analysis of goodness that was objectionable to Hobbes's contemporaries, though they saw this aspect much less clearly than its relativism. His analysis reduces "good" and "evil," which are intuitively value-laden terms, to terms that are value free. For most people, the fact that someone desires something does not mean that that thing is good. For most people in the United States until recently, some of the most desired things were the things thought to be evil, say, alcoholic beverages and certain kinds of sexual activities. The traditional view was that in addition to being an intrinsic property of things (like being red or being square), goodness and evil were a different kind of property. They were not physical properties, but moral or nonnatural properties. What Hobbes's analyses say, in effect, is that good and evil belong to the physical world, not some other world. Good and evil are closer to appetite and aversion and pleasantness and unpleasantness than to justice and injustice (L 6.3–8; see also L 9). In a word, his analyses of good and evil are naturalistic. Today there are naturalistic theories of goodness that are also theories of morality. But, for Hobbes, goodness is not a moral concept. Desire is morally neutral. In Hobbes's moral theory, the key concept is law, as we will see in the next chapter.

So far, we have seen how Hobbes's definitions gave the appearance of being relational or relativistic and naturalistic. These qualities follow from his definition of "good." In addition, Hobbes believes that goodness has another quality. (Later, I will say why I think this quality does not follow from his definition.) This quality, which is as objectionable as the others, is that all desires and everything people think is good are egoistic. He says, "every man's end [is] . . . some good to himself," "For by necessity of nature every man doth in all his voluntary actions intend some good unto himself," and "of the voluntary acts of every man, the object is some *good to himself*" (EL 5.4, 16.6; L 14.8; see also L 15.16). These quotations give the impression that Hobbes thinks that people act always to satisfy only themselves. However, what he says does not entail that each person desires only his own good, but only that the things each person desires must include something that is good for himself. According to this view, the charitable work of Mother Teresa could never be explained by the proposition that Mother Teresa wanted to help other people. That proposition is either incomplete or false. She could never act simply on this desire, because it does not contain herself as part of its object. What could have motivated her to act is the desire expressed in this proposition: Mother Teresa desired to ensure that she would get to heaven and thought that helping other people would achieve that goal (satisfy that desire). In addition to the textual evidence, there is also anecdotal evidence that Hobbes held that all actions are self-interested. His biographer John Aubrey reports that once during a walk Hobbes gave a beggar some money. Hobbes's companion, Jasper Mayne, said, "Would you have done this if it had not been Christ's command?" Hobbes replied, "Yes; because I was in pain to consider the miserable condition of the old man, and now my alms, giving him some relief, does also ease me." In short, Hobbes gave alms, purportedly, because he desired to ease his own discomfort. His description of his action sounds like that of a man who will say whatever is necessary to hold onto his thesis.

Hobbes's egoism seems to go against the way that many people think about their own motives for acting. Parents give up doing things they want to do for the sake of their children; firemen risk their lives to save others. Although parents and firemen also think that they have a duty to perform these actions, they do not think that they (always) act as they do because they desire to do their duty. Egoism, it seems, has nothing to do with their behavior.

These alleged counterexamples might be true; I don't know. But I don't think they are decisive refutations of Hobbes's view, because he can give a satisfactory account of these examples, based on his own principles. He can deny the alleged fact that parents, firemen, and others are not acting from a desire to do their duty or to avoid the pain of looking irresponsible or cowardly. Like physicists who can deny the alleged fact that colors are in objects because they have a theory that can explain color properties, Hobbes can deny that any action is purely selfless because his principles can account for apparent cases of selflessness.

One reason that many people resist accepting Hobbes's egoism or any egoistic theory is that they believe that it denies that any behavior is altruistic, and this seems to undermine morality. In fact it does not. Even on an egoistic view, there is an important difference between a person who helps the needy and the person who does not. The action of the former person helps the community and is praiseworthy, and the action of the latter person does not help the community and is not praiseworthy.

I suspect that Hobbes thought that egoism followed from his definition of "good" as "being desired," and that he thought that since "x is good" implicitly contains a reference to the subject with the desire, "someone desires x," every desire is self-interested. But that inference simply is not valid. For a desire to be self-interested, it is not enough that the person be the thing with the desire; rather, the person with the desire must be part of the content of the desire. It is consistent to hold that something is good if and only if it is desired and that some desires do not have the person with the desire as part of the content of what is desired.

It might seem that Hobbes's theory cannot explain standard judgments like this: P desires to use a narcotic x (which will injure his health), and x is not good for him. P might even know this, and say, "I desire x and I know that x is not good for me." According to Hobbes's definition, P's statement, as formulated, is contradictory. It means, "I desire x and I know that I do not desire x" and that entails "I desire x and it is not the case that I desire x." However, Hobbes has the resources to show that what P means is not contradictory, by filling out what is elliptically expressed by P. Sometimes Hobbes helps himself to something close to the standard distinction between short- and long-term goods (DH 11.14; L 6.57). A short-term good lasts a short time; a long-term good lasts a long time or is made up of many, consecutive, short-term goods. Sometimes a short-term good produces long-term consequences that are not good because they are not desired. So what P means by his original, contradictory statement is the following consistent proposition: "I desire x now, and I know that I do not desire the long-term consequences of x."[3]

In at least one place, Hobbes seems to use the word "good" in a way not consistent with his definition of it. In his proof of the fourth law of nature, "Be grateful," Hobbes uses the premise, "For no man giveth but with intention of good to himself." If that phrase means only, "For no man giveth but with his own desire to give," then it is not clear how it contributes to the proof (L 15.16; see also EL 14.2 and 15.1; and LN: 273). What Hobbes actually means by his premise is not that every action is caused by a desire, but that people always act from their own self-interest. This way of putting the matter may be misleading because "self-interest" is sometimes understood in two ways: (a) what people are interested in getting for themselves (what they desire for themselves) and (b) what is in their interest (what will contribute to a long and happy life). A person who is interested in having a certain amount of crack cocaine – this is sense (a) – is not acting in his self-interest in sense (b). This point also applies to nations. In early 2003, the President of the United States was saying in effect, "It is in the self-interest of the United States to attack Iraq (because Iraq harbors terrorists and has weapons of mass destruction that could be used against the United States)." In fact, the attack may have been against the interests of the United States. If that is true, then the President was interested in having the United States attack, but it was against the interest of the United States to attack.

Perhaps Hobbes is conflating (a) and (b). He may think that since everyone (almost) always desires to preserve his life (an instance of (a)), everyone (almost) always wants what will contribute to a long and happy life (an instance of (b)). The conflation is easy in this case because people usually are interested in having a long life and usually it is in their self-interest to have a long life. The problem is that Hobbes mistakenly thinks that every instance of (a) is necessarily an instance of (b).

When Hobbes says, "the greatest good for each is his own preservation . . . [because] nature is so arranged that all desire good for themselves," he seems to be conflating his stipulative sense of "good" with the ordinary sense of "good" (DH 11.6). By his stipulative definition of "good," everyone desires their own good whatever they desire. His semantics has everything to do with its truth, and nature has nothing to do with it. Nature is so arranged that people usually, not always, desire their self-preservation and usually, not always, their self-preservation is good. Even Hobbes sometimes recognizes that "the pains of life can be so great that . . . they may lead men to number death among the goods" (DH 11.6).

Our discussion of Hobbes's definition of "good" began with my quoting his remark that whatever is "the object of any man's appetite" is good. This quotation may slightly misrepresent Hobbes's view because he also says that the object of any man's appetite is whatever "he for his part calleth *good*" (L 6.7). Perhaps the phrase, "calleth *good*" is supposed to signal a hedge. If so, then Hobbes means that what a person calls "good" is not necessarily good. He is often represented as being content that what is good is whatever a person desires. In any case, he was merely describing what he thought was true about humans and not what he wished were true. In fact he loathed the consequences of the variability of goodness; for this variability causes conflict among people in the state of nature. Later we shall see how he gets rid of the conflict.

THE STATE OF NATURE

The state of nature is "the natural condition of mankind" (L 13). It has often been misunderstood to be the condition human beings were in when they were first created. But Hobbes, in *Leviathan*, denied that that is what he thought: "It may peradventure be thought there never was a time nor condition of war as this; and I believe it was never generally so, over all the world" (L 13.11). All for naught it seems, because his enemy, Bishop John Bramhall, misunderstood him: "The primogenious and most natural state of mankind was in Adam before his fall, that is, the state of innocence" (Bramhall 1658: 568), as have others since him. Hobbes's aspiration in philosophy was to construct complicated phenomena from simpler phenomena by deducing necessary propositions from other necessary propositions, which ultimately come from definitions. (See Chapter 5.) So, Hobbes begins with severely limited conceptual tools. Apropos his moral and political philosophy, he begins with two concepts, that of human beings and that of the state of nature, both of which are atemporal. He does not begin with the historically earliest period of human existence, but with the idea of what it is to be a human being in a condition in which there are no laws at all.

In other words, the state of nature should be understood in the first instance as a concept used in a thought experiment (cf. Pasquino 2001). If we begin with Hobbes's concept of the state of nature, it should be easy to reach the conclusion that he wants, namely, a general war of all against all. The state of nature is the condition of human beings when they are subject to no laws. (P1) follows from this:

> (P1) If a person is in the state of nature, then he is subject to no laws at all.

Reasoning semantically about the consequent of (P1), that is, about what law is, we infer:

> (P2) If a person is subject to no laws at all, then he has a right to all things.

(P2) is necessarily true because a law by definition takes away some right. This is implicit in the definition of law given in *Dialogue Between a Philosopher and a Student of the Common Laws*: "the command of him or them that have the sovereign power, given to those that be his or their subjects, declaring publicly and plainly . . . what they must forbear to do" (DPS 26). If a person must forbear doing *A*, then he has lost the right to do *A*.

If we now reason semantically about the consequent of (P2), we infer:

> (P3) If a person has a right to all things, then he has the right to anything that any other person has, including that other person's life.

(P4) follows from (P1) to (P3),

> (P4) If a person is in the state of nature, then he has the right to anything that another person has, including that other person's life.

Again, the underlying reason for (P4) is that since law restricts behavior, life without law is completely unrestricted.[4] (P4) would not pose a problem for human beings if everyone were absolutely altruistic. But people are not altruistic most of the time.

Hobbes does not need everyone to be altruistic most of the time. He can generate a war of all against all as long as human beings desire to live, the resources necessary for living are scarce and the population is dense enough to put people in contact with each other.

Hobbes does not mention either density or scarcity explicitly, although he alludes to scarcity when he refers to something "they cannot both enjoy" (L 13.3). The reason this is not a reference to scarcity is that even in a land flowing with milk and honey, aggressive people would come into conflict as long as one person was aggressive enough or stupid enough to want every object that someone else wanted. Given the desire for self-preservation, this condition inevitably leads to war.

Unfortunately, Hobbes does not deduce the universal condition of war in the state of nature from the modest principles of a desire to live, density, and scarcity. Rather he begins with equality.

EQUALITY

Hobbes says that in the state of nature, people are roughly equal, in both physical strength and intelligence, in the only dimension that really matters, ability to kill another person. He grants that some people are smarter than other people and some are physically stronger than others, "yet when all is reckoned together, the difference between man and man is not so considerable" as regards the likelihood of living a long time, because "the weakest has strength enough to kill the strongest, either by secret machination or by confederacy with others that are in like danger" (L 13.1). In the latter part of this quotation, Hobbes is thinking primarily of physical strength by itself as an equalizer. He then goes on to claim that there is "yet a greater equality amongst men than that of strength." People are roughly equal in intelligence. His justification for this claim is a bit odd: "for there is not ordinarily a greater sign of the equal distribution of anything than that every man is contented with his share" (L 13.2). One might well think that Hobbes is joking. Surely, he knew that there are great differences in intelligence. Those who think they are significantly more intelligent than most other human beings often press this point.

However, if Hobbes is joking[5] and actually thinks that there are large differences in intelligence, then his subsequent argument has a problem. He wants to argue that because people are roughly equal, there are no naturally superior people who have a natural right to govern in virtue of their superiority, *pace* Aristotle. So the existence of a naturally superior human being would seem to undermine his argument that a government rests on a covenant in which people give up their rights to another. Without equality, Hobbes cannot prove any of the laws of nature. This issue will be discussed more fully below.

In any case, I think that there is another reason why Hobbes believes in the general equality of human beings. He, like Descartes, thought that the key to scientific progress was not genius but method. From the right definitions, he claimed in *De corpore*, which will be discussed in Chapter 5, all knowledge is deducible. Descartes in *Rules for the Direction of the Mind* and in his *Meditations* had a different methodology. The important point is that they both thought that method, not natural talent, was what was crucial to scientific progress.

Whether humans are as equal as Hobbes indicates here, let's take him at his word because he uses equality in the next step of developing his moral philosophy. When people are competing for an object that cannot be shared, from "this equal ability ariseth equality of hope in the attaining of our end" (L 13.3). This is ambiguous. It means either (a) everyone thinks his chance of success is 50 percent or (b) for n people, each thinks his chance of success is 1 divided by n. It is also possible that (c) for any two people x and y, x's hope = y's hope. (They might each think that they have an 80 percent chance of success, or even 100 percent chance!) But I do not think Hobbes had (c) in mind. On any of these interpretations, what Hobbes says seems to be a non sequitur. Concerning (a), it obviously does not follow that each of the twenty-five people who know that he or she is roughly equal with the others will think that he or she has a 50 percent chance of success. Concerning (b), equal hope does not follow from equal ability. A pessimist rates his chances at less than 1 divided by n, and an optimist at more than that.

Hobbes's comment, "And therefore if any two men desire the same thing, which nevertheless they cannot both enjoy, they become enemies" (L 13.3), suggests that he has (a) in mind, because he wants to prove that every person is at war with everyone else, not just that there is war when two people exist together. So Hobbes really needs to argue from (b). However, (b) has its problems, as far as Hobbes's goals are concerned. If ten, twenty-five or 100 people are competing for the same moderately desirable object (and each is roughly equal in hope), then, even though their chances are equal, 10 percent, 4 percent or 1 percent, respectively, each will be disinclined to compete with the others because the chances of success are so low. Whether they will actually compete or not depends in part on how irrationally aggressive they are, or how great their needs are, and possibly other things. Not enough is known about the situation to say roundly what people would do, but enough is known to say that mere equality of chance or hope of getting the object is not sufficient to generate conflict.

Hobbes returns to the matter of equality two chapters later into *Leviathan*, when he deduces the ninth law of nature, against pride. What is important about this proof is that although he reaffirms his belief in the equality of all individuals, he also thinks that it is not crucial to his case that all people actually are equal. He says,

> For there are very few so foolish that had not rather govern themselves than be governed by others . . . If nature therefore hath made men equal that equality is to be acknowledged; or if nature have made men unequal, yet because men that think themselves equal will not enter into conditions of peace, but upon equal terms, such equality must be admitted. And therefore for the ninth law of nature, I put this, *that every man acknowledge another for his equal.*
>
> (L 15.21; see also DC 3.13)

Hobbes's political philosophy would have been stronger, I think, if in his chapter on the state of nature he had said that it does not matter whether people are actually equal or only think themselves equal. Moreover, I think his philosophy would have been stronger if he had recognized that people want "equal terms" not because they think their strength and intelligence is effectively equal to everyone else's but because each person thinks he deserves equal respect and equal regard, independently of whether or not he is as smart or as strong as others. At the Putney Debates of 1647, Colonel Rainborough, arguing for the rights of ordinary soldiers, said,

> I think that the poorest he that is in England hath a life to live, as the greatest he; and therefore, truly sir, I think it's clear, that every man that is to live under a government ought first to own by his own consent to put himself under that government; and I do think that the poorest man in England is not at all bound in a strict sense to that government that he hath not had a voice to put himself under.
>
> (Woodhouse 1992: 53)

Many people would prefer to die fighting than to live as slaves because of their sense of their own intrinsic worth. So a better foundation for the equality of human beings concerns their right to equal regard. But Hobbes could not have used this for his foundation, because "equal regard" is a normative notion, and he wants equality to be a natural and nonnormative property of people.

However this may be, competition can arise in the state of nature in some of the ways we have already described that do not depend on equality; and they are causes of war. Think of the nations that have fought over water, pasture, farm or oil. Competition results from scarcity and a density of population that puts people in contact with each other.

Whether competition derives from equality or some other source, Hobbes thinks that it lays the groundwork for another cause of war, "diffidence," that is, distrust. Since a person P1 knows that a person P2 is in competition for objects, P1 knows that it is rational for P2 to try to attack P1 preemptively in order to gain an advantage. This makes P1 diffident of P2 (L 13.4).

The circumstances of diffidence make things even worse than Hobbes indicates. P1 has the same reason to attack P2 preemptively that P2 has to attack P1; and P2 knows that P1 knows (or is likely to think) that P1 has a reason to attack P2 preemptively. So P2 has even greater reason to attack P1 preemptively. This in turn gives P1 more reason to attack P2 preemptively, ad infinitum. Although Hobbes says that diffidence, growing out of competition, is a second cause of war (L 13.4), it is more precise to say that competition, which itself may give rise to war, causes war by causing diffidence, which gives rise to a greater likelihood of war. Since competition causes diffidence, diffidence is not a second cause of war but a second way that competition causes war.

Another cause of war, a third cause by Hobbes's numbering, arises from the nature of some people, those who "taking pleasure in contemplating their own power in the acts of conquest . . . pursue farther than their security requires" (L 13.4). Glory seekers are warmongers. Moreover, their existence requires everyone else to be suspicious of them, and hence to be in a state of war. So whether or not one seeks glory for oneself, glory causes everyone to be at war with everyone else.

Although glory is one source of unwarranted aggression, some aggressiveness seems to be a brute fact and may spring from nothing other than itself. Unmotivated aggressiveness is just as bad as any other. Hobbes uses this fact in *De cive* to construct another argument that proves that if human beings lived without the protection of any laws whatsoever, then they would surely be in a state in which everyone would have to fear everyone. Surprisingly he does not repeat this argument in *Leviathan* or any other work. The heart of the argument is this:

The Great Fear and Danger Argument

(1) Some people are dangerous in the state of nature.
(2) It is not possible to know which people are dangerous.
   Therefore,
(3) It is necessary for a person to be afraid of everyone in the state of nature.[6]

The Great Fear and Danger Argument is so called, not because great fear is needed but because it is a great argument. It is great because it is so simple, compelling, and extendable to many other situations. Its premises are modest or logically weak. Premise (1) is uncontroversial. It can be verified either through an analysis of the nature of human beings or empirically. Many people "at the same time have appetites for the same thing," so they are in competition with other people (DC 1.6). Some people think they are better than others and thus want to dominate them, and the others need to fight back, sometimes by launching an attack preemptively (DC 1.5). When people are under the protection of a government, the danger from these people is greatly reduced because the fear of punishment checks their behavior. But The Great Fear and Danger Argument presupposes that there is no government to protect people. Premise (2) is equally easy to verify. People come into the world knowing nothing, and their ability to learn is finite and restricted to what they sense. Under these conditions it is necessary for a person to be afraid of everyone in the state of nature. This argument gets Hobbes all he needs from the state of nature.

Let's consider some of the corollaries of The Great Fear and Danger Argument within twenty-first-century American, and possibly European, society. Almost all schools have "Stranger Danger" programs for grammar-school children, who are taught in effect the following argument:

(1) Some strangers are dangerous to children.
(2) It is not possible to know which strangers are dangerous.
   Therefore,

(3) It is necessary for a child to be afraid of every stranger.

Policemen stop drivers with the following argument in mind:

(1) Some drivers are dangerous to policemen.
(2) It is not possible to know which drivers are dangerous.
Therefore,
(3) It is necessary for a policeman to be afraid of every driver.

Similar arguments can be constructed for feminists and minorities and other groups. I have been told that firefighters have their own version of it: some fires are dangerous.

In addition to the familiar three causes of war listed in Chapter 13 of *Leviathan*, Hobbes gives another list in Chapter 17:

(1) People "are continually in competition for honour and dignity."
(2) People compare themselves with others and want to be the one most eminent.
(3) People who think they are "wiser and abler to govern the public better than the rest" compete with each other.
(4) Through speech, people are able to make what is good look like it is evil and what is evil look like what is good.
(5) People need "a common power to keep them in awe and to direct their actions to the common benefit" and that power does not always exist or function as it should.

(L 17.7–12)

Hobbes believes that the proofs explained so far follow necessarily from various definitions. He realizes that some people may not be able to appreciate the force of these a priori arguments; so, he also offers a proof from experience. He says that anyone who arms himself when he takes a journey, anyone who locks his doors when he goes to sleep, and anyone who locks his chests in his own house accuses mankind. Hobbes turns the knife of the argument when he points out that to lock one's chests is to accuse one's children and one's servants (L 13.10). I think that his claim is too strong and unnecessarily so. There's a difference between accusing someone ("I think you are guilty of X") and being suspicious of someone ("It is possible that you may do X"). As The Great Fear and Danger Argument so nicely illustrates, universal fear does not require universal danger.

I said earlier that the state of nature should be considered first of all a concept in a thought experiment in order to resist the temptation of thinking that Hobbes is making a claim about primeval human beings. But concepts can be instantiated by various actual conditions, and Hobbes mentions three of them. One is the condition of savages. He thinks that "many places in America . . . have no government at all, and live at this day in that brutish manner, as I said before" (L 13.11). Another is the condition of national governments with each other: "[K]ings and persons of sovereign authority, because of their independency, are in continual jealousies, . . . having their weapons pointing and their eyes fixed on one another, that is, their forts, garrisons, and guns upon the frontiers of their kingdoms, and continual spies upon their neighbors, which is a posture of war" (L 13.12). The third instantiation of the state of nature is civil war. To some extent this was the instantiation that exercised Hobbes most. The English Civil War caused Hobbes to go into exile, depleted the nation's wealth, and shocked the people when a paralegal government beheaded King Charles I.

Hobbes summarizes his view of the state of nature in one of the most famous passages in philosophy:

In such condition [the state of nature] there is no place for industry, because the fruit thereof is uncertain; and consequently no culture of the earth; no navigation, nor use of the commodities that may be imported by sea; no commodious building; no instruments of moving and removing such things as require much force; no knowledge of the face of the earth; no account of time; no arts; no letters; no society; and which is worst of all, continual fear, and danger of violent death; and the life of man, solitary, poor, nasty, brutish and short.

(L 13.9)

What Hobbes is describing is the condition of war, which he defines as follows:

WAR consisteth not in battle only, or the act of fighting, but in a tract of time, wherein the will to contend by battle is sufficiently known; and therefore the notion of *time* is to be considered in the nature of war, as it is in the nature of weather. For as the nature of foul weather lieth not in a shower or two of rain, but in an inclination thereto of many days together, so the nature of war consisteth not in actual fighting, but in the known disposition thereto during all the time there is no assurance to the contrary. All other time is PEACE.

(L 13.8; EL 14.11)

One reason this passage is interesting involves the fact that Western philosophers traditionally have thought that one term of a pair of contradictories or contraries was better than the other.[7] This is crystal clear for the pairs, good and evil, and almost as clear for the pairs being and nonbeing, and male and female. It may be less clear for the pairs infinite and finite and rest and motion. The ancient Greeks preferred finitude to infinity because what is finite is complete and the infinite seemed incomplete; but Western medieval philosophers preferred infinity to finitude, because finitude was less than the greatest. Both the ancient Greeks and medieval philosophers preferred rest to motion, but preferred action, which might be seen as a kind of motion, to inaction. Often, though not universally, for a pair of contradictory terms, the term T that was considered better was usually defined directly and the other was defined simply as not-T.[8] Although logicians would not say that atomic sentences are better than molecular sentences, one might feel that atomic sentences are better because molecular sentences depend on atomic sentences. An atomic proposition is one in which no proper part is a proposition. A molecular proposition is not an atomic proposition. Often, though not always, definitions like this suggest that the favored term has something that the other term lacks. As regards the distinction between war and peace, it is natural to make peace the favored term and to say that it is the presence of tranquility or cooperation or something else, and that war is its absence. But Hobbes opposes this tradition. He reverses the normal priority of war and peace, and makes war, if not the favored term, at least the primary one. War, for Hobbes, is the natural condition of human beings. It is the presence of the will to "contend by battle." Peace is the time remaining. Later we will see that Hobbes also reverses the normal ordering of justice and injustice. Injustice is not keeping a covenant. Justice is not injustice.[9]

Hobbes's purpose in beginning with the concept of the state of nature was to show that human life is unlivable without government and that government must be strong enough to guarantee that it does not dissolve and send people back to the state of nature, although inevitably it will, because "nothing can be immortal which mortals make" (L 29.1). So, at the end of Chapter 13 of *Leviathan*, the question becomes "How can one move from the war of the state of nature to the peace of a civil state?" Hobbes says that it happens through a combination of the passions, which motivate people to get out of the state of nature, and reason, which shows people how to do it (L 13.13). The passions are fear of death, the desire to lead a comfortable life, and the hope that it is possible to achieve it. Surprisingly, little is said about these passions in his next chapter. Reason is prominent insofar as reasoning is displayed in the deduction of the laws of nature.

Hobbes's description of the state of nature as a state of war fits many international situations. Between the late 1940s and the early 1980s, the United States and the Soviet Union were said to be in a state of "cold war;" this meant that each feared that the other would attack and was prepared to attack the other if necessary, even though virtually no violence between Americans and Soviets occurred. As I

was writing the first draft of this chapter, the President of the
United States was threatening to invade Iraq and topple from power
Saddam Hussein. Although a formal declaration of war had not
been made, and although one might have considered the number
of sorties that American jet fighters had flown against Iraqi ground
installations to be below the threshold of war, the United States was
de facto at war. One might think that the conflict between the
United States and Iraq disconfirms Hobbes's claim that "individuals" in the state of nature are equal for all intent and purposes.
Although I sympathize with this view, there is something to be said
for the view that notwithstanding the awesome power of the
United States, that power is "equalized" over an extended period of
time. A small group of terrorists injured the United States greatly by
flying three passenger jet planes into three buildings. The United
States needed to devote extensive resources for "homeland
defense." Also, after the United States built up armed forces on the
border of Iraq in 2003, both North Korea and Iran decided to
restart their nuclear programs. The American show of force actually
weakened it so much that unfriendly nations were willing and able
to act in a way that the United States would not otherwise have
tolerated. As I am writing this final draft of this chapter, the United
States is considering redeploying some of its troops in South Korea
to Iraq, another sign of military weakness. And none of this mentions the fact that, despite American rhetoric, the opinion of the
United Nations, which has virtually no military power to speak of,
was important to the United States, because deep and widespread
opposition to the American policy against Iraq could have dire
economic consequences for the United States. Even if the United
States defeats Iraq handily, it could lose economic wars with other
nations if they unite to deprive the United States of natural
resources and favorable trade relations.[10]

How accurate is Hobbes's description of the state of nature as
applied to individuals? I think that if there were indeed no laws at
all, then with a little scarcity, and enough time, people would

descend into a condition where life was solitary, poor, nasty, brutish, and short. But I think that before many people reached that condition, they would certainly begin to form civil states, and this process would possibly not fit Hobbes's theory. First, experience does not afford people equal prudence. Some people learn from their mistakes and some don't, as numerous episodes of The Simpsons illustrate. Second, to some extent Hobbes considers physical strength and intelligence separately. This leaves out some important actual cases. Some people are both physically weak and seriously stupid. Although many of these people would die before or not long after becoming adults, there are some lower limits on how much strength and intelligence a person needs to survive, and these are far below the combined strength and intelligence of some other people. The weak, stupid people are natural subjects, in contrast with the physically strong and enormously intelligent people, who are natural leaders or sovereigns. Suppose one of them, Hercules, captures someone who is strong but stupid and someone weak and intelligent. Each captive could be kept in a pit or bound with ropes. During their captivity, Hercules could explain to the captives that it is to their advantage to make him their leader. The intelligent but weak captive would readily understand that his chances of survival are better if he obeys Hercules than they are if he goes it alone. And it would not take much intelligence for the stupid person to understand the same thing. If that person were so stupid as not to agree, Hercules could kill him and capture another, possibly with the help of the cunning of an intelligent person who has thrown in with Hercules. It would not take long to find someone smart enough to see the benefits of accepting Hercules as his leader and strong enough to benefit Hercules and his confederates. Once a few people have committed to Hercules, others would see the benefit of doing so because of Hercules's growing strength, and thus a state would emerge. What is important about this scenario is that Hercules would be a natural sovereign, someone who has a better claim than other people to be the leader. This contradicts Hobbes's view that all people are equal in the state of nature. I have not discussed any covenant that might have been made between Hercules and his subjects, because it is not necessary for my point. However, it would be easy enough to argue that Hercules and his subjects would have good reason to agree to a covenant on unequal terms. Hercules would give up less than his subjects because of his superior talents and would gain other advantages from his subjects. His subjects would give up some of their rights in exchange for greater protection and other benefits. The total amount of benefits distributed to Hercules and his subjects would be possible because civil states generate value (L 13.9).

Suppose a defender of Hobbes objects that it is only an accident that the stronger more intelligent person successfully captured a weaker or more stupid person. Sometimes the weaker or more stupid person will, with or without luck, kill the Hercules-like person. Such events do not disprove my point. All that is needed are some cases in which one person has a natural claim to leadership over other people, because Hobbes's theory cannot allow this. And there are other more serious counterexamples. Hobbes concedes that during a civil war people in the area are in a state of nature. However, it is obvious that in a civil war, there are armies that as a practical matter have overwhelming power over individuals. In these cases, the armies or the leader of the army are unequal to individual people. And it makes sense for them to align themselves with that naturally superior being.

THE RIGHT OF NATURE

Near the end of Chapter 13, when Hobbes is emphasizing the fact that the state of nature is a "war of every man against every other man," he says that during war "nothing can be unjust" (L 13.13). Moreover:

> The notions of right and wrong, justice and injustice, have there no place. Where there is no common power, there is no law; where no

law, no injustice. Force and fraud are in war the two cardinal virtues. Justice and injustice are none of the faculties neither of the body nor mind. These are qualities that relate to men in society, not in solitude.

(L 13.13)

This is a very strong statement, and difficult to reconcile with other things that Hobbes says, for example, in the next chapter, which deals with the laws of nature:

Covenants entered into by fear, in the condition of mere nature, are obligatory. For example, if I covenant to pay a ransom or service for my life to an enemy, I am bound by it. For it is a contract, wherein one receiveth the benefit of life, the other is to receive money or service for it . . . Therefore, prisoners of war, if trusted with the payment of their ransom, are obliged to pay it . . .

(L 14.27)

The easiest way to handle this apparent inconsistency is to interpret Hobbes as thinking of the state of nature in two different ways. The first or primary state of nature is the one discussed so far. It is the state of nature with no laws of any kind whatsoever. The second or secondary state of nature is the state of nature with the laws of nature added to it. The secondary state of nature is still a state of nature because it continues to be a condition of war, although the war need not be one of each individual against every other individual. The laws of nature permit temporary confederacies and other unions of convenience. The secondary state of nature is a condition intermediate between the primary state of nature and a civil state. Positing two states of nature in order to make sense of Hobbes's text is also consonant with Hobbes's synthetic method. He wants to begin with simple concepts or propositions and then add to them in order to see what these additions generate.

The state of nature gives a person the right of nature, which is the liberty each person has to use his own power as he wishes "for the preservation of his . . . life" (L 14.1; DC 1.9; cf. EL

14.7–10). The quoted phrase is important because it means that the right of nature is not unlimited right.[11] This limitation is effectively removed by what Hobbes says next: each man has the liberty of doing whatever he wants, which "in his own judgment and reason" he thinks provides the best means of achieving it (L 14.1). What Hobbes is doing here is moving from *what is the case* (what does preserve one's life) to *what someone* thinks *is the case* (what a person thinks or judges will preserve himself). Let's call this movement "the slide" from objectivity to subjectivity. Hobbes uses the slide in other crucial points in his philosophy. For example, later he slides from the objective fact that the sovereign is supposed to preserve the lives of his subjects to the subjective fact that the sovereign alone should judge what preserves the lives of his subjects. I think this slide is part of a general shift from objectivity to subjectivity in modern philosophy that is easily found in Descartes, Locke, Berkeley, and Hume.

The slide to the proposition that everyone has the right to do what seems best "in his own judgment and reason" justifies a person's doing things that do not achieve that end. If someone thinks that eating a radioactive candy bar will preserve his life, then he has the right to eat it, even though it will produce a painful death.

LIBERTY

The state of nature is a condition of unrestricted liberty. And liberty is "the absence of external impediments" (L 14.2; see also 21.1). For Hobbes, both animate and inanimate things can have liberty in the same sense. A river that runs unimpeded by a dam and other obstacles has as much liberty as a human being unimpeded by walls and other obstacles. Because it is odd to talk about rivers having liberty, Hobbes's position sounds better if his point is made using "free" and its cognates: an undammed river runs freely, just as a range animal or a doe or a human in the wild.

Liberty, as Hobbes defines it, is compatible with necessity. Recall that Hobbes is a determinist. Every event, and this includes every action, has a cause. If the immediate cause of some human action is some event internal to the person, then the action is free. If an external event is the immediate cause of an event, for example, the wind blowing a person down the street, then the event is not an action of the person. On Hobbes's criterion of freedom, a person whose actions are caused by a brain tumor or by a psychotic compulsion is still free because the immediate cause of action is internal. So Hobbes's view needs some refining, something to the effect that an event is a free human action just in case its immediate cause is some normal desire of a human being. Of course, this requires an explanation of "normal," something like, "not caused by a physical defect." It would then be debated what a physical defect is. It may be easy enough to get people to agree that behavior caused by a desire caused by a brain tumor is not normal and hence not an action.[12] But what about a chemical imbalance in the brain? The more an abnormal brain chemistry erases guilt, the more human beings are treated as machines. (See also Chapter 2.)

THE DEFINITION OF THE LAW OF NATURE

In The Elements of Law, Natural and Politic and De cive, Hobbes does not define "law of nature," but he does make clear that they are precepts and not in themselves genuine laws (EL 15.1). In De cive, he defines it as "the Dictate of right reason about what should be done or not done for the longest possible preservation of life and limb" (DC 2.1). In Leviathan, the nature of the laws of nature is not so clear. He defines a law of nature (lex naturalis) as

> [a] a precept or general rule, [b] found out by reason, [c] by which a man is forbidden [d] to do that which is destructive of his life, or taketh away the means of preserving the same, and to omit that by which he thinketh it may be best preserved.
>
> (L 14.3)

The letters I have inserted into the text indicate the four elements of the definition. The first is the easiest to understand. A precept or rule is a proposition that guides action. There are basically two kinds of precepts: counsels and commands (L 6.55). A counsel is a speech act in which the speaker expresses to an addressee a way of acting that the speaker believes will benefit the addressee. If a speaker S counsels an addressee A to do an action C, A is not obligated to do C. A can take it or leave it.[13] In contrast, a command is a speech act in which the speaker S expresses to an addressee A a way of acting that S believes will benefit S, according to Hobbes. A command creates an obligation on A in virtue of S's authority over A. Now, it would seem that in virtue of its name, a law of nature is a law, and hence a precept or rule that is given by a person who has authority. But who is or could be commanding a law of nature in the state of nature? The primary state of nature is a condition in which there is no authority of any kind. The secondary state of nature, which contains the state of nature, does not contain any human person or institution with authority to issue commands or make laws. There seems to be no alternative to God being the one who commands the law of nature. However, the proper place to consider this question is in connection with clause [c]. (We will get to [b] in a moment.) Unfortunately, clause [c] does not contain a clear answer to our question. It is cast in the despicable passive voice; it says that a person "is forbidden" but it does not say who is doing the forbidding. Any hope that the Latin version of *Leviathan* will resolve the indeterminacy is dashed as soon as one reads that a law of nature is a precept or general rule by which "prohibetur" ("it is prohibited"), with no mention of who or what is doing the prohibiting.

There are three plausible ways of resolving the indeterminacy of the passive construction:

(i)   Each person commands himself to preserve his life. The problem with this interpretation is that "x commands y" expresses an irreflexive relation. No one can command one's self, because, as Hobbes says, anyone who commands someone to do something can also release that person from the command. So, "commanding one's self" is an empty verbal form, the husk of a command.

(ii) The second way to interpret [c] is to hold that reason commands the law. This interpretation is supported in the English version by the fact that shortly after the definition Hobbes says that in the state of nature "every one is governed by his own reason" (L 14.4). The problem with this interpretation is that according to Hobbes, reason does not do anything. Hobbes downgrades reason's traditional high status by saying that it is nothing else than the addition and subtraction of the consequences of general names agreed upon for the marking and signifying of our thoughts (L 5.2). (This will be discussed in more detail in Chapter 5.) Reason sets no goals, neither preservation of life nor destruction of life. Goals are determined by desires; reason is used to figure out the means to satisfy those desires.

(iii) The third interpretation of [c] is that God commands the laws of nature. One advantage of this interpretation is that God certainly seems to have the authority to make commands. Also, Hobbes sometimes says that God commands them, for example, the laws of nature are "delivered in the word of God that by right commandeth all things" (L 15.41). In Chapter 31, "Of the Kingdom of God by Nature," Hobbes says part of the "knowledge of civil duty" is to know what the laws of God are, and these laws of God he identifies as the laws of nature (L 31.1). Further, when Hobbes distinguishes the ways in which God declares his laws, the first is "by the dictates of *natural reason*" (L 31.3). This claim explicitly connects condition [c] with condition [b]. Several objections can be raised against (iii). The first is that *The Elements of Law, Natural and Politic* and *De cive* seem to answer the question, "Who commands laws of nature," by denying the presupposition that they are laws. In these two works, as mentioned above, Hobbes is clear that the laws of nature in themselves are counsels. Whose counsels? Possibly each person counsels herself. Alternatively, reason could command the laws of nature because "*true reason is a certain law*" (DC 1.1). There are replies to both of these suggestions. The problem with the latter one, that reason commands and is a law, is that this view is at odds with the idea of reason as reckoning in *Leviathan*. Reckoning tells one how to achieve a goal that one has; it does not suggest or command one to have any goal. The problem with the former suggestion is that the language of *Leviathan* suggests that Hobbes changed his mind about the character of the laws of nature. If the laws of nature are counsels, then they are not obligatory. Some scholars think that the fact that the laws of nature obligate (only) *in foro interno* (L 15.36) means that they do not obligate. But even if that view is inherently contradictory – obligations that are not obligations – counsels do not even obligate *in foro interno* by virtue of the fact that they are counsels, not laws or commands.

Those who do not think that the laws of nature are laws often quote the last paragraph of Chapter 15 of *Leviathan* in defense of their position:

> These dictates of reason men use to call by the name of laws, but improperly; for they are but conclusions or theorems concerning what conduceth to the conservation and defence of themselves; whereas laws, properly, is the word of him that by right hath command over others. But yet if we consider the same theorems as delivered in the word of God that by right commandeth all things, then are they properly called.
>
> (L 15.41; cf. DC "Preface")

A proponent of (iii) will claim that the objector is misreading this passage. Notice, he will say, that the subject of the first sentence is not "The laws of nature" but "These dictates of reason." The difference is enormous. A law and a counsel, discovered by reason, are both dictates. A dictate is the content of either a law or counsel. It is propositional in form. For example, "that you seek peace" or "that you lay down your right to all things." These propositions do not in themselves guide action at all, any more than the proposition, "that dogs have four feet" does. Propositions are merely descriptive. Propositions can be made action-guiding by adding a certain formula or a force to them. They can be commanded or counseled. Thus, someone might say "I command that you seek peace" or "I counsel that you seek peace." Commands and counsels are neither true nor false, but obeyed or disobeyed, or followed or not followed, respectively.

Moreover, since Hobbes says, "These dictates men use to call by the name of laws, but improperly," he is presupposing that he is not using the name "law" improperly, and this correctness of usage is one of his principal methodological goals. If he thought that not only men in the past, but he too, used the phrase "law of nature" improperly, he would have said something like, "These dictates I (like men before me) call 'laws' but improperly . . ."

The last paragraph of Chapter 15 contains more evidence for interpretation (iii). Hobbes says, "But yet if we consider the same theorems as delivered in the word of God that by right commandeth all things, then are they properly called *laws*" (L 15.41). And, to repeat, Hobbes said that God does declare his law by the dictates of natural reason (L 31.3). I can imagine someone wanting, not so much more evidence that Hobbes says that the laws of nature are God's laws, but a better reason to believe that they are God's laws. I don't think any good reason can be given. More to the point, Hobbes would not have tried to give any better reason because he, like virtually every other intellectual before the Glorious Revolution, did not think one was necessary. John Selden, a friend of Hobbes and one who is sometimes thought to be an atheist, said in private, "I cannot fancy to myself what the law of nature means, but the law of God" (quoted from Martinich 1992: 381, n. 10). Hobbes himself said, "there is no doubt but they [the laws of nature] are the law of God" (L 33.22) and "There is no doubt but they [the laws of nature] were made laws by God himself" (L 42.37). Sometimes a philosopher does not prove a proposition because no one disputes it.

(iv) The fourth interpretation is that "is commanded" is used loosely or metaphorically. The phrase, "a law of nature" grammatically requires someone to make or command it. But since no one and nothing actually commands a law of nature, some circumlocution is necessary to get around that grammatical requirement. Hobbes solved the problem by using the passive voice. A problem with this interpretation is that Hobbes professedly will have no truck with metaphors in science: metaphors "can never be true grounds of any ratiocination" (L 4.4).

(v) A fifth interpretation may be considered a supplement to (iv). Hobbes could not make up his mind whether the laws of nature were genuine laws or merely counsels. So he spoke of them in two ways, sometimes suggesting that they were genuine laws and sometimes suggesting that they were not. My reservation about this interpretation is that although Hobbes says the laws of nature "conduceth to the conservation and defense" of people (which is true if they are laws), he never explicitly says that they are counsels.

Fortunately, we can continue with the exposition of the laws of nature without definitively settling this question. The next element of the definition of a law of nature to consider is [b], the phrase "found out by reason." Natural-law theorists typically hold that people know the laws of nature either because they are innate ("written on the heart") or deduced. Hobbes thinks that they are not innate because all knowledge arises from sensation; the phrase "written on the heart" is a metaphor that means that almost everyone is able to know them (EL 10.7; L 36.6 and 42.37), and they come to know them by reason.

Coming to know the laws of nature by reason satisfies the standard requirement that a law be promulgated. This is a requirement because laws are supposed to guide the conduct of people and people cannot be expected to guide their conduct by something of which they are ignorant. What makes condition [b] difficult is the question of the exact relation between the definition of a law of nature, the laws of nature themselves, and the actual way that the laws are derived. Are they deduced? And if they are, what is the form of the deduction? Let's put this matter aside until after [d] is discussed because the interpretation of [d] is material to the deductions.

The main issue is whether the last clause, the one following "and," adds something substantial to the first clause. I am referring to this clause: "to do that which is destructive of his life, or taketh away the means of preserving the same, *and* to omit that by which he thinketh it may be best preserved." (The disjunctive clause is not problematic.)

According to one interpretation, the content of every law is two-fold or conjunctive. One part forbids doing something that takes away life; the other part forbids not doing what a person thinks will preserve it. I think the conjunction is not important because the second conjunct, omitting what preserves a life, is an instance of the first conjunct. That is, since omitting what a person thinks will preserve his life is one of the particular ways that the first conjunct forbids in general, it is not necessary to think of the laws as having a conjunctive structure.

THE DEDUCTION OF THE LAWS OF NATURE

We can now take on the major task of explaining how the laws of nature are to be deduced. In *The Elements of Law, Natural and Politic* Hobbes neatly connects the first law with his point that people are equal in the state of nature: "[I]t is supposed from the equality of strength and other natural faculties of men, that no man is of might sufficient, to assure himself for any long time, of preserving himself thereby, whilst he remaineth in the state of hostility and war"

(EL 14.14; DC 1.15 and 2.3). Hence, a man should seek peace as far as possible *and* defend himself against those who will not make peace. The conjunctive nature of the first law of nature is even more pronounced in *De cive*: "[P]eace is to be sought after, where it may be found; and where not, there to provide ourselves for helps of war" (DC 2.1). The law as formulated in these two early works has led many scholars to think that the first law as formulated in *Leviathan* is also conjunctive. But a close reading of *Leviathan* shows that that is not so.

Hobbes says, "And consequently it is a precept, or general rule of reason *that every man ought to endeavor peace, as far as he has hope of obtaining it; and when he cannot obtain it, that he may seek and use all the helps and advantages of war*" (L 14.4). Although the phrase, "a precept, or general rule of reason" suggests that everything italicized is the first law, Hobbes's next sentence rules out that reading: "The first branch of which rule containeth the first and fundamental law of nature, which is *to seek peace and follow it*. The second [branch], the sum of the right of nature, which is *by all means we can to defend ourselves*" (L 14.4). The two branches that Hobbes is referring to are the two italicized conjuncts of the precept or general rule. Recall that although all laws are precepts and rules, not all precepts and rules are laws. And Hobbes is saying that only the part about peace is "the first and fundamental law of nature;" the rest of the precept and general rule is "the sum of the right of nature."

Let's now consider the proof of the first law.

[In the state of nature] no man is of might sufficient, to assure himself for any long time, of preserving himself thereby . . .; reason therefore dictateth to every man for his own good, to seek after peace, as far forth as there is hope to attain the same; and to strengthen himself with all the help he can procure, for his own defense against those, from whom such peace cannot be obtained; and to do all those things which necessarily conduce thereunto.

(EL 14.14)

In this passage from The Elements of Law, Natural and Politic, Hobbes grounds peace in equality: "[N]o man is of might sufficient, to . . . [preserve] himself." He does the same in De cive: people cannot "expect any lasting preservation . . . by reason of that equality of power . . . [Therefore] to seek peace" is the law of nature (DC 1.15; see also EL 14.14).

The proof in Leviathan is different. It seems to depend on the essence of the right of nature: "[B]ecause the condition of man . . . is a condition of war of every one against every one . . . it followeth that in such a condition every man has a right to every thing, even to one another's body. . . . And consequently . . . *every man ought to endeavor peace, as far as he has hope of obtaining it*" (L 14.4). Here the argument turns, not on equality, but on the danger of war. If equality were the only way to generate war, then this point would be unimportant, but we have seen that there are other ways of generating conflict, for example, from competition, diffidence, and glory. (See "Equality", pp. 65–77 above.)

One way to represent Hobbes's argument uses indirect proof:

To prove: a person endeavors peace

(1) A person does not do what is destructive of his life. (Content of the definition of the law of nature.)
(2) A person does not endeavor peace. (Supposition for *reductio*.)
(3) If a person does not endeavor peace, then a person does what is destructive of his life. (From the definition of "not endeavoring peace.")
(4) A person does what is destructive of his life. (From 3 and 2 by *modus ponens*.)
(5) A person does what is destructive of his life and a person does not do what is destructive of his life. (From 4 and 1 by conjunction.)
(6) Therefore, a person endeavors peace. (From 5 by *reductio ad absurdum*.)

QED

For the sake of simplicity, propositions (2) and (3) leave out certain qualifying phrases, such as "as far as he has hope of obtaining it," but these omissions do not change the substance of the argument. Also, notice that the premises and the conclusion are propositions, not imperatives ("Seek peace"), or performative utterances ("I command/counsel that you seek peace"). Proofs prove propositions by performing operations on propositions. Imperatives and performative utterances are not themselves propositions and hence neither true nor false. The command, "close the door" may be obeyed or disobeyed, but it is neither true nor false. The force of an imperative is separable from the proposition it is attached to. (Of course, a proposition could be generated from a command, for example, "You close the door," but that is not to the point.)

If the pattern of proof of the first law of nature is accepted, then the proofs of the other laws of nature are straightforward. The same general pattern of *reductio ad absurdum* can be used. Here's a proof of the second law:

To prove: a person is willing (when others are too) to lay down his right to all things

(1) A person endeavors peace. (First law of nature.)
(2) It is not the case that a person is willing (when others are too) to lay down his right to all things. (Supposition for *reductio*.)
(3) If it is not the case that a person is willing (when others are too) to lay down his right to all things, then there is no reason for other people to lay down their right to all things. (Analytic.)
(4) If there is no reason for other people to lay down their right to all things, then a person does not try to get out of the state of nature. (Analytic.)
(5) If a person does not try to get out of the state of nature, then he remains in the state of nature. (Analytic.)
(6) If a person remains in the state of nature, then he does not endeavor peace. (Analytic.)

(7) A person does not endeavor peace. (From 2 and 3–6 by four uses of *modus ponens*.)

(8) A person endeavors peace and does not endeavor peace. (From 1 and 7 by conjunction.)

(9) A person is willing (when others are too) to lay down his right to all things. (From 8 by *reductio ad absurdum*.)

QED

This proof is tedious and more explicit than Hobbes's text. But propositions (3)–(6) are supposed to show the conceptual connections between laying down one's rights and the state of nature, peace, and the means to peace.

In *Leviathan*, Hobbes pauses at this point to consider the main concept in the second law, namely, that of laying down a right, and then to introduce some additional concepts that will be important to the third law of nature.

To lay down a right, for Hobbes, is to lose that right. There are two ways to do this. One is to renounce it; the other is to transfer it. To renounce a right to *x* is to stand out of the way of anyone else using or taking *x*. In the state of nature, to renounce a right is not to give anyone else any additional right since everyone already has a right to everything. Renouncing a right to *x* simply removes one impediment to the use of *x* by other people (L 14.6–7). I think that Hobbes has no special interest in the concept of renouncing a right. He mentions it primarily to help clarify the other way of laying down a right, that is, transferring a right.

Transferring a right is not merely standing out of the way of others and removing an impediment. It is intending that some particular person (or persons) benefit from that action. There are three ways to transfer a right: by gift, by contract, and by covenant. First, when a person gives a gift, he intends the person to whom he gives it to keep and enjoy it. But once the transference of the gift occurs, the donor does not have any responsibility to ensure that the receiver keeps and enjoys it. If a donor gives someone a book as a present, she does not have any responsibility to make sure that the book is not stolen or damaged. In giving the gift, the donor alienates her right to it and thereby terminates her responsibilities for it. Second, concerning transferring a right by contract, suppose one person P1 makes the following contract with another person P2: P1 will transfer his right to $100 to P2 if and only if P2 transfers to P1 his right to a particular horse. Again, once the transfer has occurred (including the delivery of the required objects), P1 and P2 no longer have any responsibility to ensure that the receiver keeps and enjoys what was acquired. In contracting, people alienate their rights, with no obligation to act in some specified way in the future. The third way of transferring a right is similar to contracting, but is slightly more complicated. Sometimes people make an agreement that calls for future performance by one or both parties. While most people informally call this "a contract," Hobbes wants to use either the term "pact" (*pactum*) or the term "covenant" as a technical term for this kind of transferring (L 14.11). The nonchalant way that Hobbes introduces this concept belies its importance. I think that Hobbes chose "covenant" for political reasons. The Scots and the English, the first by the National Covenant and the second by the Solemn League and Covenant, had covenanted to defend the king, but members of both groups supported fighting against the king and finally executing him, actions that Hobbes condemned.

Also, the origin of a civil state or government depends on a pact or covenant, namely, a pact or covenant among people who become subjects by mutually transferring some of their rights to a sovereign.[14] This transfer of right would seem to be completed as soon as the required utterance, ritual, or sign occurs (L 14.14). However, the subjects acquire an obligation to help the sovereign govern as long as the sovereign exists. The reason seems to depend on Hobbes's principle that "Whoever has a right to the end has a right to the means," the "Right-to-Means Principle." When a subject transfers his right to govern himself to the sovereign, the subject acquires the obligation to ensure that the sovereign can use the right, as long as the sovereign has that right.

Since Hobbes often appeals to the Right-to-Means Principle, it makes sense to realize that it seems to be false. Suppose something that belongs to no one is potentially available to several people. That is, suppose a meteorite falls to earth, equidistant from two or more people, on unowned land. (The people are members of a civil state.) Both have a right to the meteorite, but neither has a right to kill the other to get it, even if that is the only way for either to get it. A more mundane example is that everyone in the United States has a right to buy a Hummer, but no one has a right to the means necessary for buying that vehicle if the means necessary is the robbing of a bank.

It might seem that although the Right-to-Means Principle is false for liberty rights, like the two just described, the principle is true for claim rights; that is, it is true for those rights in which the person with the right has a claim against other people to secure that right. Suppose an institution bestows a claim right to decent housing on every member of the institution. Then, one might infer, any member without decent housing has a right to get decent housing by any means necessary. But this inference is too strong. The claim right to decent housing means that there is an obligation on someone or something to provide a means by which the person with the claim right can have housing. But, the person with the claim right cannot use any means necessary to exercise that right. If the only way that one member could get decent housing is by evicting someone else with the same right, neither the member nor the institution would have the right to evict that person.

Although the Right-to-Means Principle is too strong as stated, a weaker principle seems to be true: the "Some-Right-to-Means Principle" says that if someone P1 has a claim right to something O, then someone or something P2 has an obligation to use some specifiable means to ensure that P1 can exercise P1's right to O. If Patty has a right to decent housing, created by the United States

Congress, then the United States Congress has an obligation to raise funds to pay for decent housing for Patty.

So, what is crucial to the concept of covenanting is that the person transferring his right to another acquires an obligation to provide certain specifiable means that will enable the recipient of the right to enjoy the right he has been given. This is a special kind of obligation, because obligation is created whenever a person lays down a right, whether it is by transferring or renouncing.

Hobbes says, "And when a man hath in either manner abandoned or granted away his right, then is he said to be OBLIGED or BOUND, . . . and that he *ought*, and it is DUTY" (L 14.7). His use here of the phrase "then is he said to be" may sound like a hedge. A cruel and unscrupulous person who gives one million dollars to a charity in order to accumulate accolades *is said to be* a humanitarian, especially by the trustees of the charity, even when they and most other people know that he is not. But I don't think that Hobbes is using the phrase as a hedge.[15] He often uses the phrase "is said to be X" when there is no question that he is talking about X. His view, I believe, is that having an obligation is simply a consequence of the transfer. That is, "x lays down a right to y" entails "x has an obligation and duty and ought to act in some specific way." Having an obligation does not hook a person up with some nonnatural or quasi-natural moral property or anything that is obligation itself.[16] If a person lays down his right to something, then he ought to do something. That is part of the meaning of "ought." There is nothing more to the matter than that. Obligations are supposed to bind people, but the bonds are weak because they get their strength, "not from their own nature (for nothing is more easily broken than a man's word)," but from "fear of some evil consequence upon the rupture" (L 14.7). Because obligations in themselves are weak, the sovereign will have to have power to make sure that citizens fulfill their obligations.

Some scholars, intent on maintaining that the laws of nature are merely prudential and not obligatory, try to explain away Hobbes's assertion that a person laying down his right is "OBLIGED" by appealing to a distinction between having an obligation and being obliged. The victim of an armed robber, it is said, is obliged to hand over her money because of the threat of violence, but there is no obligation to do so. However, this sense of "obliged" does not fit Hobbes's use of the word. For him, to be obliged is to have an obligation. This is clear from Latin versions of *Leviathan* and *De cive*, where for "is obliged" Hobbes uses the appropriate form of *debere* or *obligare*, both of which relate to having an obligation, not to be obliged in some special sense (DC 2.14 and L 14.7).

In the passage being considered, *Leviathan* Chapter 14, paragraph 7, Hobbes also claims that if someone does not do his duty as required by laying down his right, then that person has committed an injustice. That is, injustice could arise even if there were only two laws of nature, and no government existed. Further, there are other reasons for thinking that a person or an action can be just or unjust in the state of nature, but these are best considered in connection with the third law of nature.

Let's first consider a possible problem left over from our discussion of equality. I claimed that Hobbes did not need to maintain that everyone in the state of nature is equal in order to show that it is a war of each against all. And I mentioned that in his proof of the ninth law of nature Hobbes points out that one should treat everyone as if they were equal even if they are not. The possible problem to consider is whether abandoning the proposition that everyone is equal undermines his argument for the second law. Indeed, if people are unequal in ability, then the "be contented with so much liberty against other men as he would allow other men against himself" no longer holds (L 14.5). However, that result is not devastating because a weaker but adequate form of the second law is probable.

It is rational *ceteris paribus* for a person threatened with death to make a covenant with one or more people, some of whom may be stronger or more intelligent, on unequal terms. If the choice is between dying and giving some people two votes instead of one or transferring 50 percent of one's wealth instead of 10 percent, the unequal terms are rational.

So, the second law of nature could be framed in this way: That a man be willing, when others are so too, as far forth as for peace and defense of himself he shall think it necessary, to lay down this right to all things, and be contented with so much liberty against other men as he needs to survive. (I leave the proof as an exercise.)

We will now consider the third law of nature. Hobbes says that if people do not perform their covenants, then "covenants are in vain and but empty words; and the right of all men to all things remaining, we are still in the condition of war" (L 15.1). The underlying argument seems to be this: suppose that people did not (ever) perform their covenants made (supposition for the reduction). Then covenants would not really exist ("vain and empty words"); and if covenants did not really exist, then people could not transfer (any part of) their right to all things (second law of nature); and people would not seek peace. But this latter proposition contradicts the first law of nature. Therefore, people perform their covenants.

I think that Hobbes's argument is unsound, because, covenants are not the only way to transfer rights; they can also be transferred through a gift (L 14.12). Hence, Hobbes's proof of the third law is defective. However, the defect is easily repaired by circumventing the second law of nature. The third follows from the first law of nature and an analysis of the conditions necessary for a covenant:

To prove: a person keeps his covenants
(1) A person seeks peace. (First law of nature.)
(2) If a person does not keep his covenants, then he does not seek peace. (Analytic.)
    Therefore,
(3) A person keeps his covenants. (From 2 and 1 by modus tollens and double negation.)

No defense of (2) should be necessary. A person who does not keep his covenant angers the other party, and anger leads to fighting. And notice that equality of persons is not used as a premise.

Hobbes claims that the third law is "the fountain and original of JUSTICE" (L 15.2). This is odd because he already claimed in his discussion of the second law that a person can be unjust if he does not fulfill his duty when he lays down a right (L 13.7). And this duty does not depend on the existence of a covenant. If a person renounces a right or transfers one by a gift, then he acts unjustly if he tries to repossess the right. However, whether justice were to arise from the second or the third law of nature, there would be a serious problem with understanding Hobbes's views, for he also wrote that in the state of nature "nothing can be unjust." He continues: "[T]he notions of right and wrong, justice and injustice, have there no place. Where there is no common power, there is no law; where no law, no injustice" (L 13.13). He repeats this view later: "Therefore before the names of just and unjust can have place, there must be some coercive power to compel men equally to the performance of their covenants by the terror of some punishment greater than the benefit they expect by the breach of their covenant" (L 15.3). I wish that my distinction between the primary and secondary state of nature could help us here, but it does not because Hobbes emphasizes that the problem is the lack of a common power, and not just any common power. He specifically says that there is no such power "before the erection of the commonwealth" (L 15.3). I don't know of any wholly satisfactory answer to this problem. An ameliorating comment is that Hobbes is exaggerating when he says that there is no justice or injustice before the existence of a common power. But it is obvious how weak this comment is. (On the issue of whether the laws of nature bind in the state of nature, see below.)

One final question about justice in the state of nature might be asked: can people be just or unjust if people make no covenants? On first sight it would appear that the answer must be negative. However, because of the way Hobbes defines "just" and "unjust," a person who makes no covenants ends up being a just person by default. He defines "injustice" as "the not performance of covenant" and then "justice" as "whatever is not injustice."[17] So anyone who makes no covenant does not not [sic] perform a covenant and hence is not unjust and hence is just.

LAWS AND PROPOSITIONAL FORM

Before we continue with the other laws of nature, let me add to my earlier discussion about the grammatical form of laws. Laws, that is, sentences that regulate behavior, either take the imperative mood, "Do not exceed the speed limit," or contain a modal word that indicates what is prohibited, "People under twenty-one may [must] not drink alcoholic beverages," and "Everyone riding on a motorcycle must wear a helmet." As such, they are neither true nor false. This is obvious for the sentences in the imperative mood, but it also holds for the sentences with the modal verb. They express what is to be done, not what is or is not done. For the most part, Hobbes expresses the laws of nature in the subjunctive,[18] which may be used for commands but is also used for precepts more broadly. It is plausible that the laws[19] that Hobbes purports to prove are propositional in form, as one would expect the conclusion of a proof to be. This is true of the following laws: 2–5, 7–13, 15–17, 19, and 20 (L R&C 5). Only four laws, 1, 6, 14, and 18, are not of this form. Because it is natural to put laws into the imperative or to insert some modal element and Hobbes did not put most of his laws into that form, it is plausible that he did so intentionally and that when he did use the imperative or modal form, he unwittingly slipped into the more natural forms.

Why did Hobbes prefer the propositional form? The answer needs to be conjectural. One conjecture holds that he did it because he thought the laws of nature were not really laws. I don't find this conjecture compelling because Hobbes needs the laws of nature to move people to act in order to get out of the state of nature. So they must be of the form of a command or counsel. My own guess is that the laws are propositional because (1) they are being deduced and Hobbes only knew about deducing propositions from propositions; and (2) the force of the laws does not come from their propositional content, but from the person who issues the laws. Recall that commands and counsels have two parts: a propositional part and a "force" part. The force with which the proposition is expressed depends upon whether the speaker has authority over the addressee or not and whether the proposition is offered for the good of the speaker or the good of the addressee.[20]

The fact that the propositions of the laws of nature benefit the addressee suggests that they are counsels. But counsels can be taken or ignored. What Hobbes needs is something about the laws of nature that will motivate people to act. Those who think the laws of nature are laws and hence commands think that fear of punishment is the motivation. Many of those who think they are counsels think, roughly, that the knowledge that following them satisfies their desires is the motivation. The question of whether the laws of nature are laws or not remains open.

OTHER LAWS OF NATURE

From the fourth law on, most of the laws of nature sketch a conventional morality. The fourth law of nature is that a person who receives a gift from another person not cause that person to regret giving it (L 15.16). The ungracious behavior that would cause a person to regret giving a gift would directly incline the donor to not make peace with the ingrate. And there is another reason to avoid being ungracious. A donor may give someone a gift in order to show that person that he can be trusted and is willing to engage in mutual help, both of which are quasi-necessary conditions for making a covenant that creates a government. This point can be made more strongly.

In my discussion of the third law of nature, I said that Hobbes's own proof of it was defective because he did not consider the possibility that rights can be transferred by gift. This fact can be used in constructing a way that governments can be created. If person A sees that person B is transferring his right to person S, then person A may transfer her right to govern herself to person S, because A will see that A is more likely to be protected from others if S has the power of S, B and A. A is not covenanting with either S or B, and is not transferring her right on the condition that B transfers his right. A is imitating B's behavior because A sees that it is in A's self-interest to do so. This process could occur indefinitely, and the more often it does occur, the more reason a person has to join in. The reason that B would begin the gift-giving process is that B sees that his life has a better chance of being preserved if he transfers his right to S. And B has the hope that S will act kindly towards B because B hopes that S will observe the fourth law of nature, that a person who receives a benefit from another through a gift should not cause the giver to regret his action.

The fifth law is "COMPLAISANCE" (cooperativeness) "that every man strive to accommodate himself to the rest" (L 15.17).[21] This law does not depend on equality. Accommodation contributes to peace, *ceteris paribus*, whether the complaisant person is superior or inferior to the other. The sixth law is "PARDON," that a person forgive another person for past offences when that person repents and desires forgiveness. The seventh law is that punishment is justified by only the prospect of correcting the offender or deterring others from committing the same crime. In particular, Hobbes objects to taking pleasure in hurting another person, because it is pointless. These latter two laws also do not depend on equality.

I will mention only some of the remaining laws of nature to give some sense of their range and conventionality: the eleventh is that a judge is to treat all parties equally. The fourteenth is that when things cannot "be divided nor enjoyed in common," the law of nature holds that the question of ownership should be decided by lots; primogeniture is a natural form of lots. The seventeenth is that no man is to be his own judge; the eighteenth is that no man with an interest in the outcome of a dispute is to be a judge (L 15.21, 23,

31–2). Hobbes says that there are other laws of nature that pertain to "the destruction of particular men, as drunkenness, and all other parts of intemperance;" but he does not enumerate them because they are not directly related to political philosophy (L 15.34).

WHEN DO THE LAWS APPLY?

Do the laws of nature operate in the state of nature? It would seem that they have to because if they do not, then the first three would not operate, and hence there would be no way for people to get out of the state of nature, and one purpose of those laws is to enable people to get out of it. Further, as indicated above, Hobbes mentions other situations in which people have obligations in the state of nature, and they can only have obligations if at least the second law of nature is operating (L 14.27). Also, his position that covenants in the state of nature are not strengthened by oaths presupposes that there are such covenants (L 14.31).

ETERNAL NATURAL LAWS

The laws of nature are eternal for at least two reasons: (a) Their negations can never be laws, because the laws are necessary truths that follow from the definition of "a law of nature" (L 15.38); and (b) they did not come into being at any time. Reason (b) actually follows from (a). Necessary truths of any kind, such as the laws of arithmetic or geometry, are eternal. The laws of God can be divided into two groups, natural and positive. The positive ones come into being at some particular time for some particular group of people, for example, the Israelites. But the laws of nature hold for all people for all time.

However, the fact that the laws of nature are eternal does not entail that a person who knows them always has to act on them. If after making a covenant, a person discovers that some new danger has arisen which would jeopardize his life if he were to fulfill his covenant, then that person is released from his obligation (L 14.18). This suggests that there are other situations in the state of nature when a person must fulfill his covenant in the state of nature. This is confirmed by Hobbes's example of a man who covenants to pay ransom: "Covenants entered into by fear, in the condition of mere nature, are obligatory. For example, if I covenant to pay a ransom or service for my life to an enemy, I am bound by it. For it is a contract, . . . and consequently, where no other law (as in the condition of mere nature) forbiddeth the performance, the covenant is valid" (L 14.27; see also EL 15.13). Unfortunately, as I have mentioned before, Hobbes seems to contradict himself. In a marginal note, he writes that the laws of nature oblige "only where there is security" (L 15.36). And, since the state of nature is a war of all against all, it seems that one is never secure and hence that one never has to fulfill his covenant.

I don't know of an honest way to make Hobbes consistent. I think more weight should be given to the position that it is possible to be obliged in the state of nature for the reason mentioned above: if it is impossible to make covenants in the state of nature, then it is impossible to get out of it by covenanting to form a government. One might think that this can be gotten around by holding that such a covenant is not really made in the state of nature because the sovereign-making covenant is simultaneous with the creation of the government and hence is outside of the state of nature. This ploy will not work. Hobbes realized that covenants take time. One often covenants to create a government before the type of government is settled. The type of government calls for separate negotiation. If a majority agrees about the type of government, it is put into effect. If a majority does not agree, then the covenanters return to the state of nature. In either case, a covenant by which the people were obligated existed.

THE FOOL

There is another threat to the operation of the laws of nature. The book of Psalms refers to the fool who says in his heart that there is no God. Hobbes modernizes the fool to have him say that "there is no such thing as justice" (L 15.4).[22] The fool holds that since every person is committed to preserving himself, if a conflict arises between acting "justly" and acting in his own self-interest, reason dictates that the fool should act in his own self-interest. And the fool claims that his view is supported by reason itself. The fool acknowledges that a person who acts in his own self-interest and does not keep his covenant will be said to be unjust, but that is unimportant, because he will actually not be unjust. What is important, according to the fool, is achieving the goal of staying alive and, if possible, living comfortably. So, if a person could get to heaven "by unjust violence," he should.[23]

Hobbes clearly thinks that the fool is a fool, but how he shows that the fool's reasoning is defective is notoriously obscure. An example of the difficulties is that although we have just seen Hobbes report that the fool denies that justice exists, shortly later the fool seems to presuppose justice exists when he advances an argument for his view:

(1) If justice is something good, then it never conflicts with reason.
(2) Reason sometimes dictates that one not keep one's covenant.
(3) Justice is something good.
      Therefore,
(4) Sometimes it is just not to keep one's covenant.

My guess is that the fool feels justified in using (3) because his opponents are committed to (3). So, although the fool may think that (3) is false, he is able to use it against his opponents. The fool does not mention that Hobbes defined injustice as not keeping one's covenants (L 15.2); and that proposition contradicts (4). Presumably the fool thinks that the contradiction is a *reductio ad absurdum* argument against the view that covenants must always be kept because he is challenging Hobbes's position about the relationship between justice, covenant-keeping, and reason.

Hobbes himself does not seem to appeal to his definition of injustice in responding to the fool. He seems to reject the fool's argument because he thinks that (2) is false. Reason never dictates that one should not keep one's covenants. The third law of nature, which is prescribed by reason, makes this clear (L 15.5). Most people do not think that reason makes this prescription. They argue, in the spirit of the fool, as follows:

(F1) There are situations in which a person can achieve a great gain by acting unjustly without any fear of being detected.

(F2) In such a case, reason dictates that the person act unjustly. Therefore,

(F3) It is not against reason for a person to act unjustly.

Hobbes should reject this argument because (F1) is not a necessary proposition. For him, it is a matter of chance or accident that a person's unjust act is not discovered. In other words, (F1) is contingent and depends on experience to be known. Hobbes actually puts the point more strongly, claiming (improbably) that success in a devious action is always due to luck: "[W]hen a man doth a thing, which notwithstanding anything can be foreseen and reckoned on tendeth to his own destruction, howsoever some accident, which he could not expect, arriving may turn it to his benefit; yet such events do not make it reasonably or wisely done" (L 15. 5).

In the situation discussed above, the fool is trying hard not to be foolish. He is choosing to act unjustly in a situation, in which he thinks the chances of detection are virtually nil. He does what he can to make sure that his unjust action will not be detected. I think the essence of Hobbes's answer is, as mentioned above, the rejection of (F2). Although I cannot be sure, I think that Hobbes's answer to the fool can be made more explicit in terms of the conditions required for proving that something is rational. Hobbes is giving a science of morality and politics and, according to his understanding, science consists of necessarily true propositions, and necessarily true propositions are either definitions or follow from definitions. These necessarily true propositions are not statements of what experience teaches. So, the fool cannot justify his position on the basis of what consequences are likely to follow, as shown by experience. He needs to provide a justification that consists of propositions that are necessarily true. And it is this that he cannot provide and does not even try to provide. Hobbes deduced to his satisfaction how following the laws of nature contributes to peace and hence survival. The fact that a person's experience will lead him to think that he can foresee that breaking a law will not adversely affect him does not give him the certainty that comes from knowing necessarily true propositions. So *reason* cannot justify ever breaking a law of nature, because reason has shown that breaking them leads to war and war to death.

There is a second kind of case that Hobbes considers. It is much easier to handle than the one we have been discussing. In this second kind of case ("Secondly") (L 15.5), the fool is really foolish. He tells people that "he thinks it reason to deceive those that help him;" and after committing an unjust action he "declareth that he thinks he may reason to do so" (L 15.5). It is obviously irrational for a person to tell people that he or she thinks that it is reasonable to deceive people in part because in the state of nature a person needs "confederates" to survive, and people are not going to help a gabbing fool. Worse, people will not accept such a person "into any society that unite themselves for peace and defence" unless that society itself makes a mistake (L 15.5).

Hobbes's answer to the fool is obscure. There are many interpretations of it, some of which will be discussed in Chapter 7, "Hobbes Today."

To return to the second law of nature for a moment, Hobbes says that the law of the gospel is *"Whatsoever you require that others should do to you, that do ye to them"* and that it is the same as what is often called the negative golden rule, *"quod tibi fieri non vis, alteri ne feceris* [What you do not want done to you, do not do to another]" (L 14.5; cf. 17.2). What he says is the law of the gospel is not in fact the precept that is in the gospels. The gospel precept turns on how a person *wants* to be treated, not on what a person is *required* to do. Jesus taught, "Do unto others as you would want others to do to you." It is no part of the golden rule that a person imposes requirements on others.[24] Someone has pointed out that there is a platinum rule: "Do unto others as they would like done unto them."

CONCLUSION

Hobbes's moral philosophy underpins his political philosophy. Without a civil state, a robust moral life is impossible. Hobbes tries to get his reader to realize this through the thought experiment of the state of nature. If absolutely no laws existed, no behavior would be immoral. People would act in mutually destructive ways for several reasons. If resources were scarce, everyone would compete for them, because life is so highly valued. Also, some people have a natural tendency to dominate others. Everyone who recognized the conflict generated by competition and potential domination would be suspicious of everyone else and be inclined to launch preemptive attacks against others. Since everyone knows that others are or could be thinking the same thing, they need to be all the more suspicious and inclined to preemption. Finally, some people try to dominate others for the glory that goes with it. The result, in short, is war.

The only way out of this condition is to rely on the fear of death and the ability to find a solution through reason. The solution can be extracted from the laws of nature, which are discovered by reason. If people consider that they cannot live very long by depending on their own strength, then they see that they all need to make peace (the first law of nature). The only way to make peace is to lay down some rights (the second law). Laying down rights is only reasonable if people make and keep their covenants. The principal covenant is the sovereign-making covenant, and this belongs to political philosophy, the topic of the next chapter.

FURTHER READING

Gauthier, D. (1969) The Logic of Leviathan, Oxford: Clarendon Press. A classic work that argues that Leviathan contains a theory of authorization of a sovereign, in contrast with a theory that requires subjects to alienate their rights.

Kavka, G. (1986) Hobbesian Moral and Political Theory, Princeton, N.J.: Princeton University Press. An important and sophisticated philosophical work that uses Hobbes's views as the starting point for a cogent moral and political theory.

Lloyd, S. A. (1992) Ideals as Interests in Hobbes's Leviathan, Cambridge: Cambridge University Press. An important book that argues that Hobbesian people have interests that override the fear of death, many of which are based in religion.

Four

Political Philosophy

THE ORIGIN OF A COMMONWEALTH

Political philosophy might be defined as the study of the nature of government.[1] There are two basic views about government. The first is that government is natural to human beings. In addition to his definition of a human being as a rational animal, Aristotle also defined a human being as a political animal. This was the dominant view in the seventeenth century. The second basic view is that government is artificial. This is Hobbes's view. He thinks that human beings by nature are not fit for society and as such cannot be said to be naturally political. I think that Hobbes is mistaken. Even if we grant that humans are not fit for society, the fact that they need it to survive is sufficient, in my opinion, to make humans political animals by nature. Ignoring my opinion, let's consider a consequence of Hobbes's view. If government is not natural to human beings and they are born with complete liberty, what justifies the existence of a government? In other words, what justifies taking away some or all of the liberty of people not guilty of a crime? If some powerful entity merely threatens and bullies subjects to behave in a certain way, that entity is not a sovereign[2] and the people do not live under a government. The underlying theme of much of what Hobbes says about politics and government concerns the justification of government. Historically, this is not surprising, since he wrote his political works during the years when the authority of the king was being questioned and many people were making pronouncements about when subjects had an obligation to obey their sovereign and when they did not.

In each of his three books on political theory, Hobbes describes how a civil state arises from the state of nature. Each new description becomes a bit more sophisticated than the earlier ones. In the first of these, The Elements of Law, Natural and Politic, Hobbes says that in the state of nature, "every man's right (howsoever he is inclined to peace) of doing whatsoever seemeth good in his own eyes, remaineth with him still, as the necessary means of his preservation." He continues: "And therefore till there be security amongst men for the keeping of the law of nature one towards another, men are still in the estate of war" (EL 19.1). The only way to achieve this security is by each member of a group to unite:

> the making of union consisteth in this, that every man by covenant oblige himself to some one and the same man or to some one and the same council, by them all named and determined, to do those actions, which the said man or council shall command them to do; and to do no action which he or they shall forbid, or command them not to do.
>
> (EL 19.7)

Uniting this way by covenant creates the obligation in the subject such that he resigns "his strength and means to him, whom he covenanteth to obey" (EL 19.7). The result of this process is that men are united "as one person" (EL 19.7).

In his second work of political philosophy, De cive, Hobbes makes his account more sophisticated by saying something about this person:

> Now union thus made is called a city or civil society; and also a civil person. For when there is one will of all men, it is to be esteemed for one person; and by the word one, it is to be known and distinguished from all particular men, as having its own rights and properties. . . . A city therefore (that we may define it), is one person.
>
> (DC 5.9)

Hobbes has just drawn a sharp distinction between the individual persons who covenanted and the civil person, which is the same as the city, the civil society or the civil state. But Hobbes does not say what the relationship is between the civil person and the sovereign. On this latter point, it needs to be mentioned that Hobbes does not clearly divide the civil person from the sovereign (cf. Skinner 2002: 177–208). In distinguishing the citizens from the civil person, Hobbes says, "neither any one citizen, nor all of them together (if we except him, whose will stands for the will of all), is to be accounted the city" (DC 5.9). The crucial part of this quotation is within the parentheses. It seems that for Hobbes the city or civil person would have to be the same as the sovereign; otherwise there would be no reason for Hobbes to "except him, whose will stands for the will of all." On this view, the sovereign is not just the government but also the civil state itself. It points to the view of King Louis XIV, who allegedly said, "I am the state." But if the sovereign is the state and the sovereign has all of "the power and right of commanding," it seems that because the subjects have alienated their power and right to him, his actions are only his actions and not those of the subjects. So the subject would have a right to complain about his treatment. We will continue this thought when we discuss the origin of the civil state in *Leviathan*.

For now, let's look at Hobbes's description of the origin of the state in *De cive*. Hobbes makes clearer here than he does in the *Elements of Law* why people must transfer their rights to one person. Suppose they did not. It is likely in this circumstance that people would have different opinions about the appropriate means to achieve their goals. With everyone acting on their own desires and judgments, the efforts of each would clash with at least some of the others. This creates a problem; they are not using effective means to achieve their goal. Another possibility, less likely than the previous one, is that the people would all agree on some occasion about the means to achieve their goal; they would use those means and succeed in achieving their goal. However, even if they do succeed, they will soon come into conflict with each other because of the "diversity of wits and counsels, or emulation and envy" that people possess. Notice that what makes temporary success in achieving self-preservation is the unity of means, in the short run. It was lack of unity of means that caused failure in the first circumstance (DC 5.4, 5.6; see also L 17.4, 17.5). So long-term self-preservation requires a permanent entity that consequently has a unity of means at its disposal. The only thing that satisfies this description is a single "will of all men," which results when the many submit their "wills . . . to the will of one man or council" (DC 5.6, 5.7). Hobbes continues:

> Now union thus made is called a city or civil society; and also a civil person. For when there is one will of all men, it is to be esteemed for one person; and by the word *one*, it is to be known and distinguished from all particular men, as having its own rights and properties.
>
> (DC 5.9)

Hobbes does not say what the relation between the sovereign and the civil person is. The phrase, "distinguished from all particular men" suggests that the civil person is not the sovereign since a king would seem to be a particular man. (We will return to this issue later.)

Given that the sovereign needs effective means to achieve the goal of self-preservation in the long run and that these means come from the subjects, we might ask what means the sovereign has available to him. It's plausible that the subjects supply the means. In *De cive*, Hobbes sometimes says that subjects convey "the right of . . . [their] strength and faculties" (DC 5.8; also DC 5.11). But then he says that "because no man can transfer his power in a natural manner," what the subject actually does is to part "with his right of resisting" (DC 5.11). He said the same thing in *The Elements of Law*:

> And because it is impossible for any man really to transfer his own strength to another, . . . it is to be understood: that to transfer a man's power and strength, is no more but to lay by or relinquish his

own right of resisting him to whom he so transferreth it . . .
[The subjects] resign . . . [their] strength and means to him
[the sovereign].

(EL 19.7)

Now I don't see how relinquishing one's right of resisting is any
less problematic than transferring one's strength. If a person can
choose not to resist his sovereign's commands, he can choose to
obey his sovereign's commands. But there is another, more interesting problem. The will not to resist the sovereign is not enough to
generate the kind of power needed to make a civil state work.
Suppose A (who we will see is the sovereign) has to protect B by
fighting C because B has transferred his strength and faculties to A.
It seems that more is required of B than simply not resisting A! B
needs to pitch in and help. B can hardly justify his standing aside by
saying that he, as agreed, was not resisting A. Intuitively, if B has
transferred his strength to A, then B has an obligation to help A win
the fight in some active way. The same holds for cases in which
many people have transferred their right to A. If A is protecting B_1,
B_2, . . . B_n, then several of the Bs, enough to vanquish C easily, need
to help in some way.

Who decides which Bs are to help, and how? The only sensible
answer is, "The sovereign, A, of course." Otherwise the battle very
likely would not be won. People "join their strengths together
against a common enemy;" and subjects "resign . . . [their] strength
and means to him [the sovereign]" (EL 19.7; see also 19.6). I think
this is the best way to understand what Hobbes had in mind.

Three aspects of our discussion of the origin of a civil state in The
Elements of Law and De cive might be singled out for special notice:
first, the nature of the civil person; second, the relation of the
actions of the sovereign to the subjects; and third, the nature of
transferring rights to the sovereign. All three of these topics are
treated in Leviathan, though not, I think, successfully.

PERSONS

In *Leviathan*, Hobbes discusses the nature of the civil person between Chapter 15, which contains proofs of most of the laws of nature, and Chapter 17, "Of the Causes, Generation, and Definition of a Commonwealth." This placement of Chapter 16, "Of Persons, Authors, and Things Personated," will seem odd unless one understands that after he completed the revised version of *De cive* in 1647, Hobbes came to believe that his theory of the origin of the civil state required a more sophisticated treatment of civil persons in order to be cogent.[3]

In the Middle Ages, a definition of a person had become standard and it continued to be used by religious thinkers in the seventeenth century: a person is an individual substance of a rational nature. Hobbes's own definition seems to have no connection with the standard one. He says, "A person is he *whose words or actions are considered, either as his own, or as representing the words or actions of another man, or of any other thing to whom they are attributed, whether truly or by fiction*" (L 16.1). However, in *An Answer to Bishop Bramhall's Book, 'The Catching of the Leviathan'*, he justifies his definition of "person" on the basis of its usage in Latin: "Of this definition there can be no other proof than from the use of that word, in such Latin authors as were esteemed the most skilful in their own language, of which number was Cicero" (BB 310). He then quotes a passage from Cicero consistent with his usage: "*persona est, cui verba et actiones hominum attribuuntur vel suae vel alienae: si suae, persona naturalis est; si alienae, fictitia est* [A person is he to whom the words and actions of men are attributed, either his own or others: if his own, the person is natural, if another's, then he is artificial] (DH 15.1). According to Hobbes's definition, a person, it seems, is always a human being.

There are two basic kinds of persons, natural persons and artificial ones. A natural person owns his own actions. His behavior is to be attributed to him as his own action. For purposes of exposition, I am distinguishing between behavior and action. "Behavior" will refer to voluntary bodily motions. Usually, a person's behavior is identical with his actions. If A's behavior consists of walking across the room, then A's action is that of walking across the room; or as Hobbes might say, A owns the action of walking across the room.

Now consider a different kind of case, one in which a person's behavior is not his action and hence not owned by him. Suppose A is a real-estate agent who has been hired by B to bid on a house. A's behavior consists of putting certain words and numbers on a piece of paper and handing it to C, the owner of a house. In this case, A's behavior constitutes the action of B's bidding to purchase a house, because, by hiring A, B authorized A's behavior in that regard. It is B's action, even if B is asleep or otherwise unaware of exactly what A is doing, because A is "representing the words or actions of" B. In this kind of case, Hobbes says that A is a "feigned or artificial person" (L 16.2). Presumably, Hobbes wants A, the representative of B, to be the artificial person because it would be very odd to say that the natural human being, B, the person who is buying the house, is an artificial person.

But there are other cases in which it is odd to hold that the representative is the artificial person, although this is exactly what Hobbes does hold. Let's consider a second case in which a natural person's behavior results in an action being attributed to something else, a thing that is not a natural person. Suppose A represents a hospital and thus conducts business for that hospital. A is again a feigned or artificial person, and his behavior (as justified by the terms of his employment) does not constitute his own actions. Rather the actions are owned by and attributed to the hospital. Hobbes ends up with the odd view that the agent A is an artificial person, the agent personates the hospital and bears its person, even though the hospital is no kind of person. This last way of talking does not fit our own. We say that the hospital is an artificial person. But that is not Hobbes's view in Leviathan.

Hobbes seemed to sense some problem with this definition. He changed his way of talking about hospitals and persons in De homine. In that book his definition of a person seems to entail that the hospital is an artificial person: "*a person is he to whom the words and actions of men are attributed, either his own or another's; if his own, the person is natural; if another's, it is artificial*" (DH 15.1).[4] Since words and actions are attributed to a hospital, the hospital is a person. Temples and bridges get the same treatment (DH 15.4). The human beings who act on behalf of these artificial persons "bear" that person but are not identical with that person.

Unfortunately, Hobbes seems to revert to the theory of *Leviathan* in the late 1660s. In his reply to a criticism of Bramhall, Hobbes writes, "A *person* (Latin, *persona*) signifies an intelligent substance, that acteth any thing in his own or another's name, or by his own or another's authority" (BB 310; see also 311, and the discussion below in Chapter 7).

In his explanation of the notion of a person in *Leviathan*, Hobbes exploits the etymology of the Latin word *persona*. *Persona* denotes the mask of an actor in a theatrical production (L 16.3; see also DH 15.1). His main point is that as an actor a person is not responsible for his own words and movements; rather, the author is responsible for them. His purpose in saying this, which he does not disclose at this point, is to make the sovereign a mere actor and his subjects the authors of the sovereign's actions. This position undermines any attempt by subjects to criticize the behavior of the sovereign, for the subjects would be complaining, not about the sovereign's actions, but their own. Hobbes explains this very clearly in *De homine*:

> whatsoever be done by [the sovereign] . . . they [the subjects] themselves will hold it as an action of each and every one of them, each and every one will be the author of the actions that the man or group [that is sovereign] may take; and therefore he [a subject] cannot complain of any of their actions without complaining of himself.
>
> (DH 15.3)

AUTHORIZATION AND ALIENATION

If the sovereign were an actor and nothing more, then the sovereign would seem not to have any authority over his subjects, any more than an actor, strictly, has any authority over what words his character will speak.[5] So Hobbes has to explain how an actor gets authority. I think he tries to do this in two ways. The first occurs in his discussion of artificial persons. In effect, he offers the following reasoning (L 16.4):

(1) An actor S [a sovereign] acts according to the authority he received from the author A [the subjects of the sovereign].
(2) S has authority from A. (From 1.)
(3) S has authority over A. (From 2.)

I think his reasoning is flawed; (3) does not follow from (2). The change of prepositions from "from" to "over" creates an unjustified logical leap. If A gives S the authority for something, then A is superior to S with respect to that thing. S acts with authority but does not have authority over A. One might object that a person A may give another person B the authority to keep A locked up until A recovers from some addiction. The addict may say to his chosen caretaker, "I authorize you to care for me until my addiction is cured. Under no circumstances are you to obey what I say once you accept this authority until I have made a total recovery." In this case, the objection continues, B acquires authority over A as the result of A's authorization of B: B has authority from A and over A. I disagree with the supposed facts of this case. I think that in cases of weak-willed, compulsive or otherwise incompetent people, the people alienate their rights to make decisions for themselves with the hope that they will recover their competence and be given back the rights they have alienated. The incompetent person may use the word "authorize" but in fact is transferring or otherwise alienating certain rights to the caretaker. If a case like this occurred in the state of nature, then A would hope that B would give A's rights back to A as a gift. As long as B has the right to make all the decisions for A, A is the slave of B.

In civil states, the circumstances in which a person can give up his or her rights to make decisions about health or finances are highly circumscribed because the value of freedom is so high, and the possible danger of severe harm is so great. Because these laws vary from state to state, there is no general answer to give about how these laws fit or do not fit the case of the addict or incompetent person. However, for any particular case, I would look for a plausible explanation of how the person A either does not alienate A's rights or is not authorizing B, even if A uses the word "authorizes."

This brings us to Hobbes's second attempt in *Leviathan* to explain how a sovereign gets authority over subjects. It results from a confusion involving the concept of transferring or giving up a right and authorization of an artificial person. To transfer a right is to lay down that right, to alienate or lose that right, as described in the preceding chapter. This is quite different from authorization. For one person A to authorize another person B to act for A with respect to something X, is for A to give B the authority to act for A with respect to X. Obviously (according to me), for this to occur, A must have a right to X and thus could not have transferred or otherwise laid down the right. It makes no sense for Jane Doe to give anyone the authority to act with respect to the automobile she sold last weekend, because in selling it Jane Doe laid down her right to control the object (cf. Skinner 2002: 206).

Hobbes's conflation of authorization and alienation occurs because Hobbes harnesses two disparate theories of sovereignty. His original theory, which appears in the *Elements of Law, Natural and Politic* and *De cive*, is a theory of alienation, according to which subjects lose their rights by transferring them to the sovereign. The second is his modified theory, presented for the first time in *Leviathan*, which theory adds the concept of authorization to the original theory. This can be made clear by considering the proposition that Hobbes says each person in effect expresses when becoming a subject of a commonwealth.

I authorize and give up my right of governing myself to this man, or.
to this assembly of men, on this condition: that thou give up thy right
to him and authorize all his actions in like manner.

(L 17.13)

There are two obscurities in this sovereign-making formula. One is
that it is not clear how broadly the phrase, "my right of governing
myself," should be construed. Does it include everything a person
might do since anything a person might do is related to how he is
governed? It might seem that it does. So it would apply to someone's deciding whether to eat a hot dog or not. The sovereign
would have the authority to outlaw the eating of hot dogs. He
would not need to give a reason, because the sovereign decides
what the proper means to achieving peace are and he might think
that giving reasons might jeopardize peace. But suppose he did give
a reason: hot dogs are unhealthy, they cause subjects to be
unhealthy, which weakens them and thereby weakens the civil
state. Even if the subject thought this were a poor reason, he could
not legitimately argue with the sovereign because the subject
would have given up his right to judge what will promote life and
safety and what will not. By the Right-to-Means Principle, the subject must obey the sovereign, and by the Objective-to-Subjective
Slide (both discussed in Chapter 3), only the sovereign's judgment
counts (L 18.8). So the sovereign's right seems to be unrestricted.

As powerful as this reasoning seems, Hobbes has left himself
open to an equally powerful counterargument. Earlier in *Leviathan*,
he said that there are "some rights which no man can be understood by any words, or other signs, to have abandoned or transferred." Whenever a man lays down a right, he does it "for some
other good he hopeth for" (L 14.8). These rights certainly
include the right to resist assault and imprisonment, because the
goal of laying down a right is the preservation of a person's life
and "the means of so preserving life as not to be weary of it"
(L 14.8). Therefore, even if a person seems to lay down these rights

"he is not to be understood as if he meant it" (L 14.8; see also 14.29).

Let's consider the range of these inalienable rights still further. Since the right to life is a right that belongs to a person by the right of nature, each person is the judge of when that right is in danger. This slide from objectivity (the person has the right to x) to subjectivity (each person judges what the means are to the right to x) with respect to each subject's rights conflicts with the sovereign's slide from objectivity (the goal of the sovereign is to preserve the life of the subjects) to subjectivity (only the sovereign can judge what will preserve the life of the subjects). In practice, the sovereign usually prevails because of his power, but "might" does not solve the theoretical problem of right. Hobbes never reconciled this tension between inalienable human rights and sovereign rights but used one part of it or the other, as it suited his purposes at the moment.

It would be nice if I could step in and counsel Hobbes about which of these poles of tension he should have opted for, but I can't. This is part of the human condition: people need government to live a decent life; the default mode is to obey the sovereign in order to allow the sovereign to help his subjects have a decent life. In doubtful cases subjects give the sovereign the benefit of the doubt. But sometimes subjects have to take a stand against the sovereign, even to the point of overthrowing the sovereign. Finally, the line between the doubtful cases and the cases when the subject or citizen must stand against the sovereign is fuzzy.

Let's now consider the second obscurity in the sovereign-making formula. It concerns the phrase, "I authorize and give up." I have already argued that there is a conflict between "A authorizing B to do C" and "A transferring or giving up his right to do C to B." In order for A to authorize B to do something, A must have and retain the right to that thing. If A's authorization of B to do C resulted in A's loss of the right to do C, then B's behavior would result not in an action of A, but would be B's own action. If A loses the right to a bicycle by gifting it to B and B sells it, B gets the money, not A. It is absurd for *A* to say, "I give you B this bicycle and authorize you to sell it." B could rightly reply, "What do you mean 'authorize'? If you give it to me, you have no say over what I do with it."

It might be urged that although alienation and authorization are often incompatible, they are not always. (This is essentially the claim made earlier in the discussion about an addict or other incompetent person "authorizing" someone to make decisions for him or her.) Suppose *A* says, "I give you this bicycle, but I do not authorize you to sell it." In this case, it seems to me, *A* has not given the bicycle to B as a simple gift, but has made a conditional coven- ant: *A* gives the bicycle to B in exchange for B's promise not to sell it. The same covenant would be made with these words: "I give you B this bicycle on the condition that if you want to sell (or otherwise dispose of) it, then you give it back to me." In neither formulation does the word "authorize" or anything synonymous with it occur; and, in fact, authorization is not operating. None of B's behavior comes to be "owned" by *A* as the result of B's accepting and using the bicycle.

The conflict between authorizing and alienating is reflected in the ungrammatical syntax of the sovereign-making formula: "I authorize and give up my right of governing myself." Both "author- ize" and "give up" require objects. The object of "give up" is "my right of governing myself." But "authorize" has no object. Hobbes presumably wants "my right of governing myself" to do double duty as the object of "authorize," but that does not work because "authorize" needs a phrase that denotes an action, not a phrase that denotes a right. Moreover, if "my right of governing myself" were transformed into the grammatically right kind of phrase, the con- flict between authorization and alienation would be crystal clear: "I authorize you to govern myself and I give up my right of governing myself." Compare this with "I, *A*, authorize you B to represent me in buying a house and I give up my right of buying a house." Well, which is it? If B comes back with a contract for *A*, *A* might say, "Don't you recall? I gave up my right to buy a house." At this point,

B may think he can decisively show *A* that *A* is wrong. B says. "You gave up your right for *you* to buy a house, not your right for *me* to buy you a house." However, *A* has the final word: "I know I did not give up my right *for you to buy me a house*. But this is a right that you must exercise not me. If you buy me a house, then *you* buy me a house. And I will be very grateful to you. But *your buying me a house* is not my buying a house with you representing me."

I don't think that there is any way to resolve the contradiction between authorization and alienation because Hobbes wants to have things both ways. On the one hand, he wants authorization because he wants the sovereign to be an artificial person, so that the sovereign represents his subjects; and he wants the sovereign to represent his subjects because he does not want the sovereign to be accountable to his subjects. On the other hand, he wants alienation because he needs the subjects to give up their rights to govern themselves because he wants the sovereign to have unchallengeable authority over his subjects.

Did Hobbes really have no other way to resolve this problem? No, I think he did. For the sake of discussion, let's give Hobbes his theory of alienation and see whether in Hobbes's philosophy there is any effective check on the actions of the sovereign. In Chapter 30, "Of the Office of the Sovereign Representative," Hobbes says that the "office" of the sovereign, that is, the duty of the sovereign, is "the procuration of the safety of the people," and that by "safety" he does not mean "a bare preservation, but also all other contentments of life" (L 30.1; see also DC 13.2). This requires the sovereign to ensure that justice is done, not just for the rich but for the poor as well. For equity is "a precept of the law of nature," and as such a sovereign is as subject to it "as any of the meanest of his people" (L 30.15).[6] So the sovereign has duties, even though those duties are not owed to his subjects (cf. Sorell 2004).

The sovereign "is obliged by the law of nature, and to render an account thereof to God, the Author of that law" (L 30.1). Most scholars do not take seriously Hobbes's talk about the laws of nature being the laws of God. They think that, at best, Hobbes says this as a sop to the people. I take Hobbes at his word, partially because that is the default mode of interpretation – if the literal meaning is the plausible meaning of a text, then that is the right interpretation to make – but partially because Hobbes needs some kind of constraint on the actions of the sovereign, if there is to be any hope of the sovereign fulfilling his duties. Since Hobbes does not want the sovereign to have any duties to his subjects, he has no alternative but to emphasize the sovereign's duties to God.

The sovereign is under the same laws of nature that any human being is in the state of nature. They dictate to

> the consciences of sovereign princes and sovereign assemblies; there being no court of natural justice, but in the conscience only, where not man, but God reigneth, whose laws, such of them as oblige all mankind, in respect of God, as he is the author of nature, are *natural*; and in respect of the same God, as he is King of kings, are *laws*.
>
> (L 30.30)

So serious is Hobbes about the duties of a sovereign that he seems to abandon his official theory of goodness as what-is-desired to make his point. He says, "A good law is that which is *needful*, for the *good of the people*" (L 30.20), the good of the people being safety. Hobbes is not saying that a good law is one that he or the sovereign or someone else desires. A good law is by definition something that is needed: "And therefore a law that is not needful, having not the true end of a law, is not good" (L 30.1).[7]

In addition to looking out for the interests of the subjects, Hobbes wants the laws of nature to protect the rights of the sovereign. It is against the law of nature to transfer his rights to anyone else since this either returns people to the state of nature or threatens to. Hobbes is probably commenting on Charles I's signing of the Triennial Act (1641), by which he gave up his right to call and dismiss parliaments at his will. It is also the sovereign's duty to instruct his subjects about their duties in order to prevent them from being "seduced and drawn to resist him" (L 30.3). It is not beyond the capacity of ordinary people to understand their duties. They are "so consonant to reason that any unprejudiced man needs no more to learn it than to hear" them (L 30.6). Hobbes then explains these duties by correlating them with the Ten Commandments. Just as the first commandment says that people should not acknowledge false gods, the subjects are to acknowledge no one as sovereign except their own sovereign. As the second commandment says that there is to be no worship of graven images, subjects are not to praise their fellow subjects, except with the permission of the sovereign; and so on (L 30.7–8; see also 30.9–13).

It would be hard to prove that authorization is more important to Hobbes's theory in Leviathan than alienation. But he does try to wring as much out of authorization as possible. In Chapter 21 of Leviathan he argues that by the sovereign-making formula, a subject alienates no rights at all! He says that "the consent of a subject to sovereign power is contained in these words, *I authorize, or take upon me, all his actions,*" and that in these words, "there is no restriction at all" on a person's liberty (L 21.14). If there is no restriction at all on a person's liberty then absolutely no rights have been given up. And notice that the wording of the sovereign-making formula just given is not the same as the formula presented in Leviathan Chapter 17. In this new formula, nothing at all is said about alienation, about giving up "*my right of governing myself*" (L 17.13).[8] Let's waive any objection that can be made on the basis of this omission, in order to see how Hobbes eventually restricts the liberty of the subject.

According to Hobbes, a subject does not alienate the right to defend, feed, medicate himself "or any other thing without which he cannot live" according to the new formula (L 21.12). Hence the subject has no obligation to obey a sovereign who commands him not to do these things. Also, the new formula does not cause the subject to alienate his right not to kill another person. But, and this is an important "but," the subject does have an "obligation . . . upon the command of the sovereign" to obey the sovereign when refusing to obey "frustrates the end for which the sovereignty was ordained" (L 21.15). That is, the restriction of liberty or alienation of rights and the acquisition of obligation does not come directly from the new sovereign-making formula: "[T]he obligation a man may sometimes have . . . dependeth not on the words of our submission, but on the intention, which is to be understood by the end thereof" (L 21.15). That is, obligation comes indirectly, and depends on the Right-to-Means Principle: he who wills the end has the obligation to use the means necessary to that end. Thus, for example, one subject A cannot defend another subject B against the sovereign because doing so is "destructive of the very essence [end] of government" (L 21.17). A has an obligation to kill B because killing B is a necessary means to the end or goal of government, according to the judgment of the sovereign.

It might seem that Hobbes's position that the obligation to obey the sovereign arises from the subject's ends depends on an argument that equivocates on two senses of "ought." There is the moral or categorical "ought," according to which "one ought to do X" entails "one has an obligation to do X." And there is the conditional "ought" according to which, "if one wants or intends to achieve an end E, and doing M is necessary for getting E then one ought to do M." So, if one intends to go from Maribor to Ljubljana and taking a train is necessary to do that, then one ought to take the train. In this conditional sense, the fact that someone ought to do something does not mean that one has an obligation to do it. If one wants to inherit one's grandfather's estate and it is necessary to kill one's father to get it, then one ought to kill him, even though, far from having an obligation to kill him, one has the obligation not to kill him. Now, it might seem that Hobbes is arguing as follows:

(1) If one wants to make peace and obeying the sovereign is necessary for making peace, then one ought to obey the sovereign.

(2) One does want to make peace and obeying the sovereign is necessary for making peace.
Therefore,

(3) One ought to obey the sovereign. (From 1 and 2 by modus ponens.)
Therefore,

(4) One has an obligation to obey the sovereign. (From 3, by the meaning of "ought.")

And this argument seems to be invalid because the inference from (3) to (4) is invalid. The "ought" in (1) is the conditional "ought," not the categorical "ought" of obligation. It cannot be the "ought" of obligation because obligation arises only by laying down one's right and Hobbes's point about authorization in Chapter 21, paragraph 10, is precisely that one does not lay down any right in entering into the sovereign-making covenant.

I have been hedging my remarks about whether Hobbes is equivocating and arguing invalidly with the phrases "it might seem" and "this argument seems" because Hobbes might reply (and I think he may be right to do so) that the difference between a moral "ought" and a nonmoral "ought" is not the difference between a categorical and a conditional "ought." Morality is the system of rules or behavior that contributes to the happiness and wellbeing of individuals and communities; it is essentially conditional or related to attaining an end. So the moral "ought" does not have a meaning different from the nonmoral "ought;" the difference is merely nominal or one of usage. The moral "ought" consists of all of those uses of "ought" that relate to happiness and wellbeing. There is no categorical "ought," and no moral actions that ought to be done for their own sake. For Hobbes, the moral laws are the laws of nature, and the first law of nature is to make peace in order to preserve one's life. All the other laws of nature are related in some way or other to the same end of preserving one's life.

Even if Hobbes cannot choose between authorization and

alienation and get everything he wants, we may ask, "Which concept is the correct one to use in political philosophy?" The answer is both, as long as each is restricted in the right way. Citizens authorize a government to act for them with respect to specific issues such as safety from both internal and external foes. (In the United States, the citizens originally authorized two different kinds of governments, a national government and state governments, to take care of different aspects of life, in order to protect against tyranny. And it separated certain powers in the national government for the same reason.) Authorization is not *carte blanche* authority. Also, because acting for someone in some regard requires resources, citizens alienate either part of their wealth or labor to the government. But they do not (or should not) alienate basic, human rights as set down in documents like the Bill of Rights. The founders of the United States provided for procedures and agencies within the government itself to protect people against the possible abuse of their rights. However, if these procedures and agencies fail, then the citizens have the natural right to resist and, if necessary, to overthrow the government. There is no need to write this right of resistance into the Constitution because that right is more basic than the Constitution and not protected by the Constitution. The Constitution is designed to forestall the need to revolt, not to protect the right to revolt.

SOVEREIGNTY BY ACQUISITION

Hobbes distinguishes two ways in which sovereignty comes into existence: sovereignty by institution and sovereignty by acquisition. Like Hobbes, I have silently been explaining his theory in the terms appropriate to sovereignty by institution, that is, sovereignty that begins when a group of people freely creates a government. Discussing sovereignty by institution presents the essence of government more clearly than the other way in which sovereignty originates, sovereignty by acquisition, even though most governments are established through sovereignty by acquisition or conquest. The reason that it is not objectionable not to have focused on sovereignty by acquisition is that it enjoys the same rights and authority as sovereignty by institution (L 20.14).[9]

The only difference between the two kinds of sovereignty concerns the historical origin or contingent facts about the circumstances that caused people to create the sovereign: the covenant that creates a sovereign by institution is caused by the mutual fear each covenanter has towards his fellow covenanters, while the covenant that creates a sovereign by acquisition is caused by the fear the covenanter has of the person he makes sovereign (L 20.2).[10] To think that this difference of origin makes a difference to the nature of the sovereign is to commit a genetic fallacy, the fallacy of thinking that if two things have different origins, then they have different essential properties.

Sovereignty by acquisition can be divided into two types: patriarchy and despotism. Again, the basis for the distinction is the contingent facts surrounding the origin. Patriarchy is the sovereignty that a parent has over his or her children. It arises as soon as a child becomes competent to make a decision about whether to take the parent as a sovereign or not. Theoretically, the child can choose death to subjection, but this never happens in fact.[11] Either children make an explicit covenant with their parents, or they do so implicitly ("by other sufficient arguments declared") (L 20.4). By accepting the protection of their parents, children imply that they accept their sovereignty.

This account needs to be supplemented or refined to take care of two possible complications. The first concerns the fact that "patriarchy" is a misnomer. The claim of a mother over a child is usually prior to the claim of a father for two reasons: one is that the mother is always sure who her child is and a father is not (L 20.5). The other is that the mother is more often physically in control of the child: "[S]eeing the infant is first in the power of the mother, so as she may either nourish or expose it; if she nourish it, it oweth its life to the mother, and is therefore obliged to obey her rather than any other" (L 20.5).[12] This may sound cold-blooded, but Hobbes may want to make it sound cold-blooded in order to remind the reader of how horrible the state of nature is. Similarly, he may give the mother the primary claim to dominion for the same reason and not because he was enlightened on feminist issues.

The other possible complication in the account of patriarchy as sovereignty by acquisition is the fact that children become subjects of their parents one by one; so they don't seem to have anyone with whom to covenant. Given what Hobbes said in Chapter 17, a child cannot covenant with his parent (or parents), because a sovereign is not a party to a sovereign-making covenant. There are a couple of ways Hobbes might have handled this case. First, if the parent is already sovereign over a spouse, some children, or other people, such as servants, the soon-to-be-subject child could implicitly covenant with them. Hobbes himself puts a slight obstacle in the way of this solution because he says a small family is not a commonwealth (L 20.15). (He would have been better off if he had distinguished between weak commonwealths of a few members and stronger ones.) If, however, there is no one else for the child to covenant with, Hobbes could have allowed for sovereignty by gift. The child could have unilaterally authorized a parent to act for him (or transferred his right of governing himself to the parent) without any other person doing the same, with the hope that the now sovereign parent would keep the fourth law of nature: not to give the benefactor, the child, "reasonable cause to repent of his good will" (L 15.16).

Let's now consider how Hobbes might have treated, and to a large extent did treat, despotism. He says that dominion is "acquired to the victor when the vanquished, to avoid the present stroke of death, covenanteth either in express words or by other sufficient signs of the will that so long as his life and the liberty of his body is allowed him, the victor shall have the use therefore at his pleasure" (L 20.10). If only one person is being conquered the case can be treated just as the case of the single child was. The vanquished would covenant with the other subjects to authorize the sovereign to act for him (or to transfer his right to the sovereign): "It is not therefore the victory that giveth the right of dominion over the vanquished, but his own covenant" (L 20.11).[13] Alternatively, the sole vanquished person could give the conqueror the gift of government, as suggested for a single child.

Another problem with Hobbes's account of despotism arises because he says, "nor is the victor obliged by an enemy's rendering himself, without promise of life, to spare him for this his yielding to discretion, which obliges not the victor longer than in his own discretion he shall think fit" (L 20.11).[14] This passage gives the impression that the conqueror may promise to spare the life of the vanquished person. Since this promise applies to the future, it means that the conqueror may make a covenant with the vanquished. But this seems to contradict the entire thrust of Hobbes's theory up to this point. If the conqueror can acquire an obligation to a subject, then the conqueror has duties to the subject, and the subject can blame the conqueror for actions that the subject judges jeopardize his life. The correct reply to this supposed problem, I think, is that since the conqueror is not the sovereign of the defeated person, the conqueror can make a promise to the enemy without that promise making the conqueror the sovereign of the enemy. That is, the promise is a nonsovereign-making covenant between two people in the state of nature; one is a natural person A, the other is a sovereign, not the sovereign of A. To become a sovereign through a sovereign-making covenant is to acquire the job of preserving a person, but to acquire the duty of preserving a person, say, through a promise, is not thereby to become that person's sovereign.

THE PROPERTIES OF A SOVEREIGN

Given that sovereignty is the same whether it is by institution or acquisition, what properties does it have? The most important one is absoluteness. The sovereign controls all the political power there is in the government, and he has authority to control every aspect of life (L 20.16–19). This entails that a sovereign cannot act unjustly towards a subject, because everything the sovereign does is authorized by the subject; "and consequently he that complaineth of injury from his sovereign complaineth of that whereof he himself is author; and therefore [he] ought not to accuse any man but himself" (L 18.6). A related property is permanence or lack of "forfeiture" (L 18.4). His subjects cannot legitimately take sovereignty away from their sovereign. Hobbes obviously is thinking about the illegitimate removal of Charles I's sovereignty during the crisis of 1641–2, when the Parliament in effect took away many of the traditional powers of the king. Although illegitimate, successful revolution is a way in which sovereignty is lost. A sovereign can also lose his sovereignty by abandoning it, as some Englishmen claimed James II did in 1688, or by having it destroyed by external attack.

The sovereign is also the judge of all controversies between his subjects, because all controversies are disagreements about propositions, and he is the judge of the truth of all propositions (L 18.11–12). In particular, the sovereign is the judge of which opinions are offensive and jeopardize peace, and hence the sovereign controls what gets published and what does not. Hobbes justifies this position with a blatantly invalid argument: "And though in matter of doctrine nothing ought to be regarded but the truth; yet this is not repugnant to regulating of the same peace. For doctrine repugnant to peace can no more be true than peace and concord can be against the law of nature" (L 18.9).

In this instance, Hobbes is sliding from subjectivity to objectivity. He seems to think that if the sovereign judges a proposition to be false, as he has a right to do, then it is false. But this is, at best, to conflate two different criteria of truth. The basic criterion of truth is something objective, like fitting the facts or corresponding to a fact. Two plus two equals four, and the earth is the third planet from the sun, independently of whether anybody judges it to be true.

However, in practical life, people set up institutional or conventional ways of settling possible disputes about truth. The truth about scoring and fouling in competitive sports is decided by referees and umpires. If an umpire calls a runner out in baseball, then it is an institutional fact and hence an institutional truth that the runner is out, even if it is not true according to the basic and objective criterion of truth that the runner was out.[15] Within a commonwealth, the decision of the sovereign is the institutional criterion of truth. A sovereign may decide that it is a truth that all property ultimately belongs to the sovereign. Those who preach the doctrine that not all property does ultimately belong to the sovereign may hold a "doctrine repugnant to peace" and a doctrine that does not satisfy the institutional criterion of truth. But from that it does not follow, as Hobbes seems to suggest, that that doctrine is not objectively true (L 18.9).

From the sovereign's power to judge the truth of all propositions, it also follows that he is the judge of all judicial controversies; he judges guilt and innocence and determines who is to be rewarded and how. He also decides ownership of property. No doubt thinking of disputes like those about Ship Money and Forced Loans during the reign of Charles I, Hobbes holds that the king is the ultimate owner of all property (L 18.11). Similarly, thinking of Charles's wars against the Scots in the late 1630s, Hobbes says that the sovereign is the judge of when and against whom a nation should go to war (L 18.12).

A summary of the most important of the sovereign's properties, those described above and those discussed earlier in this chapter, is revealing: the sovereign is absolute. He is all-powerful insofar as he has all the political power there is. He is all-just in the sense that he makes the laws and judges who keeps and breaks them. He is all-good in the sense that he is the only one authorized to reward people and hence judge them to be good. He is a savior in the sense that he saves his subjects from the threat of death in the state of nature (L 38.15). In short, Hobbes attributes godlike qualities to the sovereign. When he defines the sovereign as a "mortal god," I think he means it rather more seriously than is suggested by the commentaries of many scholars. From the late sixteenth century until the late nineteenth century, there was a gradual and seemingly inexorable drift away from a belief in a divine god and towards a human god in the form of the state. Hobbes is one of the most important figures in the history of that drift, although I think he did not abandon the belief in "immortal God" (L 17.13).

POLITICAL LIBERTY

Various ironic aspects of Hobbes's philosophy have already been pointed out. He thinks that nature is artificial, that machines are alive, and that human beings are machines. Immediately after arguing that a sovereign's power and authority is absolute over his subjects, Hobbes argues that subjects have a great deal of freedom because "no commonwealth in the world . . . [has] rules enough to set down for the regulating of all the actions and words of men (as being a thing impossible)" (L 21.6). He then adds that it is "very absurd for men to clamour as they do for the liberty they so manifestly enjoy", because they have "freedom from chains and prisons" (L 21.6). Hobbes is wrong about how little an absolute sovereign can command. An absolute sovereign can command that no one is to do anything except, say, work, eat at specified times, and sleep at specified times. Such a command may be difficult to enforce and it would soon weaken the state, but these drawbacks are not to the point, namely, that absolute sovereigns are able to limit the freedom of subjects horribly.

In addition to this personal freedom, which exists because subjects are not in prison or in chains, Hobbes talks about a kind of freedom or liberty that the civil state has. It is the same kind of freedom that individual people have in the state of nature. Civil states are not protected by anything other than their own power and hence they "live in the condition of a perpetual war and upon the confines of battle, with their frontiers armed and cannons planted against their neighbors round about" (L 21.8). In this regard, republics are no freer than any other form of government. It is unfortunate, according to Hobbes, that ancient writers such as Aristotle and Cicero have perverted the minds of people to think that there is less freedom in monarchies than there is in democracies (L 21.9). Hobbes is largely right about the relations between states. One of the few principles of international relations is that your enemy is on your border. The long-standing unprotected borders between the United States and Canada and Mexico (and recently among other countries) are exceptions to an old rule. The U.S. immigration officers that currently patrol the Mexican border are not on the lookout for Mexican enemies of the United States but for enemies, particularly terrorists, who may enter the United States through Mexico.

In the wake of the horrors of dictators in the twentieth century, it is easy to find the following words offensive:

> the greatest [incommodity] that in any form of government can possibly happen to the people in general is scarce sensible in respect of the miseries and horrible calamities that accompany a civil war . . . or that the greatest pressure of sovereign governors proceedeth not from any delight or profit they can expect in the damage or weakening of their subjects . . ., but in the restiveness of themselves that, unwillingly contributing to their own defense, make it necessary for their governors to draw from them what they can in time of peace, [in order] that they may have means on any emergent occasion or sudden need to resist or take advantage on their enemies.
>
> (L 18.20)

THE DISSOLUTION OF THE COMMONWEALTH

Nothing human lasts forever. So no commonwealth does either. Hobbes considers various causes of dissolution. In *Leviathan*, Hobbes begins with structural imperfections in the civil state (L 29.2). Of these, the first is "*that a man to obtain a kingdom is sometimes content with less power than to the peace and defense of the commonwealth is necessarily required*" (L 29.3; see also 30.3). For Hobbes, it is a defect in the civil state if a sovereign has anything less than absolute authority over his subjects. Hobbes is probably thinking in particular of Charles I, who had laid down some of his authority in his "King's Answer to the Nineteen Propositions" in June, 1642. Charles was hoping to prevent a civil war, but in fact it emboldened his opponents, and civil war broke out about a month later. Although Hobbes mentions William I's dispensing of the power to judge ecclesiastics, he probably is also thinking of Charles: "[W]hen the exercise of the power is laid by . . . [it] disposeth great numbers of men, when occasion is presented, to rebel" (L 29.3). A related poisonous doctrine is that sovereign power is divisible into more than one branch of government (L 29.12). These are "mixed governments," in which one part might levy money, another legislate laws, and still another see that they are carried out (L 29.16 and 12.5).

The second of the structural causes of dissolution is "the poison of seditious doctrines, whereof one is that every private man is judge of good and evil actions" (L 29.6; see also DC 12.1, 12.6). Hobbes observes that this doctrine is true in the state of nature, but it is also one of the causes of war in that state because different judgments bring people into conflict. Hobbes observes that in entering a civil state subjects give up their right to judge good and evil. "The measure of good and evil actions becomes the civil law; and the judge [is] the legislator, who is always representative of the commonwealth" (L 29.6; see also DC 12.1). He can certainly say this. But someone can point out that he also said there are certain things that a person can never give up, even if it appears that he is giving them up (L 14.8), and it is plausible that one should never give up every right to judge what is good and evil since judgments about the most important good, life, and the most important evil, death, often need to be made suddenly. In fact, people do retain a large part of their right to judge good and evil since virtually all their daily choices are made with that right. Hobbes is exaggerating when he says that subjects who judge about good and evil, "are aspiring to be Kings" (DC 12.1). They need not be aspiring to judge the good and evil of anyone other than themselves.

Another poisonous doctrine is that people have freedom to follow their private conscience. For Hobbes, conscience is judgment about good and evil and "the law is the public conscience by which he [the subject] hath already taken to be guided" (L 29.7). (See also Chaper 7.)

It was part of Roman law and widely accepted in England that the sovereign is above the law. It seems that this has to be the case because if he were subject to the law, then someone could judge him and whoever can be judged is not sovereign. So, the doctrine that the sovereign is subject to the law is poisonous (L 29.9 and DC 12.4).

The next poisonous doctrine is the proposition that private people have property rights independent of the sovereign (L 29.10). A few decades later, John Locke promoted this view. According to him, property is acquired in the state of nature by "mixing" one's labor with an object. In contrast, Hobbes denied that the conditions are suitable for having property without the protection of a sovereign: "Tell me, then, where this property came to you from, if not the commonwealth? And from where did it come to the commonwealth, except that each man transferred his right to the commonwealth?" (DC 12.7).

Hobbes considers the poisonous doctrines just described to pose the greatest danger to a commonwealth. But there are others, for example, "the difficulty of raising money for the necessary uses of the commonwealth" (L 29.18). This was in fact one of the prime causes of the English Civil War. Charles was deprived of the revenue that Parliament usually provided to a new king. His later efforts to get money were unpopular, especially his attempt to have the Short Parliament (1640) give him money to wage war against the Scots. It is also dangerous for a private person to have great popularity, and dangerous for one city – Hobbes is thinking of London – to have the wealth to raise its own army (L 29.21).

THE VALUE OF HOBBES'S PHILOSOPHY

My extensive criticisms of Hobbes's theory may give the false impression that there is nothing valuable in it. But there are many valuable things in it. To name just a few of these: Hobbes is right that if there were no laws at all, human life would be short and intolerable. We may think, like Rousseau, that people have a natural inclination to goodness and cooperation and that society corrupts people, but in fact, most of our goodness and cooperative spirit is the result of enculturation. Even with the elaborate social conditioning that we go through, all of us are occasionally tempted to act in various antisocial ways. What constrains us is fear of punishment by the State or pain from a bad conscience, which itself is the result of training. If all laws were abolished, it would not take long for first a few people and then everyone to act out of narrow self-interest and many to become predators. I say "everyone" because those who did not act in these ways would soon be dead. So, as much as we praise freedom, we should respect necessary laws.

Laws require people to alienate some of their rights and governments to represent us in various ways. But Hobbes was wrong to think that the government represents us with respect to the things that we alienate. What we alienate, some property and time, is the cost of having the government represent us in other matters. Although citizens are remarkably tolerant of bad government, the government's right of representation is revocable.

On many matters, Hobbes's views are useful because he presents powerful arguments that need to be refuted, and our search for the proper refutation may lead to the correct, constructive view of government.

CONCLUSION

In The Elements of Law, Natural and Politic and De cive, Hobbes's theory is that governments come into existence when people make a covenant, according to which all the parties transfer many of their rights, each transferring the same rights, to someone, who thereby becomes the sovereign, for the purpose of protecting them from threats to life and limb. In Leviathan, Hobbes complicates his theory at the same time as he makes it more subtle. Governments do not seem to be completely alien and intimidating to their subjects. The sovereign represents the subjects because they have authorized him to act on their behalf. Instead of figuring out the differences between what a subject alienates and what he authorizes a sovereign to do, Hobbes conflates the concepts and says that the subjects "authorize and give up [alienate]" something.

In any case, historically governments are created through covenants occasionally when the people fear each other (sovereignty by institution), but usually when they fear the very entity that they make their sovereign (sovereignty by acquisition). For Hobbes, sovereignty is absolute. The sovereign has all the political power in the State, and has authority over every aspect of life even though each person retains a right to self-preservation. As powerful as the State is, it is not immortal, for everything that humans create is mortal.

FURTHER READING

Braybrooke, D. (2001) Natural Law Modernized, Toronto: University of Toronto Press. A sophisticated treatment of Hobbes's political philosophy that locates him in the tradition of natural law.

Hampton, Jean (1986) Hobbes and the Social Contract Tradition, Cambridge: Cambridge University Press. It's a sophisticated piece of philosophy that finds tensions and contradictions in Hobbes's views and tries to state the best theory that can be derived from his text.

Hobbes, T. (1647) De cive in Man and Citizen, B. Gert (ed.) (1991) Indianapolis, Ind.: Hackett Publishing Co., pp. 87–386. A slightly earlier, more concise statement of Hobbes's political philosophy than the one in Leviathan.

Hobbes, T. (1668) An Answer to Bishop Bramhall's Book, 'The Catching of the Leviathan', in English Works, W. Molesworth (ed.) Vol. 4.

Five

Science, language, and logic are interlocking concepts in Hobbes's philosophy. Science is a set of true sentences or propositions of a language. It consists of two parts. The first part is a set of definitions, which are in effect axioms (cf. DCo 3.9). The second part is all of the sentences that are entailed by those definitions either directly or indirectly (cf. Hanson 1990). The inferences from definitions or from intermediate sentences (theorems) to other theorems are calculations or reckonings of words, just as adding and subtracting numbers are. The calculation of words is reasoning (L 5.2); the study of reasoning is logic. Science, language, and logic, then, form a tight cluster of concepts.

Since science consists of sentences, Hobbes's theory of language will be discussed before his theories of logic and science.

THE BASIC UNITS OF LANGUAGE

In the late twentieth century, one of the principal debates in the philosophy of language was whether words or sentences were the basic unit of language. The argument for sentences is that the most basic function of language is to express a thought, and the smallest linguistic unit that can express a complete thought is a sentence. The argument for words is that sentences depend on words because they are made up of words, and the meaning of a sentence is a function of the meanings of its words. To some extent, Hobbes appreciated both positions. When he talks about language itself, he begins with the meanings of individual words. However, when he talks about how language is used for communication, he presents an inchoate theory of speech acts, which takes the actions performed using complete sentences as the primary linguistic unit.

Sometimes he seems to combine both views. When he talks about how language is used in science, he explicitly says that definitions are "prior" to the names they contain: "[S]ince a definition is an explication of a composite name through resolution, and the process goes from the simples to the composites, the definitions must be understood before the composite names" (DCo 6.15). So, simple names are prior to composite names because the latter are complex, but the simple names depend upon definitions, which are sentences and hence complex!

In *De homine*, the last installment of his general philosophy, Hobbes considered the possibility that sentences were the basic unit of language, but opted for the view that words were basic because sentences are made up of words (cf. DH 10.1). He thought of words as being more fundamental for another reason, namely, that words solve the first problem that a person has who wants to do philosophy. Human beings do not have in themselves the concentration and memory necessary to go beyond what they can gather from their sense experience. Sense experience excludes reasoning, which requires some device that will help a person recall experiences to mind in a reliable way. Reliable recall is achieved, according to Hobbes, by the use of some kind of mark or token that jogs the memory. Without further explanation, Hobbes defines a mark as a sensible thing "employed by our own decision, so that at the sensation of these things, thoughts can be recalled to the mind, similar to those thoughts for the sake of which they were summoned" (DCo 2.1). The phrase "employed by our own decision" ("*arbitrio nostro adhibitas*") means that the marks are arbitrary. There is no natural similarity between the mark for a thing and the thing itself. The mark for a tree is not the image of a tree; the musical notation for a C major is not a sample tone of C major and does not resemble it in any other way. Hobbes does not explain why people choose arbitrary marks to aid their memory rather than something that has a natural similitude to the thing to be remembered. One might think that the marks have to be arbitrary because they are words, and words, as everyone knows, do not resemble what they stand for, except perhaps for some onomatopoeia, like "bow-wow;" and even those have an arbitrary element, because French dogs bark "ouah ouah" – more precisely, the words in French for a dog barking are not the same as the words in English for a dog barking. Similar comments could be made about the sounds of other animals. French cows say "meuh;" Croatian cows say "muuu." French frogs say "coa-coa;" Croatian frogs say "kre-kre."[1] However, most of this is irrelevant because it is based on the false premise that Hobbes thinks that marks are words. Hobbes is not yet talking about *words*. He is talking about how a given individual can remember and organize his experience reliably.

The reason that people need marks is that they cannot rely on the memory of a tree to recall a tree or the memory of a dog's bark to recall a dog's bark. But this raises the question again. Why should an arbitrary mark be a more reliable mnemonic device than something that shares the same pictorial or auditory property with the thing to be remembered? Suppose you did not have a language, but wanted to remember a sunset. Would you picture to yourself the multicolored clouds illuminated by the orange-ish yellow sun that slowly slips beneath the horizon or would you invent some phrase, say, "bluck smuck riggersment" to remember it?

But let's give Hobbes his arbitrary marks. He says that they alone would not be especially helpful to human beings, because even if an individual were quite talented scientifically and discovered all sorts of things for himself using his arbitrary marks, all of his efforts would perish with him when he died. In contrast, if every-one used the same arbitrary marks, then knowledge could be passed from one generation to the next (DCo 2.2). In other words, marks need to become signs. Signs, Hobbes says, are "*the antecedents of consequences and the consequences of antecedents, since we generally experience*

them in a similar way preceding or following one another in a similar fashion"
(DCo 2.2).

This definition is completely general in the sense that it applies
to the arbitrary signs that will supersede the "marks" used for
remembering things and to nonarbitrary signs. The nonarbitrary
signs are natural signs, like dark clouds preceding rain and, conversely, like the rain (or wet trees and ground) that follows dark
clouds. Hobbes's example is interesting because even though he
recognizes natural signs, he must not think that they are easy to
remember, because, if they were, he would not have argued directly
from the nature of human memory to the necessity for marks. I
think that almost everyone can remember that dark clouds precede
rain without the help of words.

But of the two kinds of signs, arbitrary and nonarbitary, Hobbes
cares more about the arbitrary ones. While marks were instituted
for each person's own memory, signs are instituted for the sake of
others. One person uses the arbitrary sign of a barber pole in front
of a building as a sign that haircuts are given inside.

The function of signs explains why as a matter of fact they must
be arbitrary. Everyone who wants to talk to another person needs to
be able to be understood by them. A person cannot produce sounds
that would give someone else either a picture of something or an
odor with the kind of specificity that communication would require.
A person could act out some scenes, but how would the observer
know that the person was acting out something and not merely
doing what he appeared to be doing. Ignoring the problems with
French-speaking dogs and English-speaking dogs, some sounds
could be imitated with the hope that they would be recognized as
recalling earlier instances of those sounds or the animals that produced them, but, again, the resemblance is marginal, the number of
sounds that could be imitated small, and the likelihood that the
observer would recognize the message or recognize the utterance
as a message would be even smaller.

The situation would be improved if the person could draw the observer a picture or a series of pictures. But this is impossible, given Hobbes's belief that human beings are naturally unsocial. One would be risking life and limb to present a picture that expressed, "Let's be friends." Even if people were sociable, the limits on their ability to draw would greatly restrict what they could say. How could one draw the following? "Tomorrow, just before sunrise, let's hunt the lion we saw the day before yesterday." Linguistic communication is easier to generate if arbitrary sounds could be employed. (My guess is that Hobbes began with the knowledge that words are arbitrary signs, and then inferred that marks must be arbitrary.)

NAMES

Here is Hobbes's definition of a name:

> A name is a human vocal sound employed by a decision of man, so that there might be a mark [a] by which a thought similar to a previous thought might be aroused in the mind, and [b] which, ordered in speech and uttered to others, might be a sign to them that such a thought either previously occurred or did not occur in the speaker.
>
> (DCo 2.4)

The inserted letters in brackets indicate that names serve both of the functions he has discussed: those of marks (memory) and of signs (communication), and he holds that the function of marks is prior to that of signs, because "they would serve a man as a memory aid even if he existed alone in the world" (DCo 2.3).

[a] It is highly doubtful whether what Hobbes says about marks is true. If a person were all alone and wanted to remember something because his memory is not good enough to remember the thing directly, how could an arbitrary mark help him? Suppose the person tied a string around his finger with the intention of having it remind him to explore the far side of an island. On the next day, he looks at the string. If his memory is not good enough to

remember that yesterday he wanted to explore the island today, how is the string supposed to help, given that the string adds one more thing to be remembered? It is as if a person who wanted to carry water in a leaking bucket, devised the scheme to first pour the water into a second leaking bucket and then into the first one. More, not less, water would be lost by this method.

[b] As signs, names signify some idea that the speaker wants to convey to his audience. Hobbes, as mentioned above, seems to have the view that the smallest complete unit for linguistic communication is either a sentence or a speech act. The Latin word he uses, "oratio," can be understood to mean either. For linguistic communication, the single vocal sound (vox) "man" is not sufficient to convey a thought. For "man" might be simply the beginning of a word, say, "manageable." Without knowing the complete expression, it is not justified to think that "man" is a word and not merely a syllable of a longer word. Hobbes's point sounds similar to one made famous by Gottlob Frege: it is only in the context of a sentence that a word has a sense.

In order to convey a thought, the first name uttered must be completed by another name, a predicate, to yield, say, "Man is an animal." Of course, people are able to convey a complete thought with a single word, for example, "Fire," but these should be understood as derived from more explicit linguistic forms and not as primary ones. If the vocal sound "Fire" actually were first used to mean "There's a fire in here" or "Let's get out of here because there is a fire in here," then it is obvious from these translations that "Fire" expressed a complete thought, and did not simply name a fire. What would be the point of someone naming a fire if a fire threatened to kill or maim him and his fellows? What is needed is action. The use of "fire" in the circumstances imagined makes sense only if it is part of a useful and complete thought.

Because Hobbes is a nominalist – the only thing universal is a name – he thinks that concrete names are logically prior to abstract names (DCo 2.9).[2] The concrete name "hot" names every hot body. Such bodies are hot by virtue of some cause or property. A property is an abstraction, which is named by the abstract name. The name of the property of hot things is "hotness." According to him, infinitives are also abstract names, for example, "to be hot": "abstract names denote the cause of a concrete name, not the thing itself" (DCo 3.3: "*Nomina autem abstracta causam nominis concreti denotant, non ipsam rem*"). Concrete names are logically prior to abstract ones because concrete names form primary propositions, while abstract names would not exist without concrete ones (DCo 3.4).

Names denotes four basic kinds of things: bodies,[3] accidents, phantasms, and names. Absurdity results when a name that denotes one of these kinds is coupled with a name that denotes one of the other kinds. Hobbes likes to illustrate these absurdities with propositions from Aristotelian or scholastic philosophy. For example, the sentence, "Existence is a being" is absurd because "existence" is the name of an accident (the cause of a body) and "being" is the name of a body. ("Being" is the name of every body.) Another example is "The intellect understands." In this case, Hobbes is taking "the intellect" to be the name of an accident and "understands" to be the name of a body, to wit, the person who understands. An example of copulating the name of a body ("body") with the name of a phantasm ("ghost") is "A ghost is a body." Ghosts, according to Hobbes, are appearances, not bodies (L 34.3). Similarly, "Color is an object of vision" couples the name of a phantasm ("color") with the name of a body ("object of vision"). An example of coupling the name of a body with the name of a name is "A universal is a being." "A universal" is the name of all general names, for example, "all dogs" and "all circles;" the predicate, "a being" names dogs and circles (DCo 5.2–5).

An example of an absurdity that combines the name of an accident with the name of a phantasm is "Color is in the object." "Color" is the name of a phantasm; "in the object" is the name of an accident. Something in an object causes an animal, beast or man, to have the phantasm of color. Similar examples could be constructed with "light," "sight," and "sound" replacing "color." These examples are a neat linguistic way of presenting Hobbes's modernistic view that qualitative properties do not exist in the world in the same way that they are perceived by animals (DCo 5.6).

An example of an absurdity of combining a phantasm with a name is "The idea of a man is universal." The phrase, "The idea of a man," names a phantasm, and "universal" is the name of universal names, for example "all men" (DCo 5.8).

SIGNIFICATION AND DENOTATION

One of the two main semantic theories of the twentieth century, namely, that of Gottlob Frege, distinguishes between the sense and reference of words.[4] Something similar to that distinction was held by philosophers during the Middle Ages. Roughly, in the medieval version, the distinction is between some mental or conceptual feature associated with a name and the ability of the name to pick out some object or objects in the world. Words express concepts and refer to objects that fall under those concepts. In "Every human is a rational animal," the word "human" expresses the concept of a human and thus refers to each human being. Words modified in different ways, for example, "every human," "no human," "some human," and "this human," refer to different individuals or groups of individuals. Hobbes's view is no doubt owed to the medieval view as transmitted through the scholastic logic he learned at school in Oxford.

According to Hobbes, a name signifies a concept and denotes an individual object. In a sentence like, "The stone is heavy," the word "stone" signifies that the speaker is thinking of a stone and denotes the stone that the speaker is thinking about (DCo 2.5). The scope of naming should not be underestimated. There can be names for images of stones or trees or any other body. There can also be names for figments of the imagination, a unicorn, and even names for things that do not exist, for example, the word "future." "Unicorn" and "future" are names of things that do not exist. Even what is not, was not, will not, and cannot be has a name, for example, the word "impossible." And the word "nothing" is a name; it names . . . nothing (DCo 2.6).

Hobbes presents a traditional categorization of names. There are positive and negative names, such as "man" and "nonman." The words "man" and "nonman" are also a pair of contradictories. Everything is named by one or the other name, and nothing gets both names. Proper names are intended to name only one thing, such as, "this," "Homer," and "the author of the *Iliad*." They are what today might be called "singular terms" since they include demonstratives, proper names and descriptions (DCo 2.8). Common names are names that might be common to or true of more than one thing. The word "dog" is the name of every dog, taken individually, not as a collection. So is the word "moon." Many planets have moons. But even if the earth's moon were the only one, "moon" would still be a common name because it could be applied to other natural satellites of a planet if they had them. Common names are also called "universal names" because of their scope. And the name "universal" "is not the name of something existing in nature, nor of an idea or of some phantasm formed in the mind, but is always the name of some vocal sound or name" (DCo 2.9). So the word "dog" is a universal because it names many things. This is a statement of Hobbes's nominalism. Only individuals exist. Universals are names that may denote many things.

Hobbes's traditionalism in logic is evident from his treatment of "universal, particular, individual, and indefinite names." For him, an individual name ("Homer") has a definite and fixed signification and hence is the name of one thing. A name formed by prefixing "all" or "every" or "whichever" to a common name is a universal name ("every dog") (DCo 2.11). Names formed by prefixing "some" or "a certain" to a common name are particular names because, says Hobbes, they have "indefinite signification." They name something particular but signify it indefinitely in the sense that one cannot figure out who or what is being named simply by knowing the signification of the phrase. Finally, names that do not have any "quantifier" word in front of them are indefinite names.

SPEECH ACTS

Hobbes was more insightful about the *use* of language than almost any other philosopher prior to the twentieth century. His distinction between a sentence used to counsel someone and a sentence (sometimes the very same sentence) used to command someone is put to good use in *Leviathan* when he explains what a law is. A law is a command; it is to be followed because the speaker wants it to be followed. A counsel gives advice and need not be followed by the person who gets it. A command expresses what is or appears to be good for the speaker, while a counsel expresses what is supposed to be good for the addressee (EL 29.1; L 6.55, 25.4, 25.11). One can argue with Hobbes about the essential difference between the two. But that he recognized that there is an important contrast between command and counsel and made substantive use of it in his political philosophy is impressive.

At least as impressive is his recognition that religious language ought to be used to honor God, not to describe him (DC 15.18; L 3.12). This difference between two uses of language supports his sharp distinction between faith and reason. The language of reason is descriptive; the language of faith is honorific. The two cannot contradict each other precisely because language used honorifically is neither true nor false, but either appropriate or inappropriate. Some of the predicates traditionally assigned to God would be literally inconsistent with each other if they were being used descriptively (L 31.16–27). (See Chapter 6, "Religion.")

Other uses of language that Hobbes mentions are questions, requests, promises, threats, decisions, commands, and lamentations.[5] He mentions these in order to help isolate the use of language characteristic of logic. A proposition, he says, is "speech consisting of two copulated names by which the one who is speaking signifies that he conceives the name which occurs second to be the name of the same thing as the name which occurs first" (DCo 3.2).[6] One problem with this definition is that it only applies to subject-predicate propositions. The predicate of the proposition, "Ava ran a mile," is not a name, and a person who asserts it is not saying that "ran a mile" is a name of Ava. We shall see that Hobbes sometimes talks as if the most important propositions are subject-predicate ones, and sometimes talks as if conditional propositions are more important.

DEFINITIONS

Definitions are important for Hobbes because they are the most basic propositions of science. They are "first in reasoning," because nothing can be proved without them. They are "truths established by the decision of speakers and hearers, and therefore indemonstrable" (DCo 3.9). Implicit in these remarks is a tension or contradiction between the relevant importance of the speaker vis-à-vis the hearer or a problematic vagueness about who the speakers and hearers are. Suppose the speaker wants a word to mean one thing and the hearer either does not want it to mean that or thinks that it does not mean that. Who's the master? It might seem that the speaker is the master, but what if the speaker wants the word "war" to mean "a state of tranquility and happiness" and "peace" to mean "the aggressive attempt to impose one's will on another." Does the hearer have to accept these definitions? Or suppose that some speakers and hearers of a community use a word w to mean M, and other speakers and hearers of the same community use w to mean N. How does a hearer know which meaning w has if the hearer does not have prior information about how the speaker uses w? Suppose that the speaker says that by w, she means the same as the word x. How can the hearer know that the speaker means by x the same thing that she, the hearer, means by x? These are general problems connected with meaning and definition. Although Hobbes does not solve any of these problems satisfactorily, he raises interesting issues in connection with them. They are easiest to explain if for expository purposes we distinguish between technical (stipulative) definitions and descriptive ones.

A technical definition is one in which a scientist declares that he will use a word in a particular way. That way may be different from the ordinary use of the word although it often overlaps with it. Hobbes intended his definition of "philosophy" to fit the ordinary use. (See below in the section from pp. 149–50.) But his comment that "those who are looking for another philosophy are advised to look elsewhere" suggests that his definition is a technical one, and he would not change it even if it did not accord with ordinary usage (DCo 1.10, 25.1).

Also, when Hobbes lists the properties of a definition, he seems to have technical definitions in mind, as indicated by at least two of these properties. One is that a definition "removes equivocation and indeed that whole multitude of distinctions which those use who think that philosophy can be acquired by quarreling" (DCo 6.15). The other is that it is "not necessary to quarrel over whether a definition is to be admitted or not" because if the hearer ("the student") does not accept the definition, "it is the same as if he did not want to learn." Technical scientific definitions do not aim at describing how people use words but at making things clear.

It would seem that the notion of an incorrect definition would not make sense in relation to technical definitions. They are either accepted or not. Yet, Hobbes does refer to "wrong" or incorrect definitions: "So that in the right definition of names lies the first use of speech, which is the acquisition of names, and in wrong or no definitions lies the first abuse, from which proceed all false and senseless tenets." He thinks they need to be nipped in the bud because, as "reckoning proceeds," absurdities in the system will multiply (L 4.13). My guess is that an incorrect definition is one that conceals a contradiction within it. Although the concept of an absurdity will be dealt with in more detail later, for now it is appropriate to mention that absurdities often arise when people are trying to do science because scientific propositions, according to Hobbes, are necessarily true. So any mistake in a scientific system will be the negation of a necessarily true proposition, and the negation of a necessarily true proposition is a contradiction, a proposition easily called "absurd." Here's an example. Suppose that one holds the following propositions:

(1) All squares are figures with equal internal angles.
(2) All figures with equal internal angles are isosceles triangles.
(3) No square is a triangle.

(1) and (2) entail

(4) All squares are isosceles triangles.

(4) entails

(5) Some squares are triangles.

And (5) contradicts (3). In short, some definition or some proposition that follows from a definition among (1)–(3) is incorrect. (It is (2), of course.)

Given his beliefs that people use words with inconsistent meanings (L 4.24, 25.1) and use words that are literally meaningless, it is surprising that Hobbes does not rail against using words as ordinary speakers and hearers generally use words. Yet he does not. In fact, sometimes he seems to hold that scientific definitions are correct or incorrect according to whether they accord with usage. It is necessary, he says, for a person who "aspires to true knowledge to examine the definitions of former authors and either to correct them, where they are negligently set down, or to make them himself" (L 4.13; see also QLNC 396). It is plausible that Hobbes is urging scientists to learn from the discoveries of previous scientists, notwithstanding his generally negative view of actual scientific progress (L 4.12).

Hobbes does not make clear the relation between technical definitions, which the speaker has the right to stipulate, and descriptive definitions, which are determined by the community of speakers. Overall, I think his inclination is to favor technical definitions in scientific works, and scientists should look at "the definitions of former authors," not because they are bound by them, but because they may be able to build upon their results.

However the tension between technical and descriptive definitions should be worked out, Hobbes seems to be committed to one other view of definitions, a view that I think he would never abandon. For him, the sovereign resolves all disputes (DC 16.16). So if there is a dispute about the meaning of a word, no matter in what area of human discourse, it is the sovereign, not speakers and hearers generally or even scientists, who establishes the true or appropriate definition.

NECESSARY AND CONTINGENT PROPOSITIONS

It is easy to confuse two very different distinctions in Hobbes's philosophy. One concerns the necessity and contingency of events in the world. Every event that is caused occurs necessarily or is a necessary event. Whether an event is necessary or not does not depend on anyone's knowledge. Hobbes believes that all events are necessary because he is a determinist. A contingent event is one that did or did not or may or may not occur, given our limited knowledge. So although there will either be a sea battle tomorrow or there will not be one, and whichever situation turns out to be the case will necessarily be the case, the event is contingent because there is no way for us to know whether the sea battle will occur or not. The distinction between necessity and contingency belongs to metaphysics and epistemology, not to language or logic.

The other distinction is between necessary and contingent propositions. It does belong to logic or the philosophy of language: "A *proposition* is necessary when no thing can be conceived or imagined at any time, of which the *subject* is a name while the predicate is not." In "every necessary proposition, the predicate is either equivalent to the subject," as in "Man is a rational animal" or it is part of an equivalent name, for example, "Man is rational" (DCo 3.10). In contrast, a contingent proposition "is one which can sometimes be true and sometimes false," for example, "Some cats are yellow." To use one of Hobbes's examples, even if "All men are liars" is true, it would be only contingently true, because "liars" is not part of the meaning of "men" (DCo 3.10). Hobbes's definition of a contingent proposition is not completely successful because many propositions that are not necessary are always true. For example, "John F. Kennedy is President of the United States of America on January 1, 1962" is always true but is not necessary because the predicate is not part of the meaning of "John F. Kennedy."

Let this suffice for understanding Hobbes's philosophy of language. We now turn to his philosophy of science, which includes his views about logic.

THE VALUE OF PHILOSOPHY

Today, pure science, in contrast with engineering, law, and other professional disciplines, is often considered purely theoretical and thus without practical value in itself. Any practical value that comes from science, conceived in this way, is an application of science, not science itself. Philosophy is often thought of in the same way. Many philosophers in the best American universities consider specialties like business ethics or medical ethics not genuine parts of philosophy, precisely because they are applications of philosophy and not theoretical.

Hobbes conceived of science and philosophy quite differently. He did not believe in the wholly theoretical pursuit of truth. For him, philosophy should be practical (utile).

> For I do not think that the great effort that must be expended in philosophy is worthwhile in order for someone to rejoice and exult silently to himself alone over some difficulty regarding doubtful matters that had been conquered or the detection of extremely hidden paths.
>
> (DCo 1.6)

Archimedes had discovered the value of π so precisely that, given a circle with radius 10,000,000 equal parts, a quadrant of the circle would be between 15,704,225 and 15,714,285 parts. Two Dutch mathematicians, Ludovicus van Cullun and Willebrordus Snellius made the calculation even more precise (DCo 20.1). But Hobbes was not impressed with their efforts.

> [I]f we consider the benefits, which is the scope at which all speculation should aim, the improvement they have made has been little or none. For any ordinary man may much sooner and more accurately find a straight line equal to the perimeter of a circle, and consequently square the circle, by winding a small thread about a given cylinder, than any geometrician shall do the same by dividing the radius into 10,000,000 equal parts.
>
> (DCo 20.1)

Although its importance will only be discovered later, notice first that Hobbes thinks that an empirical procedure, winding a thread around a cylinder, gives a geometrical result. It is not the experimental aspect that is important, but the fact that a physical object, a string, is giving the circumference of the circle and that a physical object, when stretched, produces a straight line. For Hobbes, geometric proofs are constructions or instructions about how to make a construction.

The second thing to notice in the quotation above is that philosophy, according to Hobbes, should make human existence more comfortable. That means finding out how to measure bodies and their motions, how to move heavy weights and to build buildings, and how to navigate the seas and to map the face of the earth (DCo 1.7). Even more importantly, philosophy, in particular, moral and political philosophy, is to be valued for preventing calamities caused by people themselves, especially civil war (DCo 1.7). "Knowledge," Hobbes says, "is for the sake of power" (DCo 1.6);[7] and that power can be used to prevent the worst from happening to humans.

Hobbes, like Descartes, says that all people are roughly equal in intelligence. The difference between the developed civilizations of Europe, most of Asia, and part of Africa, and the uncivilized parts is philosophy, the right method of discovering truth. Many scholars think that Hobbes and Descartes were joking about equal intelligence. But if they were, then their emphasis on the benefits of proper methodology loses its force. If they thought that proper methodology was built on a foundation of great intelligence it seems to me that they would have said so.

THE SCOPE AND DEFINITION OF PHILOSOPHY

For Hobbes, as for other seventeenth-century intellectuals, philosophy was identical with science. (The physicist Isaac Newton was a professor of "Natural Philosophy.") Philosophy deals with "every body of which any generation can be conceived and of which a comparison can be made after any consideration of it" (DCo 1.8; see also DCo 6.13). Consequently, philosophy deals only with things that involve generation or at least have properties of which humans can have knowledge. Thus, Hobbes says, theology is not part of philosophy (DCo 1.8). God is not an object of science, Hobbes avers, because his nature cannot be known and hence cannot be described.[8] But this position is not really acceptable in light of other things he says. For example, science does not give humans knowledge of the nature of ordinary things: "[T]he principles of natural science . . . cannot teach us our own nature, nor the nature of the smallest creature living" (L 31.33). Further, since every cause is a moving cause, according to Hobbes, God moved when he created the world and hence should be an object of science. Even the fact that God is invisible to humans should not put him beyond the pale of science, both because physics considers invisible causes (DCo 6.6) and because Hobbes allows one to infer causes from effects. In fact, Hobbes infers the existence of God from the effects observable in the visible world. That is the proof for the existence of God from motion.

My guess is that Hobbes knew that little more than the existence of God could be proved through scientific reasoning and was so intent on squelching speculation about the nature of God that he exaggerated the smallness of the role God plays in science (cf. Calvin 1559: I.10.2). Human beliefs about God should be provided by the Bible and the sovereign.

In Leviathan, Hobbes divided science into two main parts. The first is natural philosophy, which consists of the "Consequences from the accidents of bodies natural" (L 9, diagram). The second is politics or civil philosophy, which consists of "Consequences from the accidents of politic bodies" (L 9, diagram). The division of philosophy in Leviathan does not fit with the tripartite scheme of philosophy that Hobbes worked out in De corpore, De homine, and De cive. Of these two ways of dividing science, the one in Leviathan makes more sense. Human beings outside of civil states are simply physical bodies. So the material in De homine does not deserve a separate volume.

Hobbes's conception of science can be made more precise by carefully considering his definition of philosophy: philosophy is "[a] the knowledge, [b] acquired through correct reasoning, [c] of effects or phenomena from the conception of their causes or generations, and also [d] of generations which could exist from the knowledge of their effects" (DCo 1.2; see also 6.1, 25.1, and L 46.1). Hobbes virtually repeats this definition in Chapter 6.1 and in Leviathan 46.1.[9] I will discuss [a] through [d] at length below.

[a] According to Hobbes, there are two kinds of factual (in contrast with scientific) knowledge: sensation and memory (L 9.1). Hobbes calls this knowledge "absolute." There are two kinds of statements or expressions of absolute knowledge, according to Hobbes, natural science and civil history (L 9.2). But these statements are not the knowledge itself (L 7.3). By dividing statements of factual knowledge into history and civil history, Hobbes is obviously thinking only of factual statements about the past, the ones in memory. It seems to me that he should not have omitted statements of fact about the present, such as, "I feel happy."

Knowledge of fact, past or present, depends upon sense experience and is common to beasts and human beings. When multiple instances of the same kind of sensation are remembered, the knowledge is experience. Because memory is fallible, experience and hence beliefs about factual information are fallible (DCo 1.2; see also L 2.4; EL 4.6; and DCo 25.8). A person might believe that "This box is red" expresses a fact, when actually, the box is white but cleverly illuminated by a red light. Many twentieth-century empiricists maintained that pure sense experiences were infallible and that many of the statements that Hobbes would call empirical are not really so. For example, "This is red" would supposedly report a pure sense experience, about which the person having it could not be mistaken. Hobbes's class of factual propositions ("This is a red box") is much broader and includes concepts that twentieth-century empiricists would have considered to some degree theoretical, including ordinary concepts like that of a box.

In most contexts, what is absolute is considered superior to what is conditional or hypothetical; so knowledge of fact sounds superior to scientific knowledge, but not according to the way Hobbes explains absolute and conditional. "Conditional" and "hypothetical" refer to the grammatical form of the proposition, for example, "If something is a human being, then it is rational." This statement does not assert the existence of a human being. It merely says that if something is the case, then something else is necessarily the case (DCo 3.10). In scientific propositions, the relationship between the antecedent of this conditional ("if . . .") and its consequent ("then . . .") is necessary, not merely by virtue of the conditional form, but by virtue of the meanings of the terms in the antecedent and consequent. The conditional, "If something is a human being, then it is rational," is a scientific proposition and necessarily true because a human being is rational, by definition. Here's another example: "If something is a circle, then the distance between its center and each point on its perimeter is the same." This statement is necessarily true, because of the necessity between the meaning of "circle" and the meaning of "the distance between." The consequent of the conditional gives either the definition of a circle or a proposition that follows from the definition of the circle (DCo 6.16).

Although he claims that scientific propositions are essentially conditional propositions and logically more basic than categorical propositions, Hobbes makes this claim after he has written about categorical syllogisms as if they were the basic form of scientific demonstration (see also DCo 6.13; cf. Hanson 1990). He does not convert what he said about categorical propositions to reasoning with conditional ones. If he had, he might have recognized that conditional propositions contribute to argument forms that categorical propositions do not, for example, *modus ponens* and *modus tollens*. He might also have noticed that conditional propositions are equivalent to certain other noncategorical propositions. "If p, then q" is equivalent to "If not q, then not p," "Not p or q" and "It is not the case that (p and not q)."

Also unfortunate is the fact that his treatment of syllogistic reasoning is perfunctory and a simplification of Aristotelian logic. He observes that a syllogism – he defines "syllogism" in such a way that only valid "syllogisms" are syllogisms – has exactly three terms, a major, minor, and middle; that nothing can be inferred from two particular propositions; and that there are various combinations of premises that can occur in syllogisms (DCo 4.2–12). His treatment is not more incisive and elaborate because he has a low opinion of the "precepts of syllogizing." The way to learn logic is to do mathematics: "[T]hey who devote their time to the demonstrations of mathematicians will learn true logic more rapidly" (DCo 4.13). What Hobbes does not seem to appreciate here is that almost no mathematical thinking is formulated in categorical syllogisms. So he owed the reader a direct account of scientific reasoning in terms of conditional propositions and mathematical reasoning.

When Hobbes discusses the correct method of science and

discusses the nature of "demonstration" ("*demonstratio*") or proof, he again talks about it in terms of categorical syllogisms:

> Any two definitions which can be compounded into a syllogism produce a conclusion which is said to be demonstrated because it is derived from principles, that is, from definitions; and the derivation or compound itself is called a proof. Similarly, if a syllogism is made from two propositions, of which one is a definition and the other a conclusion that has been previously demonstrated, then that syllogism is also said to be a demonstration.
>
> (DCo 6.16)

Although Hobbes admired the rigorous reasoning of geometry, he still conceived of chains of proof only as chains of syllogisms, and he did not insist on using the geometrical term "theorem." The word "conclusion" was precise enough (cf. Hanson 1990). Since geometry was his paradigm of science, he should have discussed geometric reasoning in detail. However, when he gets to the section on geometry in *De corpore*, he discusses basic concepts as that of point, line and figure, and then purports to prove various theorems. What he does not talk about is methodology.

I suspect that Hobbes's view that scientific propositions are conditional and true by virtue of the meanings of the component propositions was intended in part to overcome skeptical challenges to the possibility of science and indubitable knowledge. The clause that expresses the hypothesis ("if such and such"), immunizes the entire proposition against the factual falsity that might occur if the denoted object did not exist. And the semantic connection between the subject and predicate terms immunizes the entire proposition against the factual falsity of the object denoted in the antecedent not having the property denoted in the consequent. In short, a conditional proposition guards against the possibility that the object that a statement seems to be about does not exist and against the possibility that that object does not have the property it is said to have. Science, for Hobbes, is a system of hedged assertions.

If Hobbes's philosophy of science was intended to conquer skepticism, it nonetheless would not have succeeded in quieting the committed skeptic, who might ask how the person who is expressing the consequent of the conditional proposition can be certain that he is correctly remembering the meaning of the term he introduced when he was expressing the antecedent. Hobbes is assuming the reliability of memory, so scientific knowledge is no more secure from error than supposed factual knowledge is. Also, even though Descartes was only a methodological skeptic, not a practicing one, he, I think, would be dissatisfied with Hobbes's foundation for science for at least two reasons. First, it did not have an existential foundation. One of the most important aspects of Descartes's "*cogito*" is the fact that it begins with something that exists. In contrast with scholastic systems that began with self-evident conceptual truths that did not commit a person to any existing thing, for example, "everything is identical with itself" and "every object either has a particular property or it does not," Descartes begins with something in the real world. Second, Descartes thinks that fundamental truths (except perhaps the *cogito*, which is self-certifying) needed a criterion or test of their truth. For him it is clearness and distinctness. Hobbes rejects both of these aspects of Cartesian science. Hobbes holds to the classical view that science is a set of general or abstract truths, not individual truths or objects. And Hobbes knows that if one tries to use a criterion to overcome skepticism, the skeptic can always be skeptical about either the appropriateness of the criterion or the correctness of its application. In his *Objections* to Descartes's *Meditations*, Hobbes provides enough evidence that he was not gripped by skeptical doubts in the way that Descartes was. (See Chapter 1.)

[b] Let's now consider the second element of Hobbes's definition of philosophy, "acquired through correct reasoning." Just as knowledge of fact comes from sensation, scientific knowledge comes from reasoning; it is "*knowledge of the consequence of one affirmation to another*" (L 9.1).

This feature alone distinguishes science from knowledge of fact since the latter does not depend on reasoning. Reasoning, according to Hobbes, is computation, and computation adding and subtracting:

> And to compute is *to collect the sum of many things added together at the same time, or to know the remainder when one thing has been taken from another*. To reason therefore is the same as to add or to subtract.
>
> (DCo 1.2)

In *Leviathan*, he says the same thing:

> When a man *reasoneth*, he does nothing else but conceive a sum total from *addition* of parcels, or conceive a remainder, from *subtraction* of one sum from another; which (if it be done by words) is conceiving of the consequence of the names of all the parts to the name of the whole, or from the names of the whole and one part, to the name of the other part.
>
> (L 5.1)

Hobbes's illustration of computation is rather informal. Suppose someone were to observe something obscurely at a great distance. The observer cannot put any word to the object other than "a body." It has to be a body, because bodies are the only things that exist according to Hobbes. If the observer then approaches the object, she may see that the object is moving in a certain way that leads her to call the body "animate." Approaching still closer, she hears the voice of the animate body and sees evidence of intelligence; she attributes the word "rational" to it. She can then compound or compute all of her ideas and conclude that the object is a human. In other words, the observer is totaling up the ideas of rational, animate, and body, and getting the sum, human being. Subtraction of ideas is easily illustrated by thinking of the same human being moving away from the observer. When it can no longer be observed to be rational, that idea is subtracted and the observer has the idea of an animal, and when the animal moves so far away that it cannot be seen to be animate, the observer is left with the idea of a body.

Even if we accept this description of coming to see (and not to see) that something is a human being, one cannot simply generalize and say that all reasoning is addition and subtraction. What does this simple agglomeration of ideas have to do with propositional reasoning? Let's restrict the question to reasoning with categorical syllogisms. After giving a treatment of syllogistic reasoning that relies heavily on definitions of major, minor, and middle terms, and the impossibility of inferring a valid conclusion from particular premises, Hobbes begins a new section with the sentence,

> It is obvious from the preceding that a syllogism is nothing other than a collection of a sum which is made from two propositions (through a common term which is called the middle term) conjoined to one another; and thus a syllogism is an addition of three names, just as a proposition is of two.
>
> (DCo 4.6)

In fact, it is not obvious "from the preceding" how a syllogism is a collection of a sum made from two propositions. What does it mean to add "through a common term"? Consider two seemingly similar arguments:

| All humans are mortal objects. | All humans are mortal objects. |
All mortal objects are bodies.	All bodies are mortal objects.
All humans are bodies.	All humans are bodies.

Each argument is "adding through" the same term, "mortal objects." What makes the syllogism in the first column valid and the argument in the second column invalid? The laws of arithmetic will not tell us. The laws of valid syllogistic reasoning do not say anything about adding and subtracting. Here is a typical set of laws: "At least one premise must be affirmative," "If a premise is negative, the conclusion must be negative," "If a premise contains a particular premise, the conclusion must be particular," "The middle term must be distributed at least once," and "Any term that is 'distributed' in the conclusion must be distributed in a premise."

Among other ways of determining the validity of a syllogism is one that involves assigning pluses and minuses to terms and premises with rules about what combinations are valid (Sommers 1970). But there is nothing essentially additive or subtractive in these assignments or rules. The assignments or rules could have been formulated in terms of the colors red and blue or concepts of tables and chairs, or anything else.

An underlying reason why reasoning is not simply arithmetic adding and subtracting is that addition and subtraction apply to numbers, not propositions. The number 2 is added to 2 to get 4. This is essentially different from asserting, "2 plus 2 equals 4," even though that proposition states something true about the numbers 2 and 4. Individual numbers do not assert anything; they are neither true nor false. In contrast, a proposition is either true or false. To take the basic case, the object denoted by the subject of a sentence is said to have the property denoted by the predicate of that sentence. The proposition is true when the thing denoted by the subject has the property denoted by the predicate (DCo 3.7, 5.2).[10] The subject and predicate of a sentence do not add up to 2, 3, or any other number. To say that they "add" up to a sentence is to use an inapt metaphor. The point is not that reasoning is not computation; it is that reasoning is not obviously always addition and subtraction, and Hobbes gave no good reason for his readers to think so. He gives the illusion of explaining what computation is.

So far, what I have been saying about Hobbes's view of philosophy makes it essentially a linguistic affair. Science consists of a certain kind of sentence or proposition and the truth of those propositions is guaranteed by the meanings of the terms in those propositions, not in some relation to the world. The hook-up is effected by virtue of the fact that names name bodies in the world. The word "human" is the name of each human being; "white" is the name of each white thing, and "tall" is the name of each tall thing. Because words hook up to empirical objects in the world, Hobbes may be called "a term empiricist." Hobbes is not an empiricist in the sense of one who makes empirical sentences the foundations of science. Hobbes's view is intuitive. It contrasts with the dominant view in contemporary philosophy, according to which the primary way in which language hooks up with the world is through sentences. There are basic sentences ("There's a rabbit") about some observable event (a rabbit hopping by) that makes the sentence true. The hook-up is between the entire sentence and the event, not the more commonsense view that the hook-up occurs between the word "rabbit" and the rabbit.

[c] For Hobbes, there are two scientific methods: One is described in clause [c], the other in clause [d]. Clause [d], which will be discussed in more detail below, describes a method, the analytic or resolutive method, that begins with effects or phenomena and reason to their causes. Clause [c] describes the method that goes from causes to effects. It is a "synthetic" and "compositive" method because it seems to generate or give composite effects. There is some scholarly controversy about what the terms analytic and synthetic (and resolutive and compositive) mean or what Hobbes means by them (Hanson 1990). They were used by Renaissance scholastics, and it is not clear whether Hobbes meant what they meant by them, nor what those philosophers meant by them. For our purposes, it is better to ignore the Renaissance view and concentrate on Hobbes's own words and interests.

We need to begin by recalling the importance of motion for Hobbes. Everything comes to be, not to mention passing away, by virtue of motion (DCo 25.1; Jesseph 1996: 90).[11] Hence, he inferred, to understand the world is to understand how things come to be. He also thought that there must be some small number of ways that things come to be – through contact between bodies – and so the principles would be few and generative. That is, the correct scientific principles would state how things come to be.

One way to understand Hobbes's point is to think of the way that sentences might be constructed in a language. Suppose there is a set of sentence letters, A, B, . . ., Z, two propositional connectives, ~, →, and three generation rules:

(GR1)   Enter any sentence letter as a sentence.
(GR2)   If Φ is a sentence, enter ⌜ ~ Φ ⌝ as a sentence.
(GR3)   If Φ and Ψ are sentences, enter ⌜(Φ → Ψ)⌝ as a sentence.

We can then generate the following sentences:

(1)	A	by GR1
(2)	B	by GR1
(3)	~A	from 1 by GR2
(4)	(~A → B)	from 3 and 2 by GR3
(5)	((~A → B) → B)	from 4 and 2 by GR3
(6)	(((~A → B) → B) → ((~A → B) →B))	from 5 and 5 by GR3
(7)	(((~A → B) → B) → (((~A → B) → B)→ ((~A → B) →B)))	from 5 and 6 by GR3.

These generated sentences obviously become complex in a short period of time. If one thinks of the rules and lines of generation used in the generation of subsequent lines as the causes of the lines they generate, it is easy to see how Hobbes could think of the scientific method that begins with causes and explains effects as constructive. For example, the immediate causes of (7) are (5) and (6) by rule (GR3). Hobbes of course did not know anything about generative or recursive rules. I am using one aspect of contemporary linguistic theory to illustrate Hobbes's idea that causes generate effects that are seemingly more complicated than the causes.[12]

The way in which successive causes make effects more complex can also be seen in connection with constructive geometry, Hobbes's paradigmatic science. A constructive geometer has only two instruments: a compass and straightedge (unmarked ruler). The geometer has only two ways of drawing a line:[13]

(1) With the straightedge one may draw the line segment that joins any two given points, and one may extend any line indefinitely.
(2) With the compass, one may draw a circle by keeping one leg fixed at a point (the center point), extending the other leg a fixed distance from the first, and moving it until a closed plane figure is formed (a circle).

Figure 5.1 shows a generation of a line that bisects a given angle. First, a circle was drawn taking A as the center. The circle intersects the angle BAC at points B and C. Obviously, AB = AC since they are radii of the same circle. Then a circle was drawn with B as its center;

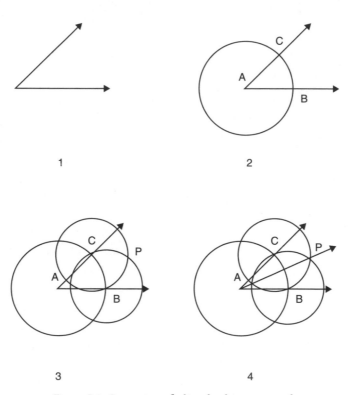

Figure 5.1 Generation of a line that bisects an angle

the radius r = BC. Then a circle was drawn with C as its center and the same radius r = BC. The two circles intersect at two points, one being P. (This is known as the Two Circle Theorem, not discussed here.) Finally, the line AP was drawn. Since the triangle PAB is congruent with the triangle PAC, the line AP bisects the angle BAC.

We now need to step back and consider a tension or contradiction in Hobbes's conception of science. On the one hand, he holds that scientific propositions are necessarily true by virtue of their meanings, and there does not need to be anything constructive in such propositions. Sentences true by virtue of their meanings are sometimes called "truisms," and truisms make no substantive assertion, for example, "All white horses are white." Simply to define a term is not to make any advance in proving something informative, and any inference drawn from a definition will be similarly uninformative. On the other hand, he holds that science says how things come to be. And if we think of constructive geometry, we see that new things, sometimes very complex, come to be. Relative to the constructions themselves, the propositions that describe the constructions may seem unimportant. This seems to be obvious from some of Hobbes's own work. Here is one of his constructions, and he peppers his scientific works with many constructions just about as complicated.

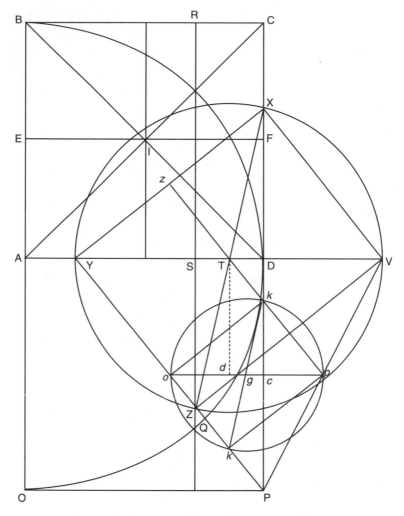

Figure 5.2 Generation of a complex geometrical figure

The construction is a physical operation and is not itself a proposition. In short, Hobbes explicates the concept of scientific thinking in terms of syllogisms consisting of definitions or propositions following from definitions; yet, his paradigmatic examples of scientific reasoning are geometric constructions.

He might have tried to reconcile the two general conceptions by discussing the relationship between the constructions and the propositions that describe the constructions and what they prove. But if he had done this, he would have been giving up the syllogistic conception of science, because the directions for constructing geometrical figures are not syllogisms. Consider two definitions of a circle. (i) A circle is a plane figure of which each point on the perimeter is equidistant from a given point inside the figure. (ii) A circle is a figure generated by placing one leg of a compass at a point with the other leg at a fixed distance from it and moving that leg until a closed plane figure is formed. The first, or analytic, definition says nothing about how it was constructed; the second, or constructive, definition does. Ideally, Hobbes is committed to giving constructive definitions of all the terms he uses in his scientific propositions. In this way, he was ahead of his time since an important part of contemporary science, especially physics and biology, says how things are constructed and how they may be constructed when they can be. But in fact few of his definitions are constructive, for example, "A human being is a rational, animate, body."

The tension or conflict between his two conceptions of science comes out within a very short space in *De homine*, his last statement of the nature of science. He says that science deals with "the truth of general propositions" (DH 10.4). He explicates "the truth of general propositions" as "the truth of consequences."[14] However, he also implies that the constructions of individual geometrical figures are either scientific propositions or at least part of science:

[M]any theorems are demonstrable about quantity, the science whereof is called geometry. Since the cause of the properties that individual figures have belong to them because we ourselves draw the lines; and since the generation of the figures depends on our will; nothing more is required to know the phenomenon peculiar to any figure whatsoever, than that we consider everything that follows from the construction that we ourselves make in the figures to be described.

(DH 10.5; see also DCo 25.1)

Since the lines that geometers draw are individual lines, individual objects or individual propositions that describe these lines seem to be part of science, contrary to what he said about generality in the preceding paragraph (DH 10.4).

I suspect that the conflict just considered, namely, the idea that the truth of general propositions depends on the truth of consequences and the inclusion of particular phenomena within science, may be connected in this way: for Hobbes,

(A) If something is a circle, then each point on its perimeter is equidistant from a point within the circle,

is equivalent to

(B) All circles are things about which each point on its perimeter is equidistant from a point within the circle.

And what seems to guarantee the truth of both of them is the semantic connection between the predicate expressions in (A) and the obviously related subject and predicate of (B). Further, (A) bears a superficial resemblance to the singular proposition, (C):

(C) If this is a circle, then each point on its perimeter is equidistant from a point within the circle.

However, as predicate logic shows, while A is in fact a universal proposition, "$(\Lambda x)(Cx \to Px)$," (C) in fact is a conditional proposition with two singular propositions as components, "$(Ct \to Pt)$." Hobbes can be excused in large part for not sensing the difference between (A) and (C), but it is surprising that he does not see the difference between his claim that scientific propositions are general and his inclusion of an individual object as a scientific phenomenon.

Although his conceptions of science as propositional and science as constructive are in tension with each other, at one point he combines them to make a claim about the relative certainty of various sciences. (However, we shall see that the claim is false.) He maintains that the propositions of geometry are necessary and a priori, precisely because we ourselves create the figures. In short, he thinks that geometry is more certain than physics. But Hobbes's argument is unsound because of factual mistakes. Some geometric figures are caused by humans, in particular, those the geometer draws using straightedge and compass. But most geometric figures are not. Every body has some geometric figure, and we do not know exactly what figures they have because we did not create them. These geometric bodies are identical with the ones of physics, which Hobbes acknowledges come from an inscrutable cause. Further, he is wrong about the objects of physics. Some of them are objects created by human geometers. That is, when a human constructs a line, circle or any other geometric object, he is also creating an object of physics. So humans do know the causes of these objects of physics.

Hobbes's mistake about the certainty of geometry gets transferred to his views about ethics and politics. He thinks that those sciences are like geometry because "we ourselves make the principles, that is, the causes of justice (namely, laws and covenants)" (DH 10.5). However, covenants for individual civil states and individual laws are what humans make. When humans know the exact cause of a civil state, they know the historical events that created it. This knowledge, obviously, belongs to history, not science. Humans do not make what is distinctively scientific about morals, namely, the laws of nature. The laws of nature are eternal and discovered by reason, not invented. Humans could not decide to make "Promote war" or "Break your covenants" laws of nature. Humans do not make the principal concepts or propositions of politics either. The nature of sovereignty, for example, is fixed and eternal. What humans invent, or one community of humans, is the convention to have the word "sovereignty" mean sovereignty. The fact that humans define "covenant," "justice" and other key terms of politics, goes no way towards showing that humans create that science, for they define the terms of every science. Certainty comes from beginning with definitions and from constructing one's own objects (DCo 25.1), no matter whether those definitions and constructions are part of geometry, politics, or physics. Hobbes thinks that certainty is not possible when one begins with effects and reasons to causes. This is the method discussed in clause [d].

[d] Analytic reasoning, it seems, begins with an actual individual effect and hypothesizes a possible cause for it. Hobbes says that this is the study of physics, but I don't see why it does not belong as much to practical geometry. For example, for some given plane figure F, one might hypothesize that it was formed with the use of a compass: one foot of the compass was placed in a fixed point, which eventually became the center of the circle; the other foot was rotated through 360 degrees. Of course there are other hypotheses. The circle may have been formed by tracing the perimeter of a circular template. Another hypothesis, which Hobbes does not seem to consider, is that the figure is not a circle at all.

But whichever hypothesis is used, the result is a true, conditional proposition: either (1) If this figure F was formed by placing one foot of the compass, etc., then F is a circle; or (2) If this figure F was formed by tracing the perimeter of a circular template, then F is a circle.[15]

The method of analysis differs from the method of synthesis in at least three ways. The first, which has just been described, is that the starting point of the scientific process is an event that is considered as an effect, not a cause. The second is that the effect is an individual thing or event, and hence the proposition that explains it is a singular proposition. This is connected with the first difference because actual effects in the world are individual: "If this figure was generated," and so on. Hobbes's willingness to explain individual effects with particular propositions seems to contradict his explicit statement that science consists of "the truth of general propositions" (DH 10.4). The third difference is that the explanation given in the antecedent of the hypothetical proposition is not necessarily the correct explanation of how the effect actually came to be. Proposition (1) is necessarily true because of the necessary relationship between the movement of a compass and a circle, even if the antecedent of (1) is false. The true explanation of the generation of the figure F might be the antecedent of proposition (2). This third difference does not mean that any false conditional proposition with a false antecedent would yield a true proposition, because the antecedent and consequent must be related semantically.

Demonstration requires that the premises entail the conclusion. When Hobbes summarizes what he accomplished in his civil science or political theory, he wrote,

> I have derived the rights of sovereign power and the duty of subjects hitherto from the principles of nature only, such as . . . consent concerning the use of words has made so, . . . known to us . . . from definitions of such words as are essential to all political reasoning.
>
> (L 32.1)

The key word here "derived," *deducta* in the Latin version, is a word of logic.

Hobbes thought of his method as geometric. According to some scholars, this means that Hobbes did not derive "conclusions," but "theorems" and that his premises did not "entail" the theorems (Hanson 1990: 591). However, Hobbes devotes an entire chapter to syllogisms in *De corpore*, the only form of reasoning that Hobbes treats explicitly (DCo 4). I think this understanding of Hobbes's method involves a false dichotomy between conclusions and theorems. Every theorem and every conclusion is entailed by its premises. Hobbes did not sharply distinguish between conclusions and theorems, if he distinguished between them at all. Knowledge or science is achieved through reasoning by beginning with "true propositions" and ending with "true conclusions" (EL 6.3).

It is also sometimes denied that "demonstration" means what it meant for Aristotle or that it is important for Hobbes. But Hobbes says in his chapter "On Method," that a "syllogism," formed from any two definitions and producing a "conclusion," is a demonstration (*demonstratio*) (DCo 6.16; cf. Hanson 1990: 618). And in general, "a demonstration is a syllogism or series of syllogisms derived from the definitions of names all the way to the final conclusion" (DCo 6.16).

THE UNITY OF SCIENCE

Another vexing issue in Hobbes's philosophy is what he means by the unity of science. Many scholars, notably Tom Sorell, think that Hobbes did not intend the three parts of his science, *De corpore*, *De homine*, and *De cive*, to be deductively connected. The principal argument for this view is that Hobbes published *De cive* first and considered it deductive. So, it cannot depend on either of the first two parts.

I think that this view confuses the order of exposition with the order of deduction. *De cive* begins with the conception of human beings in the state of nature, and, according to Hobbes's official method, with definitions that include a definition of "man" or "human being." And "man" is the topic of the second part of his science, *De homine*. If the conclusions that he draws about "man" in *De homine* were inconsistent with his definition of "man" in *De cive*, the parts of his philosophy would not be logically independent, but inconsistent with each other. It is no good to object that the conclusions about men in *De homine* do not have to include a definition of "man," because since "man" is used in *De homine*, it must be defined or else be meaningless. Moreover, men are bodies, and thus what Hobbes says about men in *De homine* has to follow from what he says about bodies in *De corpore*. I do not need to mention that Hobbes defines "man" in *De corpore* as "body, animate, rational."

The reason that Hobbes could have given for how he was able to present *De cive* first, and could have presented *De homine* first, is that each part of his science begins with definitions and he can define the basic terms of each part of science in a way that is identical with the theorems of the logically prior sciences. In *De cive*, taken alone, "Man is a rational animate body" is a definition and is explicitly defined. But in *De cive*, taken as part of *Elementa philosophiae*, "Man is a rational animate body" is a theorem. There is no contradiction between that proposition being a theorem and a definition, because those terms are relativized to a science or part of a science.

Hobbes sketched out the unbroken set of definitions and theorems that he imagined in *De corpore* 6.6:

> When, therefore, universals [words] and their causes (which are the first principles of knowledge τοδιοτι) are known, we have their definitions (which are nothing other than the explications of our simplest conceptions). For whoever correctly conceives what a place is (for example) must know its definitions: that a place is a space which is completely filled or occupied by a body. And whoever conceives what motion is must know that motion is the loss of one place and the acquisition of another. . . . After the consideration of those things which are produced from motion simpliciter, there follows the consideration of those things which the motion of one body effects in another body. . . . After physics we come to morals, in which the motions of minds are considered, namely desire, aversion, love, benevolence, hope, fear, anger, jealousy, envy, and so on. . . . That all these things ought to be investigated in the order I have said consists in the fact that physics cannot be understood unless the motion which is in the minutest parts of bodies is known and such motion of the parts [cannot be understood] unless what it is that effects motion in another thing is known, and this [cannot be understood] unless what simple motion effects is known.
>
> (DCo 6.6)

In fact, Hobbes gives a different reason for how *De cive* was able to be presented first. He says, "the motions of minds are not only known by reasoning but also by the experience of each and every person observing those motions proper to him only." Consequently, "those who have not learned the earlier part of philosophy, namely, geometry and physics, can nevertheless come to the principles of civil philosophy by the analytic method" (DC 6.7). Unfortunately, this explanation is not to the point. Hobbes is here explaining how the method of discovering a science may differ – it may come from definitions or experience – when the issue is what are the logical relations between the three parts of his philosophy.

I think what underlies the problem is Hobbes's confusion of two senses of analysis. One sense is logical. To proceed analytically is to begin with theorems and discover definitions.[16] The other sense is psychological. To proceed analytically is to begin with experience and isolate simple ideas.[17] Because of the inconsistencies, real or imagined, in Hobbes's writings, this matter, like many others, will not be settled once and for all.

CONCLUSION

Hobbes wanted to develop a theory for the new science being pioneered by people like Galileo and Harvey. He in effect developed two theories. The first is linguistic. Scientific propositions are sentences that are necessarily true by virtue of the meanings of their words. The basic propositions are definitions, and theorems are propositions that follow analytically from earlier propositions. For Hobbes, definitions have the logical form of conditional sentences: if something is X, then it is Y. Definitions hook up with reality through the names they contain, the Xs and Ys. One problem with this theory is that these definitions are also supposed to describe how causes create their effects, and it is not clear how many definitions could do that. The other theory is "hypothetical." It takes seriously the fact that many scientific propositions are hypotheses in the sense of being good guesses about how some actual effect occurred. A scientist who begins with an effect proposes a possible cause for that effect. The resulting scientific propositions are still necessarily true, but they are not certain, because one cannot be certain that the proposed cause is the actual cause of the effect.

Concerning language itself, Hobbes is a nominalist in that he thinks that universals are words. What each dog or each tree has in common is the word "dog" or "tree," respectively. The rest of his theory of language is a fairly conventional form of scholastic nominalism. His logic is similarly scholastic. As much as he criticized Aristotle and the scholastic philosophers who followed him, Hobbes adopted their syllogistic logic as his own. This was a major mistake on his part since modern science rarely uses categorical syllogisms either to discover or justify their results.

FURTHER READING

Jesseph, D. (1999) *Squaring the Circle*, Chicago, Ill.: University of Chicago Press. By far the best description of Hobbes's mathematical views and his controversies with contemporary mathematicians such as John Wallis.

Peters, R. (1967) *Hobbes* 2nd edn, Harmondsworth: Penguin. Chapter 5 contains a clear treatment of Hobbes's views about language.

Shapin, S. and S. Schaffer (1985) *Leviathan and the Air-Pump*, Princeton, N.J.: Princeton University Press. A fascinating and influential account of Hobbes's arguments with Robert Boyle.

Watkins, J. W. N. (1973) *Hobbes's System of Ideas* 2nd edn, London: Hutchinson University Library. Although slightly dated, a good introduction to Hobbes's scientific views.

Six

Religion

CULTURAL CONTEXT AND RELIGIOUS BELIEFS

Although Hobbes's political philosophy remains the most important aspect of his thought for scholars today, his views about religion have been studied intensively for more than a decade in part because of the recognition that they were important to his general philosophy and because his analyses of basic concepts of religion are philosophically interesting.[1] It is fascinating to consider such questions as whether faith in something is compatible with rationality, whether miracles are compatible with a deterministic universe, and whether revelation could occur. If nothing else, these concepts test the boundaries of our conceptions of rationality, determinism, and knowledge.

The dominant interpretation of Hobbes's view is that he was an atheist. Another interpretation with many adherents is that he was a deist. Some "atheist" and "deist" interpreters think that he was trying to undermine religion, especially the Christian religion, in *Leviathan* in his analysis of the origin of religion and in his supposedly debunking analyses of revelation, prophets, miracles, and similar concepts. Other "atheist" and "deist" interpreters think that he was trying to domesticate religion, in order to make sure that it served the interests of the civil government, as ancient Roman religion served the interests of the Roman government.

A third view holds that he was a genuine theist, although of an odd stripe. My own particular version of this view gives a great deal of weight to the scientific and political context within which

Hobbes was working and to what he said he was doing. In the seventeenth century, modern science was beginning to come up with results that were incompatible with the traditional Christian understanding of the world. To many, the choice seemed to be between accepting modern science and rejecting Christianity and accepting Christianity and rejecting modern science. Hobbes, like Pierre Gassendi, Thomas White, Robert Boyle, and to a lesser extent René Descartes, was trying to reconcile Christianity with modern science by reconceiving the traditional conceptual foundations of Christian doctrine. Negatively, for Hobbes this meant abandoning scholastic Aristotelianism. Affirmatively, it meant restricting doctrine to the literal meaning of the Bible. And he made other moves, for example, emphasizing the limitedness of human knowledge and emphasizing the difference between faith and reason. In these regards, he was a very protestant thinker. His theology was Calvinistic.

The other powerful cultural phenomenon affecting Hobbes was the adverse relation religion was having on peace and politics. Once the Reformation was well under way, Western European countries and the British Isles experienced political problems when the religion of one state was different from the religion of a neighboring state, or when the religion of the prince was different from the religion of a large part of the people. The Thirty Years War, the so-called last of the wars of religion, left many of the Western European countries weak. The English Civil War was in large part a war of religion. Hobbes's solution fit the official doctrine of England before everything began to fall apart in 1640. The monarch was an absolute sovereign and the head of the Church. It was the view of James I, but he had been dead for a quarter-century when *Leviathan* came to life.

In short, among Hobbes's timebound projects in *Leviathan*, I think that he had these two: to show that biblical Christianity was compatible with modern science, and to show that genuine Christianity was not politically destabilizing. His rather eccentric and conspicuous failure to achieve the first had led scholars to think that he was not seriously trying to succeed.[2] I will not discuss the second project further because, as interesting as it is, its philosophical value is negligible.

In addition to the cultural context, my reason for thinking that Hobbes was a Christian was his own behavior, public and private. He professed belief in the Nicene Creed and subscription to the Thirty-Nine Articles. He argued for, or professed, Calvinist theological views, a preference for episcopal government and nonpuritan worship (Martinich 1992). He attended episcopal church services, even during the Interregnum, when they were illegal, and when he was in his eighties or older and could easily have pled incapacity. He received the Eucharist from priests of the Church of England; he was attended by clergymen during a serious illness in 1647 and his final illness in 1679; and he was buried inside a church of the Church of England. If Hobbes expected people to figure out that he was of some anti-Christian bent, he should have had the decency to indicate in some straightforward way, either in personal letters to trusted friends or by his behavior in his last years when he had almost nothing to lose. Or his assistant James Weldon, who wrote about Hobbes's final days, should have reported his atheism, and the Cavendishes of Chatsworth should have disowned him, or at least have not allowed him to be buried inside a church (Martinich 1999).

Of course Hobbes could have been faking it all, Wheldon covering up, and the Cavendishes obtuse or shameless. These are logical possibilities. But to be reasonable possibilities, they must be supported, not by the skepticism nor ingeniousness of the interpreter, but by evidence sufficient to overwhelm the substantial evidence that Hobbes was what his behavior indicated him to be, a stubborn, proud, odd, but orthodox, Christian (Martinich 1992). Many scholars have been incredulous because they ignored the criteria that were laid down for terms like "orthodox" and "Calvinist." Hobbes was orthodox in doctrine according to the criterion operating in England during the late sixteenth and the seventeenth century.[3]

Although my presentation of Hobbes's religious views is influenced by my "theist" interpretation, those with a different interpretation will have no problem following what Hobbes purports to say, and they can make their own inferences to an alternative interpretation.

REVELATION, PROPHETS, AND MIRACLES

Hobbes carries out his project of reconciling Christianity with modern science by employing various tactics, as we shall see. Perhaps the most important of these is to assert that something is a fact and then to show that it is impossible for anyone to know which candidates for being that kind of fact actually are facts. People know less than they think they know. What Hobbes does is to transfer what Christians had believed to be an object of knowledge to the realm of faith. For example, he asserts that there have been true prophets, and the Bible identifies who they are and the circumstances within which they worked (BB 326). But who these true prophets were, the Israelites could not know until it was too late to do any good. For example, the king of Israel wants to know whether he should go to war against Ramoth Gilead. So he asks his four hundred prophets. They all say that he should go to war. Only one prophet, Micaiah, says that he should not, and he says this only after initially lying and saying what he knew the king wanted to hear, that he should go. As events would have it, the king, following the overwhelming majority of his prophets, went to war and was killed (L 32.7, 36.19–20). The king acted rationally. Given his belief in prophets, following the overwhelming majority of them made sense. Unfortunately for him, they were wrong, and the Israelites, but not the dead king, came to know that Micaiah was the true prophet. We might say that "true prophet" is a retrospective term; one only knows whom it should be applied to when it is too late to act on the prophet's prediction.

There are other problems with prophets. One prophet can deceive another prophet, even a true prophet (L 32.7). The implication is, if a true prophet cannot tell the true from the false, how can other people? Also, prophets often lie. God himself says this (L 36.19, quoting Jeremiah 14:14).

There are three solutions to the problem of trying to identify true prophets. One is that a person should accept those prophets that she has an obligation to believe; and the prophets a person has an obligation to believe are those the sovereign says the person should believe because the person has transferred her rights on such matters to the sovereign. The second solution is to use your reason. Reason says that one should either obey one's sovereign – this leads us back to the first solution – or follow the criteria laid down by God. This leads to the third solution, namely, follow the two criteria that the Bible laid down for true prophets. The first criterion is that the prophet should not teach anything against the established religion.[4] (People who are often aghast that the Bible says this should read Deuteronomy 13:1–5.) The second criterion is that some miracle will reveal a prophet to be a true one (L 32.7). All three solutions are interlocking, as indicated. Reason says follow the command of the sovereign; a Christian sovereign says follow the Bible; the Bible says obey the sovereign. This solution may not work for Christians under a non-Christian sovereign, but that is not Hobbes's problem. As a Christian, Hobbes would not expect a non-Christian religion ever to take over England, and none of his fellow citizens would think so either. Many of them expected Christ to return shortly.

Are the Bible's criteria effective and reliable? Do they actually separate the true prophets from the false ones? The answer depends on the ability of the criteria to give an unambiguous answer to the question, "Is this person a true prophet?" There are a couple of reasons for holding that they do not, according to the standards of Christianity. First, Hobbes in line with the standard view of the Church of England says that miracles do not occur any more

(L 32.9). They were unnecessary because all that was required for salvation, the work of Jesus and the Bible, was complete around the end of the first century.

The second is that there is no way to know whether a miracle has occurred. Let's consider this at more length. Far from denying that miracles have occurred, it is important for Hobbes to assert that they have, because the Christian religion requires them. (Alternatively, according to the debunking interpretation of Hobbes, he is showing that revelation cannot be known to have occurred because miracles cannot be known to have occurred.) But, having affirmed their existence, he shows why a person cannot know that a miracle occurred and, moreover, would be disinclined to claim to have seen a miracle.

Hobbes defines a miracle as "[a] *a work of God (besides his operation by the way of nature, ordained in the Creation)* [b] *done for the making manifest to his elect* [c] *the mission of an extraordinary minister for their salvation*" (L 37.7). Item [a] concerns the fact that Hobbes does not want the human being through whom God works a miracle to become puffed up. God is the agent, not the human instrument of the miracle. Item [b] is an aspect of his Calvinism. There is no point in working miracles for those who are not elect (L 37.6). It cannot do them any good. Item [c] concerns the fact that miracles are not pointless pyrotechnics or other forms of impressive display. They have to have a purpose related to salvation.

As nice as this definition is, it does not fit everything that Hobbes says about miracles, for example, what he says about Noah's rainbow. Because it was the first rainbow, it was an "admirable" work, that is, it was one that rarely occurs and for which a person cannot imagine a cause (L 37.4). Being the first rainbow it was rare, and Noah, not being a scientist, had no way at all of imagining a cause for the rainbow (other than God). The reason that this is a nice example is that the physics of the rainbow was discovered not very long before Hobbes wrote *Leviathan*. It is a way of showing that one can accept miracles without giving up modern science. So the rainbow was a miracle for Noah, but not for educated seventeenth-century intellectuals.[5] In general, the more a person knows about nature, the fewer kinds of things can be candidates for the miraculous. As Hobbes says, "the same thing may be a miracle to one and not to another. And thence it is that ignorant and superstitious men make great wonders of those works which other men, knowing to proceed from nature (which is not the immediate, but the ordinary work of God), admire not at all" (L 37.5). Someone who keeled over during a heated debate might in the past have been thought to have been miraculously struck down by God, but now we know it is simply too many cheeseburgers and french fries that caused a heart attack.

The example of Noah's rainbow shows how God could have worked a miracle without violating the laws of nature. Some people today believe that God miraculously saved the Hebrews from the Israelites by arranging that at just the right time a strong, natural wind would blow the water of the Red Sea so that a strip of land would be uncovered, over which the Israelites could cross to safety. So, the laws of nature are compatible with revealed religion. However, this reconciliation of science and religion is obscured because later, when Hobbes defines a miracle, he, in line with the ordinary notion of a miracle, says God's action cannot be part of the ordinary operation of nature. My guess is that Hobbes forgot what he had achieved by using the miracle of Noah.

In any case, the condition that miracles require ignorance narrows the range of possibly miraculous events. People do not like to admit their ignorance, so many will choose not to see a miracle rather than admitting that they are stumped. Hobbes describes some religious scams to drive the point home (L 37.12). But there is no need to think that Hobbes thought miracles had never occurred. They served their purpose in establishing the Old and New Covenants. Since they are not needed now, it is good that science is undermining their possibility.

The example of Noah's rainbow does not fit Hobbes's definition in another way. Item [c] requires that miracles point out a prophet. That is why the Creation, as awesome as it was, is not a miracle. Oddly enough, Hobbes says that "the destruction of all living creatures in the universal deluge" was not a miracle either (L 37.6). But if the deluge was not a miracle, why should Noah's rainbow be one since it did not reveal any prophet either. That Hobbes should apparently contradict himself within three paragraphs is disconcerting, but not atypical.

We have just seen that although true prophets existed and miracles occurred, it is difficult, if not impossible, to identify such things, until it is too late to do anyone any immediate good. What about revelation? Again, Hobbes asserts that revelation has occurred and also explains revelation in such a way that one cannot know when it occurs.

There are two kinds of revelation: direct and indirect. Direct revelation occurred when God spoke to a person without the mediation of any other human being. Of course other things can mediate the experience. God typically spoke to people in a dream or a vision. And this highlights the problem with purported cases of direct revelation. Almost every dream is nothing but a dream, and almost every vision is nothing but a mirage or hallucination. How can one tell the difference between these ordinary phantasms and the revelatory ones? There is no way. Hobbes points out that the sentence, "God appeared to me in a dream," means the same as "I dreamed that God appeared to me." Since the latter has no evidential value, neither does the former. If someone objects that he was awake when God appeared to him, Hobbes might have asked whether it is more likely that the person thought he was awake but was dreaming or whether he was awake and God appeared to him (DCo 25.9).[6]

Things are different, but no better, for indirect (true) revelation, that is, those cases in which God speaks to someone, who reports this to someone, who may or may not report it to someone, and so on. Anyone who receives a report from another human being about a revelation from God receives indirect revelation. Jews, Christians, and Muslims are the recipients of indirect revelation via a book, on the assumption that the book is a true report of a message of God. Certainly, there are cases of false indirect revelation. These are cases in which the message passed on does not begin with God but with some human being. It does not matter whether the human being that begins the chain is benighted or fraudulent. How can a human being tell the difference between the genuine and the false cases of indirect revelation? He cannot, because the recipient of true, mediate revelations is in the same epistemic situation as the recipient of false, mediate revelations. In each case, the recipient is receiving the message from another human being, and the recipient can have no way of knowing whether the informant is telling a truth or a falsehood (possibly unwittingly). Hobbes wrote:

> And consequently, when we believe that the Scriptures are the word of God, having no immediate revelation from God himself, our belief, faith, and trust is in the Church, whose word we take and acquiesce therein. And they that believe that which a prophet relates unto them in the name of God, take the word of the prophet, do honour to him, and in him trust and believe, touching the truth of what he relateth, whether it be a true or false prophet. . . . For if I should not believe all that is written by historians of the glorious acts of Alexander or Caesar, I do not think the ghost of Alexander or Caesar had any just cause to be offended or anybody else but the historian. If Livy say the gods made once a cow speak and we believe it not, [then] we distrust not God therein, but Livy.
>
> (L 7.7)

I have been emphasizing that one cannot know instances of true prophets, miracles, or revelation. But, as Hobbes indicates in the preceding quotation, one can have faith in them. Hobbes is the first major philosopher to pry faith and knowledge apart in this way, giving each a realm that does not intrude on the other.[7]

FAITH

The Greek word for faith in the New Testament is "πιστις" which means "trust in others" and which gives one "confidence, [and] assurance," according to the standard Greek dictionary by Liddell and Scott. Hobbes must have had the Greek text in mind when he wrote that to "have faith in, or trust to, or believe a man, signify the same thing, namely an opinion of the veracity of the man" (L 7.5). He says, "it is impossible to believe any person before we know what he saith, it is necessary he be one that we have heard speak" (L 43.6). He appeals to Paul of Tarsus for support: faith comes by hearing (L 43.8, quoting Romans 10:7). But he seems to be wrong about this. Although it is sometimes ill-advised to believe someone we have not heard speak firsthand, it is possible to believe what such a person said and to believe it to be true, without being acquainted with that person. A large part of history consists of just such beliefs. Such beliefs may also require faith in the person or persons who preserved the words or documents handed down to us, but that does not preclude faith in the author of the words.

It's plausible that one reason that Hobbes made this mistake is that he wants to undercut any claim of his contemporaries to put his trust in anyone other than the sovereign, either as head of the government or of the Church. This is what moves him to say that since faith "is not so much concerning the thing as the person" whom one trusts and since we have "no immediate revelation from God himself, our belief, faith, and trust is in the Church" (L 7.5, 7.7). This position offended many Christians, and undermines the grounds for belief in Christianity, as his contemporaries realized.

Hobbes probably thought that he secured faith sufficiently by asserting that "faith is the gift of God and he worketh it [faith] in each several man by such ways as it seemeth good unto himself" (L 43.7). Although Hobbes could not say it directly, he is in effect saying, "Trust God that your faith comes from God in the right way."

Although faith is not knowledge, to have faith is not to renounce one's "senses and experience" (L 32.2). Although "many things in

God's word [are] above reason" (L 32.2), in the sense that humans cannot either prove or refute them, none of them contradicts reason. If a proposition of faith seems to be inconsistent with reason, "the fault is either in our unskillful interpretation, or erroneous ratiocination" (L 32.2). Some truths of faith cannot even be understood by many humans. In such cases, a person should nonetheless commit himself to those propositions when obedience to an authority requires it (L 32.2). The authority in whom a person should have faith is her sovereign, because she transferred to him her right to make all such decisions and because God in effect said that one should. Servants, obey your masters. What if the sovereign is a non-Christian? Hobbes bites the bullet, and says that obedience is owed to a Muslim sovereign as much as to a Christian one. To deny this is to promote civil disobedience and also to violate the gospel maxim, "Do unto others as you would have them do unto you."

In addition to meaning trust in a person, the word "faith" can also mean the propositions that define a religion. For Judaism, it is the proposition that there is one God and it is Yahweh; for Islam, it is the proposition that there is no god but God [Allah] and Mohammad is his prophet. For Hobbes, the faith of Christianity is summed up in one sentence, "Jesus is the Christ." Hobbes uses this proposition in two ways. Sometimes he exploits its simplicity. It is easy to be a Christian, and Christians should not squabble about doctrine. Sometimes he exploits its power. Everything else required for belief follows from this one proposition.

There is still another sense of "faith." It is a divine gift from God (L 26.40, 43.7, 43.9). In this sense, the causes are various. God causes faith "in each several man, by such ways as it seems good unto himself" (L 43.7). One of these is by hearing the Bible read ("Faith comes by hearing" (Romans 10:17; L 29.8, 43.8)). This leads people to ask, "How do we know that the Bible is true?" Hobbes says that it is a mistake to ask that question. Since everyone believes that God is its ultimate author, the question can't sensibly be asking about authorship. And, as for knowledge that God is the author, that can be known only by "those to whom God himself hath revealed it supernaturally" (L 33.21).[8] If we weaken the meaning of the question to "Why do we believe that the Bible is the word of God?", the answer is that different people believe for different reasons (L 33.21). Some because they trust their parents or the clergymen who taught them; some believe it for the value of the moral teaching or the magnificent poetry. The appropriate question to ask, according to Hobbes, is "By what authority is the Bible made law?" and the answer to this question is quite simple. The person who makes the laws about any matter in a commonwealth has the authority to make the Bible the law, that is, the sovereign, to whom each subject has transferred his right to govern himself. This follows from the familiar premise that whoever has a right to the end has the right to the means necessary to that end. No one can deny that religion has threatened the peace on many occasions; so regulating it belongs to making peace. If individual people were free to choose the book that would serve their religion, then, because all sorts of choices would be made, a commonwealth would have no Church. For Hobbes, the Church must be "the same thing with a commonwealth of Christians . . . because it consisteth of men united in one person . . . in one Christian sovereign" (L 33.24). This view will strike many North Americans and Europeans as at least odd and perhaps abhorrent. But Hobbes was living at a time of homogenous national populations. Officially, there were no Jews in England at least until after 1654, not to mention Muslims.

We have been considering some robust concepts of revealed religions: revelation, prophets, and miracles. We will now turn to some concepts that have some claim to being logically prior: religion, superstition, and true religion.

RELIGION, SUPERSTITION, AND TRUE RELIGION

In *De cive*, Hobbes's treatment of these concepts was in line with conventional thinking of the day. Superstition, he says, is "fear of the invisible, when separated from right reason" (DC 16.1). Atheism is the absence of fear, which one believes comes from right reason. Almost every human being falls to superstition or atheism without "special assistance from God" (DC 16.1). True religion, the belief in the one God who created the universe, began with Abraham, to whom God revealed himself. Hobbes reiterated the definition of superstition when he replied to John Bramhall, who criticized him for what he said about superstition in *Leviathan* (BB 291).

It's unfortunate that Hobbes did not explain what motivated his odd description of superstition in *Leviathan*. Here is what he wrote: "Fear of power invisible, feigned by the mind, or imagined from tales publicly allowed, RELIGION; not allowed, SUPERSTITION. And when the power imagined is truly such as we imagine, TRUE RELIGION" (L 6.36). I suggest that these descriptions be rendered as follows. (For the sake of simplicity, I define the three words in the form, "x has G," rather than that of "x is G"):

"x has a religion" = df "x has an imagination of something y, the imagination is caused either by x's mind or by tales that are publicly allowed, and x believes that y is invisible and powerful, and x is afraid of y."

"x has a superstition" = df "x has an imagination of something y, the imagination is caused by tales that are not publicly allowed, and x believes that y is invisible and powerful, and x is afraid of y."

"x has a true religion" = df "x has an imagination of something y, and x believes that y is invisible and powerful, and x is afraid of y, and x's imagination of y accords with the way y is."

How are these three propositions related? Perhaps Hobbes intended the proposition about "religion" to serve as a genus for two types of religion: superstition (false religion) and true religion (Martinich 1992: 56–9). On this view, Hobbes uses the negation of "publicly allowed" as the specific difference of superstition and the negation of "feigned by the mind," as the specific difference of true religion.

This yields the sensible definition of "true religion," roughly, fear of power invisible, which is truly such as we imagine it to be.

But the resulting proposition for superstition, roughly, "fear of power invisible, not allowed" misses the mark, as a definition. In fact, it is not important whether "religion" is supposed to be the genus of the other two terms, because whether it is a species of religion or not, his description of superstition seems false, and it offended his contemporaries.

If fears of invisible powers are superstitions simply because they are "not allowed," then, Hobbes was committed to holding that Christianity and every version of Protestantism were superstitions! In seventeenth-century Spain, Protestantism was not allowed and hence a superstition, and during part of the first century, Christianity was not allowed in Rome, and hence a superstition.

Obviously, something unusual is going on here, but it may not stem from an anti-Christian attitude. Consider first that there would be something wrong with Hobbes's renderings of "superstition" even if it did not involve categorizing Christianity occasionally as a heresy. "Superstition" is intuitively at least the contrary of, and possibly the contradictory of, "true religion." But Hobbes's renderings have the consequence that something can be both a true religion and a superstition. If this is all that is going on, then the problem is not that Hobbes is being antireligious, but philosophically incompetent.

Although it is possible that Hobbes simply muffed his definition of "superstition," there are better explanations for what Hobbes was doing. He was attuned to the ways that words get used or misused. For example, he held the obviously false view that the meaning of "tyranny" was the same as the meaning of "monarchy." (Even Charles I thought that a bad monarch was a tyrant (Kenyon 1986: 18).) The only difference between these words, according to Hobbes, is usage. "Tyranny" is used by people who do not like the monarch. What underlies this difference is emotions: "[M]en give different names to one and the same thing from the difference of their own passions, as they that approve a private opinion call it opinion, but they that mislike it, heresy" (L 11.19; also 42.130).[9] In short, "heresy" is a term of abuse. "Superstition" seems to be one too. Hobbes conveys this when he says that people call "religion" whatever they worship, but "in them that worship, or fear that power otherwise than they do, superstition" (L 11.26).

Hobbes might be accused of being sardonic, but a jaundiced eye on the usage of "religion" and "superstition" in seventeenth-century England was justified by the abuse and counterabuse during the previous century, for most of which every change of sovereign meant a change in religion. The interpretation I am suggesting frees Hobbes of a philosophical blunder, ties his rendering of "superstition" to his rendering of "heresy" and illustrates his well-known view about rhetoric.

The use of terms primarily for their pejorative value is fairly widespread. Recognizing that some words are used primarily for their pejorative value is important in both daily life and in philosophy. During the Reformation, many Protestants called Roman Catholics "superstitious," Roman Catholics called the Protestants "atheists." In the 1950s, many Republicans in the U.S. called liberal Democrats "communists;" in the 1960s, many liberal Democrats and leftists called Republicans "fascists." It is not important whether the critics believed these epithets were literally true or not. What is important is to recognize when there is a discrepancy between a word's literal meaning and its use to abuse someone. *Pace* those philosophers who say that meaning is use, we can often distinguish between how words are used and what they mean. It is plausible, then, that Hobbes consciously or not was calling attention to the use of "superstition" and not defining its literal meaning.

One might think that Hobbes's definition of "religion" is also problematic. If the only two sources of a religion are feigning by the mind or acceptance of tales told, usually to children, it appears that no religion is true. There are two responses. One is that if

Hobbes did intend superstition and true religion to be species of religion, then the definition of "religion" does not suggest that there is no true religion. The other response is that, although "feigned" usually meant "invented," and Hobbes sometimes uses it in religious contexts to mean "false" or "insincere" (L 11.26, 12.6, 48.12), it could also mean simply "made," and being made is not bad for Hobbes. The sovereign is made by humans, he is called a "feigned" person (L 16.2), and no one is more prosovereign than Hobbes. The reason that the imagination needs to be made is that God is not an object of sensation.

Hobbes's description of superstition in *Leviathan* angered many of his readers. So in *De homine* (1658), Hobbes omitted a discussion of superstition and defined "religion" respectfully: "Religion is the external worship of men who sincerely honour God" (DH 14.1).

THE CAUSES OF RELIGION

A text often used to argue that Hobbes was not just a nontheist but was insinuating that all religions were superstitions or false religions occurs in Chapter 12 of *Leviathan*, "Of Religion." He says, for example: "[T]here is almost nothing that has a name that has not been esteemed . . . in one place or another, a god or devil. . . . Men, women, . . . [and] a leek, were deified" (L 12.16). In fact, this sentiment was common among the Protestant reformers. The author of the pseudonymous treatise, "On the Old and New God," points "to the inborn irreligiousness of mankind and to the great number of deities it has created" (quoted from Eire 1986: 75). Moreover, the quotation from Hobbes is taken out of context. It occurs in a passage in which Hobbes has distinguished pagan religion from true religion, and the comment about polymorphous gods applies only to pagan religions. It is no good to object that Hobbes was not serious about the distinction because that begs the question. Because of the importance of Chapter 12, a close reading of it is appropriate.

The chapter begins with a basic fact about human beings: they are the only creatures that have religion. So it must be the result of "some peculiar quality . . . not to be found in other living creatures" (L 12.1; cf. Calvin 1559: 1.3.1). "Peculiar" does not mean bizarre but something that is characteristic of something, as distinct from others. At 11.26 of *Leviathan*, Hobbes says that "the natural seed" of religion is "fear of things invisible" (cf. L 11.27). His phrase, "*religionis semen*" may have been inspired by Calvin's "*semen religionis*" (Calvin 1559: 1.4.1). At the beginning of the following chapter, he describes three causes of religion, which seem to be three things related to that natural seed. The first is that people are curious about the causes of events that affect one's "own good and evil fortune" (L 12.2; see Calvin 1559: 47). The second is that people want to identify why an event happened precisely when it did and not earlier or later (L 12.3). The third is that when a person "cannot assure himself of the true causes of things (for the causes of good and evil fortune for the most part are invisible), he supposes causes of them" that are either suggested by his own imagination or by people he accepts as authorities (L 12.4; DC 15.1). This results from the fact that humans can see far into the future, unlike other animals.

The first two causes, namely, the concern over one's own "good and evil fortune" and the desire to know exactly when something will happen, causes a person to have anxiety, to be worried about what will happen and when (L 12.5).[10] (Calvin's term for the underlying emotion of religion is "fear" (*timor*) (Calvin 1559: 1.10.2).) Each human being is like Prometheus bound, who waited each day for an eagle to rip his liver out, only to have it restored that night for another ripping the next day.

Anxiety is typically described as fear that does not have an object, and it is worse than garden-variety fears which do. This does not mean that it is more consoling to know that a lion will devour you than not to know what ill will befall you. Typically the unknown evil falls within a certain range of unknown objects; sitting in the dentist's office, one does not know whether one will need one, two or ten cavities filled, a root canal, or the extraction of two impacted wisdom teeth. People prefer to know what they need to fear, because it gives them the opportunity to plan actions that will protect them, so far as possible, from the object of fear. Consequently, people cope with their anxiety by positing "some *power* or agent *invisible*," to be the cause "either of their good or evil fortune" (L 12.6). This is the beginning of pagan religions, which some of the ancient poets said "were at first created by human fear" (L 12.6).

One might think that there is no reason to stop with pagan religions. The same explanation applies to Judaism and Christianity. So, it is inferred, Hobbes is hinting that all religions are the same. All religions are the result of unjustifiably positing invisible causes, and all equally superstitious. This interpretation would be plausible if Hobbes did not explicitly differentiate the Judeo-Christian god from "Gentile" or pagan gods (and if Calvin did not have similar things to say). Hobbes contrasts the origin of Gentile gods with that of the religion that has an "eternal, infinite, and omnipotent" God, which is "derived from the desire men have to know the causes of natural bodies" (L 12.6). Because Hobbes's distinction is generally accepted by theists, there is no reason to attribute sarcasm or innuendo to Hobbes's remark in order to explain it. If belief in an eternal, infinite, and omnipotent God were as spurious as belief in Gentile gods, then it would also be implied that the search for genuine causes is no better than any other search.

Hobbes's position that all Gentile religions are false and only one religion is true fits the view of Calvin, who wrote: "Scarcely a single person has ever been found who did not fashion for himself an idol or specter in place of God. Surely, just as waters boil up from a vast, full spring, so does an immense crowd of gods flow forth from the human mind" (Calvin 1559: 1.5.12; see also Eire 1986: 204–5).

So strong was Calvin's belief in religious corruption that he said, "And so it happens that no real piety remains in the world" (Calvin 1559: 1.4.1). Of course, it is not sensible to take his categorical statement strictly as entailing a denial of Christianity. It's the hyperbolic language of a reformer. Hobbes often sounds the same.

Hobbes's proof of an eternal, infinite, and omnipotent God is a conventional conflation of the traditional arguments from cause and effect and from motion:

> For he that from any effect he seeth come to pass should reason to the next and immediate cause thereof and from thence to the cause and immediate cause thereof and from thence to the cause of that cause and plunge himself profoundly in the pursuit of causes shall come at last to this, that there must be . . . one First Mover, that is, a first and eternal cause of all things, which is that which men mean by the name of God.
>
> (L 12.6)

Hobbes had anticipated this argument in the previous chapter:

> Curiosity or the love of the knowledge of causes draws a man from consideration of the effect to seek the cause, and again, the cause of that cause, till of necessity he must come to this thought at last that there is some cause whereof there is no former cause but is eternal.
>
> (L 11.25)

Again, there are no signs of irony or sarcasm in either passage. The proof would have struck seventeenth-century intellectuals as obviously sound. Its brevity is explained by its obviousness. It is only in a time of serious doubt about the existence of God that proofs will expand, sometimes into book length. In much of the Middle Ages, notably in Anselm of Canterbury and Thomas Aquinas, individual proofs are sometimes given in one paragraph and often in less than four or five pages.

It might be urged that Hobbes's endorsement of the argument from motion does not change the fact that all religion begins with fear of invisible power. When queried about this fact, Hobbes pointed out that it is biblical. While the "fear of a God . . . was the beginning of religion, the fear of the true God was the beginning of wisdom to the Jews and Christians" (BB 292). Hobbes is alluding to the phrase from the psalm, "The beginning of wisdom is fear of the Lord." Interpreting Hobbes's words as ironic or conveying an innuendo can be sustained only by ignoring part of the text.

In short, paragraph 6 of Chapter 12 of *Leviathan* contains two parts. The first part talks about false, pagan religion; the second part talks about true religion. This structure is repeated in the next paragraph, 7. Pagan religions produce false concepts of God when they assert that the invisible power is an incorporeal spirit, which is a contradictory concept. True religion recognizes that the infinite, omnipotent, and eternal God is "incomprehensible" (L 12.7). One reason that God is literally incomprehensible is that he was discovered by the argument from motion to be an invisible cause. Another, related reason has to do with the limits of human understanding. Because humans are finite beings, they cannot have an idea of the infinite (L 3.12).

The fact that Hobbes says that God is invisible is not problematic. Endeavors (*conatus*) and the smallest particles of matter are invisible but real. A blind man can infer the existence of fire, even though it is invisible to him, and physicists study invisible motions (EL 11.2; L 11.22; DCo 6.6).

Hobbes believes that there are four "seeds" of religion.[11] The first seed is the opinion humans have of the nature of the invisible cause, "the opinion of ghosts" (L 12.11) or "opinions concerning the nature of powers invisible" (L 12.13). Hobbes observes that "there is almost nothing that has a name that has not been esteemed amongst the Gentiles in one place or another, a god or a devil, or by their poets feigned to be animated, inhabited, or possessed by some spirit or other" (L 12.13). These things include "men, women, a bird, a crocodile, a calf, a dog, a snake, an onion, a leek" (L 12.16; see also BB 289, 292–3). But, the objection goes, seventeenth-century Christians thought that the man Jesus was God and Roman

Catholics thought that bread was God. So there is no difference between Christianity and pagan religion.

There are two replies to this objection. First, there are intelligent, theist philosophers today, who know about the beliefs of pagan religions, and know that their own beliefs fit under the same general description, and yet they still believe. The reason is that the fact that every woman, bird, crocodile, calf, dog, and virtually every human being who was ever thought to be a god was not a god does not prove that no man was a god. The fact that 1,000 arrows shot at a target miss the bull's eye does not prove that no arrow hits it. Christians traditionally thought that their religious beliefs hit the bull's eye of religious truth, while those of every other religion missed. Whether these Christians thought they had compelling arguments for their beliefs or merely faith, their knowledge of all the false religions did not undermine their religious beliefs. Similar remarks apply to orthodox Jews and fundamentalist Muslims. Christians think that all the false religions are perversions of the true religion. I am not asserting that these Christians and other theists are justified in their beliefs. I am asserting that knowledge of pagan religions is consistent with belief in the truth of one's own religion. The second reply is an anecdote. In 1961, my superannuated Latin teacher, a devout Catholic priest, had some occasion to report that until the end of World War II, the Japanese people believed that their emperor was a god. His words at one point were very close to the following: "Can you believe that anyone would be so silly as to believe that a human being was a god?" At my desk, silent I sat thinking that Roman Catholics believe exactly that, but I knew enough not to contribute that thought.

The second of the four seeds of religion is "ignorance of second causes" (L 12.11). That is, even when people have the right idea about the kinds of things that exist, they often mistake the aspect of that that has the causal power. Because Phormio won a battle for the Athenians, the Athenians thought that the cause of the victory was his being a Phormio; so the Athenians sent Phormio's son into another battle, because he had the property of being a Phormio. He was defeated (see Thucydides 3.7). In religion, a place, a bystander, or words are thought to be causes. Hobbes alludes to the Roman Catholic doctrine that the words of consecration can turn bread into the body and blood of Jesus as a mistake about what is a cause (L 12.8). Pagan founders of religion exploited the second seed of religion by attributing to their false gods the ability to effect things that belong to genuine second causes, for example, "the cause of fecundity to Venus, the cause of arts to Apollo" and so on (L 12.17).

The third seed of religion is "devotion towards what men fear" (L 12.11). For this one, Hobbes says only that worship of humans should consist only of "such expressions of their reverence as they would use towards men, gifts, petitions, thanks, submission of body, considerate addresses, sober behaviour" and so on (L 12.9). The good or natural way to worship god is with "oblations, prayers, thanks" and similar things. The bad way to worship originated among pagan religions by including the founders among the gods, by the thoughts of ignorant people that the representations of gods contained the god, by attributing human shapes to the gods, and human "faculties and passions" to the gods, such as "sense, speech, sex, [and] lust" (L 12.18). The fourth seed of religion is the "taking of things casual for prognostics" (L 12.11). People project regularities of the past to the future (L 12.10). Examples are "innumerable . . . superstitious ways of divination" such as "the priests at Delphi, Delos, Ammon, and other famous oracles" and horoscopes, necromancy and augury (L 12.19).

Overall Hobbes's description of the seeds of religion is much more negative than positive. The names of two of the seeds, opinion of ghosts and ignorance of causes, are pejorative. But this fits with the Calvinistic and more broadly reformed attitude towards human religion. Almost all religions are perversions of the one true religion. Calvin wrote, "scarcely one man in a hundred is met who fosters" true religion (Calvin 1559: 1.4.1).The reason that religions are so diverse is that these four seeds combine with "the different fancies, judgments, and passions of several men" to spawn "ceremonies so different that those which are used by one man are for the most part ridiculous to another" (L 12.11). Since God is incomprehensible, the judgments that people make about invisible powers and what they intend to do are almost always baseless. What people can do rightly is worship God, the invisible power by showing "their reverence."

The seed or seeds of religion are in themselves neither good nor bad. The kind of religion that results from them depends on how the seed is cultivated and that depends on the kind of man that begins or sustains a religion. So Hobbes introduced the distinction between the good and bad cultivations of religion (L 12.12). Bad, "Gentile" or pagan religions were "nourished and ordered [by men] . . . according to their own invention" (L 12.12). The true religion, of Abraham, Moses, and Jesus, was founded "by God's commandment and direction" (L 12.12). The purpose of both kinds of religion was to make people "more apt to obedience, laws, peace, charity, and civil society" (L 12.12).

THE CAUSES OF THE DECLINE OF RELIGION

Hobbes says that religion is discredited in four ways:

(i)　to have the wisdom of the founders suspected;
(ii)　to have the sincerity of the founders suspected;
(iii)　to have the love of the founders suspected; and
(iv)　for the founders to be "unable to show any probable token of divine revelation" (L 12.24).

The expectation that these four ways will correlate with the four causes of the rise of religion is disappointed.

Concerning (i), Hobbes says that a wise founder will presumably know the nature of the invisible powers. When a religious leader makes the doctrines of a religion contradictory, the followers will know that the doctrine cannot be true and hence that the leader does not know the nature of the invisible powers (L 12.25). The Roman Catholic Schoolmen introduced "so many contradictions and absurdities, that they acquired the reputation of being ignorant" (L 12.31).

Concerning (ii), when followers have reason to believe that their leaders do not believe in the religion, they will lose their belief. Hobbes's example of this is the decline of the ancient Roman religion and the rise of Christianity. The pagan priests led scandalous lives in contrast with those of the Apostles. Hobbes then continues the example by claiming that the Roman Catholic religion failed in England partially because priests led scandalous lives (L 12.31). (These examples could also be used to illustrate the third cause of the decline of religion.)

Concerning (iii), religious leaders will lose the love of the people when they use religion to advance their own private ends. Hobbes's first example is the sons of Samuel taking bribes and judging unjustly (L 12.30). His two other examples are contemporary:

> The Church of Rome declared necessary for salvation so many things that obviously benefited the Pope personally, for example, requiring a king to be crowned by a bishop, claiming authority to judge which births are legitimate and which not, and taking money for private Masses and indulgences.
>
> (L 12.32)

And these abuses are not restricted to the Roman Catholic Church. They exist in the Presbyterian Church, which "hath presumed most of reformation" (L 12.32). Hobbes might have mentioned that one of the chief complaints against the episcopal Church of England in 1640–1 was that the bishops and many of the clergy lived scandalous lives. That he did not mention them is especially surprising since the episcopacy had been abolished in England, and he could have played to the crowd by criticizing them by name. I suspect that he did not because he preferred episcopacy over other forms of church government.

Concerning (iv), a religion is discredited when a religious leader tries to add a doctrine to the religion without performing any miracles. Hobbes's example is the rebellion of the Israelites when Moses tried to introduce the Ten Commandments as the law of the Israelites (Exodus 32:1–2). Since Moses had not worked any miracle for forty days, the Israelites "revolted from the worship of the true God recommended to them by him [Moses] . . . So that miracles failing, faith also failed" (L 12.29). Hobbes's specific criticism is that a religious leader cannot introduce a new doctrine without a miracle. It was standard Protestant doctrine that miracles had ceased with the death of the last apostle, because all the doctrine needed for salvation was set down in the Bible. Calvin wrote: "miracles . . . [have] vanished away in order to make the new preaching of the gospel marvelous forever" (Calvin 1559: 4.9.18).

Hobbes concludes the chapter not by saying that all the changes of religion in the world stem from priests, but "unpleasing priests" (L 12.32). In doing this, he is reducing his four causes to one of the four causes of atheism, listed by Francis Bacon in "Of Atheism" (Bacon 1996: 372).

THE NATURE OF GOD AND LANGUAGE ABOUT HIM

Sometimes Hobbes seems to say that the only thing that humans know and is literally true about God is that he exists. Sometimes he seems to add two or three other things, for example, that humans know that God is eternal, omnipotent, the creator and infinite (L 12.6). His justification for saying that God exists is clear; he gives a standard, if perfunctory, proof for his existence (L 12.6). Given the proof that God is the first cause of the universe, he is justified in saying that God is the creator.

It is not as clear what grounds Hobbes has for saying that God is omnipotent. Since the universe is finite, it's possible that the creator needed only a finite power. Perhaps by "omnipotent" he meant only that God has all the power that there is, and he might have justified this on the grounds that since the relation of causality is transitive and God is the first cause, God causes everything and hence has all the power. He certainly did hold the traditional Christian belief that God is the cause of everything (QLNC 215, 245, 450).

The only kind of productive cause Hobbes recognizes is efficient causality, causes that move bodies. This suggests that God does not create the world from nothing, as other Christian philosophers held, but that God only moves something to make the universe. At the beginning of Leviathan, he says that God "made" the world, not "created" it (L Introduction 1), although in other places he says that God created the world. If Hobbes did see God only as a maker, not a creator, his view would be consonant with the opening line of Genesis. "In the beginning, when God made the heavens and the earth, the earth was a formless void and darkness covered the face of the deep, while a wind from God swept over the face of the waters." As the New Oxford Annotated Bible comments on this passage, "the text does not describe creation out of nothing." Hobbes might have been perfectly happy with primeval matter and a moving God, who ordered the matter to form the universe.

Concerning God's infiniteness, Hobbes has a clear position:

> Whatsoever we imagine is *finite*. Therefore there is no idea or conception of anything we call infinite. No man can have in his mind an image of infinite magnitude, nor conceive infinite swiftness, infinite time, or infinite force, or infinite power. When we say anything is infinite, we signify only that we are not able to conceive the ends and bounds of the thing named, having no conception of the thing, but of our own inability. And therefore the name of God is used . . . not to make us conceive him (for he is incomprehensible, and his greatness and power are unconceivable).
>
> (L 3.12)

This passage may be misleading because humans seem to have an image of God as either a large old man with a flowing white beard or perhaps a very bright light that speaks, or something else. But Hobbes's point is that humans do not get their image of God from a sensation of him, and people know, or should know, that whatever image accompanies their talk about God does not represent him. In his *Objections* to Descartes's *Meditations*, he says,

> But when I think of an angel, what comes to mind is an image, now of a flame, now of a beautiful child with wings; I feel sure that this image has no likeness to an angel, and hence that it is not the idea of an angel. But I believe that there are invisible and immaterial creatures who serve God; and we give the name 'angel' to this thing which we believe in, or suppose to exist. . . . In the same way we have no idea or image corresponding to the sacred name of God. . . . It seems, then, that there is no idea of God in us.
>
> (Hobbes 1641: 127)

So, according to this passage, humans have no image of God. Yet, speaking somewhat imprecisely, he can go on to say in the same context that it is not necessary to have an idea of something in order to think about it: "[T]he idea by means of which I imagine an angel is composed of the ideas of visible things" (Hobbes 1641: 127). Also, in other places, Hobbes holds that using words without thinking of the appropriate images is a recipe for conceptual disaster. This is an instance of Hobbes being imprecise or inconsistent.

It may seem contradictory for Hobbes to say that God is infinite and omnipotent and that humans cannot know the *nature* of God (L 12.6). To hold this position is not to give sufficient weight to the difference between knowing something about God and knowing his nature. Sometimes Hobbes seems to emphasize this difference, as when he says people have no "idea of him [God] in their mind answerable to his nature" (L 11.25). The nature of God is what is peculiar to him; it is what makes him to be God. People cannot know God's nature because they have no immediate cognition of him, if for no other reason. Hobbes, like other Christians, held that God cannot be sensed. Given his belief that God is body, because everything is a body, perhaps he was not justified in asserting that God cannot be sensed (BB 305–6, 309, 313, 383). But he seems to hold that God is a body, so subtle, that he cannot be sensed by human beings.

As evidenced by his proof of the existence of God, it is possible to know the existence of God by reason.[12] Similarly, physics has knowledge of invisible causes (DCo 6.6). Hobbes reasons to the existence of invisible causes, of motions too small to be perceived: every large motion must be made up of at least two parts. And these two parts must themselves be divisible into two parts that are motions, and so on until one reaches a motion too small to be perceived.

Also, a blind person is able to infer the existence of fire from the heat he feels, even though he cannot see it.

> For as a man that is born blind, hearing men talk of warming themselves by the fire and being brought to warm himself by the same, may easily conceive, and assure himself there is somewhat there which men call fire and is the cause of the heat he feels, but cannot imagine what it is like nor have an idea of it in his mind such as they have that see it, so also by the visible things of this world and their admirable order, a man may conceive there is a cause of them, which men call God, and yet not have an idea or image of him in his mind.
>
> (L 11.25)

Finally, and this may be the strongest point that Hobbes makes: "[T]he principles of natural science . . . are so far from teaching us anything of God's nature, as they cannot teach us our own nature, nor the nature of the smallest creature living" (L 31.33).

Concerning eternity, Hobbes needs to hold that God is eternal because if he were not, then something would have to cause him to exist, and if something caused him to exist, then that cause would be God, which contradicts the hypothesis.

It might seem that Hobbes's position that God is the first cause is contradicted by his acceptance of the principles that everything that is moved is moved by another and that every cause is in motion. Since God is the cause of the world, God must be in motion, and, it would seem, something must move God. But if something moves God, then God is not God. The flaw in this argument is the inference from "if God is in motion, then something must move God." Nothing needs to cause God to be in motion. He can simply always have been in motion. In fact, it seems that the only way for God to be God is to be in motion, because otherwise something would move God. So is being in motion part of God's nature? The answer is "No." Necessarily true propositions merely "tell us about the labels applied" to things, not what their natures are (Hobbes 1641: 2.125).

Let's now move from Chapter 12 of *Leviathan* to Chapter 31, where Hobbes considers the kind of language that should be used about God. Most philosophers before Hobbes, and even most after him, treat the language used about God as descriptive, in the same sense that scientific language is descriptive. Not only is Hobbes sensitive to the diverse uses of language, but he also recognizes that the same word or sentence might be used in different ways. The same sentence can be a command or a piece of advice. Apropos of God, the same word can be used either descriptively or honorifically. His main point is that the purpose of the language used about God in worship is honorific, not descriptive:

> And therefore, when men out of the principles of natural reason dispute of the attributes of God, they but dishonour him; for in the attributes which we give to God, we are not to consider the signification of philosophical truth, but the signification of pious intention to do him the greatest honour we are able.
>
> (L 31.33)

The words that should be applied to God have their normal descriptive meaning, but they are used primarily to honor God, not to describe him. What is said about God in order to honour him can be apt or inapt, but it is at least misleading to say that it is false. I did not say that it is at least misleading to say, "that it is not true or false" because some of what is said honorifically about God is true, and it is worth mentioning that fact for several instances.

Hobbes says, "first, it is manifest, we ought to attribute to him [God] *existence*; for no man can have the will to honour that which he thinks not to have any being" (L 31.14). Since Hobbes proved the existence of God (L 12.6), existence is something that is both literally true of God and something that should be applied to him in order to honor him. This same point applies to the second thing that he thinks should be attributed to God honorifically:

> Secondly that those philosophers who said the world, or the soul of the world, was God spake unworthily of him, . . . ; for by God is understood the cause of the world; and to say the world is God is to say there is no cause of it, that is, no God.
>
> (L 31.15)

The third attribute used to praise God is also unproblematic. "Thirdly, to say the world was not created, but eternal (seeing that which is eternal has no cause) is to deny there is a God" (L 31.16). The first three attributes are all descriptively true because of the proof of the existence of God.

The fourth attribute that Hobbes discusses amounts to having providence over creation, that is, God's having concern for human beings. In the seventeenth century, people who believed that God did not have concern for human beings were counted as atheists. Now Hobbes does not have a proof that God cares about humans, but it is part of what Christians believe and part of what ought to be said about God (L 31.17).

Although God is a body, humans should not attribute figure to him because whatever has a figure is finite, and we have already attributed infinity to God (L 31.19). The next attribute of honor is literally true. God is inconceivable. Humans should not say that they "conceive, and imagine, or have an idea of him" because they can only conceive what is finite (L 31.20).

Since God is a body, he must be a whole and he must have parts, and he must be in some place, and either be in motion or at rest. Yet, according to Hobbes, none of these things should be said about God.

> Nor to say he is in this or that *place*; for whatsoever is in place is
> bounded and finite . . . Nor that he is *moved* or *resteth*; for both
> these attributes ascribe to him place . . . And therefore when we
> ascribe to God a *will*, it is not to be understood, as that of man, for a
> *rational appetite*; but as the power by which he effecteth everything.
>
> (L 31.14–26)

To insist that all language must be used descriptively is less to comment on Hobbes's views about God than it is to criticize his view about language.

CONCLUSION

How successful was Hobbes in reconciling Christianity with modern science? I think he clearly failed, but it was a brilliant failure. Few, if any, Christian philosophers had tried to work out a case in the detail that Hobbes did, so he was exploring largely unknown territory. Many of the conceptual points he makes about revelation, prophets, miracles, and religious language are imaginative and have been adopted by later thinkers, including Christian ones. However, I think Hobbes failed in large part because I think it is impossible. But Hobbes and his contemporaries could hardly have known it. Often he did not draw the plausible consequences that critics have pointed to since the second half of the seventeenth century. Although all of his contemporary critics were certain that Hobbes had failed, they were often as blind to the plausible inferences that followed from their own beliefs. Further, their positive views about religion and its relation to science were usually no better than, and generally inferior to, Hobbes's.[13] That's why Hobbes continues to be exciting to read and to learn from, while his critics are read only by scholars from a sense of duty.

Historically, the most salient point about Hobbes's treatment of religion is that it was one of the milestones on the road from theism in the seventeenth century to deism in the eighteenth century, and towards atheism in the nineteenth century. This is the significance his work came to have; it is not in my opinion the intention that he had for it.

FURTHER READING

Curley, E. (1996) "Calvin or Hobbes, or, Hobbes as an Orthodox Christian," *Journal of the History of Philosophy* 34: 257–71. The best criticism of the interpretation of Hobbes in Martinich (1992); it is followed by Martinich's response and Curley's rejoinder.

Martinich, A. (1992) *The Two Gods of Leviathan*, Cambridge: Cambridge University Press. An argument that Hobbes was trying to reconcile modern science with Christian doctrine and show that authentic Christianity was not politically destabilizing.

—— (2001) "Interpretation and Hobbes's Political Philosophy," *Pacific Philosophical Quarterly* 82: 309–31. An explanation of the appropriate aims of interpretation, applied to Hobbes's religious views.

Seven

Hobbes Today

For more than a quarter-century, an enormous amount of first-class research has been done on the philosophy of Thomas Hobbes by scholars located in departments of philosophy, history, and political science. This represents a sea change from the situation in the preceding two-and-a-half centuries. From the end of the seventeenth century until roughly the last quarter of the twentieth, Hobbes's mathematics and natural science were largely ignored, having lost out to the tradition of Boyle and Newton. His moral and political philosophy was not so much attacked as was a distortion of it called "Hobbism." It was briefly resurrected in the first half of the nineteenth century by William Molesworth, who thought Hobbes was a utilitarian. Molesworth published Hobbes's English and Latin works. This has been the standard collected edition since that time; it is now being superseded by an edition being published by the Clarendon Press.[1]

SCHOLARSHIP BEFORE 1975

From near the end of the nineteenth century until 1970, a few works deserve to be mentioned, some of which have a continuing influence: Leo Strauss's The Political Philosophy of Thomas Hobbes: Its Basis and Genesis (1936, republished in 1952), Howard Warrender's The Political Philosophy of Hobbes (1957), Michael Oakeshott, "Introduction" to Leviathan (1946), C. B. Macpherson's The Political Theory of Possessive Individualism (1962), and David Gauthier's The Logic of Leviathan (1969) (also noteworthy are Peters (1967) and Watkins (1973)).

Leo Strauss argued in the original edition of 1936 that Hobbes was the first modern political philosopher on the grounds that he explicitly rejected "all earlier political philosophy" (Strauss 1952: xv) and grounded his theory in the natural rights of the individual, in contrast with the medieval theory of natural law. (Strauss later claimed that Machiavelli was the first modern philosopher (Strauss 1952: xv).) Although Hobbes used the language of "natural law," Strauss thought that Hobbes's concept was not the traditional one.

Perhaps more important than Strauss's claim about the origin of the concept of individual rights is his thesis about the relation between Hobbes's political philosophy and his use of modern science. Strauss wrote that they are "independent." Hobbes's moral philosophy is both modern and "pre-scientific": "The moral attitude which underlies Hobbes's political philosophy is independent of the foundation of modern science, and at least in that sense 'pre-scientific'. It is at the same time specifically modern" (Strauss 1952: 5).

Hobbes's thought was essentially humanistic, and Aristotle influenced him much more than he would admit or realize. Strauss held that Hobbes never veered from that humanist orientation. Strauss's thesis is significant because, in addition to denigrating Aristotle with some frequency, Hobbes professed to embrace the geometric method and endorsed the modern scientific view of Copernicus, Harvey, and Galileo. Part of the geometric method was the method of analysis and composition that Hobbes described in the first part of *De corpore*. Strauss's point was that this method does not yield the basic propositions of Hobbes's political philosophy, namely, that human beings are self-interested. That is, Hobbes's thesis about self-interest does not logically depend on his psychology (Strauss 1952: 3). One might object that Strauss is using a point of logic to deny that Hobbes actually thought that his psychology entailed self-interest. Hobbes, like many intelligent people, often was mistaken about what a view entails.

Strauss variously considered Hobbes an agnostic or atheist, but never a Christian (Strauss 1952: 74). In contrast, Howard Warrender thought that Hobbes was a Christian and gave the impression that his Christianity was essential to his moral and political philosophy (Warrender 1957). Warrender's thesis is an extension of A. E. Taylor's interpretation. Taylor is impressed by Hobbes's claim that a person whose acts "are in accord with right" but not done with the intention of doing right may not be a just person (Taylor 1965: 37). This is a Kantian point, as is the point that being willing to do something wrong is an "irrational attempt to will both sides of a contradiction" (Taylor 1965: 38).

For Hobbes, the laws of nature are imperatives, commands, not counsels, according to Taylor. They forbid certain actions, irrespective of a person's motivation (Taylor 1965: 40). Taylor claimed that Hobbes's "consistent deontology" is logically independent of his "egoistic moral psychology" (Taylor 1965: 45). Hobbes's ethical doctrine had "no logically necessary connection" with his psychology. The only way "to make the theory work" is to adopt "a certain kind of theism" (Taylor 1965: 37, 50). An obvious objection to Taylor's argument is the one raised against Strauss's. Even if the only way to make Hobbes's theory work is to adopt a certain kind of theism, it is not obvious that Hobbes's theory works. He may not have adopted the premises necessary to make his theory work. What Strauss, Taylor, and others need to do to make their case is to show on the basis of textual or contextual evidence that Hobbes actually argued in the way that they say he needed to argue.

J. W. N. Watkins criticized Taylor's thesis for bifurcating Hobbes's civil philosophy into "two contrasting and disconnected subsystems" (Watkins 1973: 58); that is, Hobbes had one account of the obligatoriness of the laws of nature and another account of the motivation to fulfill the laws. Taylor might have replied that he can hardly be blamed for pointing out a bifurcation that exists in Hobbes's theory. My own view is that the supposed bifurcation merely reflects the two parts of Hobbes's theory of the laws of nature. He gave separate answers to different questions: "What makes a law of nature have normative force?" (Answer: God's command), and "What motivates a person to obey the law of nature?" (Answer: the desire for self-preservation).

To return to Warrender, he was even more explicit than Taylor was that "there exists a considerable gulf between these laws [of nature] and the principles upon which Hobbes's natural man is motivated" (Warrender 1957: 274–5). Hobbes has two systems, "a system of motives and a system of obligations. The system of motives ends with the supreme principle of self-preservation . . . the system of obligations ends with the obligation to obey natural law regarded as the will of God" (Warrender 1957: 213).

The argument for the alleged system of obligations was criticized by many scholars. Watkins, for example, points out that "Hobbes's account of political authority starts out from individual needs" (Watkins 1973: 58). Although this is true, it does not show that Hobbes did not rely on some theistic premise intended to show that the laws of nature were normative. It may be the case, and I think Hobbes's text shows that it is, that Hobbes needed the premises about individual needs in order to prove the propositions that constitute the content of the laws of nature (the dictates of reason) and needed the theistic premise to hold that these propositions had the nature and force of laws. Hobbes himself argued that the same words could be used to express either a counsel or a command, depending upon the source of the words (EL 10.1; DC 14.1; L 25.4). A command comes from someone with authority who expresses what he wants done. According to Watkins, a moral system "can exist only when there is a sovereign" (Watkins 1973: 58). Watkins's view is contradicted by Hobbes's assertion that sovereigns are subject to the laws of nature in conducting international relations, where the sovereign is not a sovereign vis-à-vis other people in the state of nature.

Those who hold that Hobbes's laws of nature are merely prudential and hence not moral may be committing the fallacy of false dichotomy.[2] It is not necessary to choose between prudence and morality. The world is better if they coincide, and many Anglican moral philosophers who came after Hobbes thought that morality and self-interest do coincide (Darwall 1995: 80, 194; cf. Marshall 1985). I think these Anglicans were inspired by Hobbes's work, but either did not recognize it or could not admit to the fact because of his bad reputation. Watkins thinks that any theistic interpretation of Hobbes's laws of nature will make men "see double, and mistake their lawful sovereign" (Watkins 1973: 66). But that is not true since the sovereign, according to Hobbes, is God's representative on earth.

In his influential introduction to a 1957 edition of *Leviathan*, Michael Oakeshott rejected those interpretations that made his materialism the central aspect of Hobbes's philosophy. Instead, Oakeshott maintained that the "coherence of his philosophy . . . lies . . . in a single 'passionate thought' that pervades its parts" (Oakeshott 1957: xix). That thought is Hobbes's belief that political theory is philosophy and philosophy is reasoning (Oakeshott 1957: xx). Concretely, this means that philosophy is not theology, science or sense experience. Because reasoning is about temporally prior causes and their effects, Hobbes's philosophy is mechanistic, according to Oakeshott (Oakeshott 1957: xx–xxi). It is because reasoning is about the power of causes to produce effects that power plays a central role in Hobbes's philosophy. Civil philosophy is "precisely the application of this conception of philosophy to civil society" (Oakeshott 1957: xxvii). Thus civil philosophy will concern the generation of civil society, that is, how it arises from the nature of man (Oakeshott 1957: xxix). Although Oakeshott's interpretation is imaginative and continues to influence theorists in political science departments, philosophers tend to ignore him because his views lack the detailed critical analysis that philosophy demands.

Another important strand of Hobbes scholarship before 1975 was the Marxist interpretation of C. B. Macpherson, for whom Hobbes's conception of human beings is "really an analysis of bourgeois man" (Macpherson 1945: 170; see also Strauss 1952: 121). Human beings have "a constant drive" for "material gain" and this drive dominates "the whole character of the individual" (Macpherson 1945: 173). It is the pervasive consciousness of scarcity and the determination to avoid it that makes the Hobbesian person a bourgeois man (Macpherson 1945: 173–4). Consequently, all value is determined by the market (Macpherson 1945: 174).

To a great extent, Macpherson's theory was undermined by an article by Keith Thomas. Thomas conceded that Hobbesian man is bourgeois; but the concession is made possible by the vagueness of the term "bourgeois" (Thomas 1965: 186). For bourgeois man, the right to property is absolute and not dependent on the government. But for Hobbes, property is a consequence of government and ultimately belongs to the sovereign (Thomas 1965: 223; see L 24.5–7). As for the concept of a free market, Hobbes made no use of it. For him, coerced bargains are as legitimate as uncoerced ones (Thomas 1965: 235–6). Rather than acquisitiveness, Hobbes thought that pride was the most important characteristic of human beings (Thomas 1965: 190).

At this point, analytic philosophy still had not seriously engaged with Hobbes. The change came with the publication of David Gauthier's The Logic of Leviathan (1969). The fact that Gauthier could ask in the late 1960s, "Why write on Hobbes?", indicates that the so-called "Hobbes Industry" had not yet tooled up (Goldsmith 1991). Gauthier says that Hobbes is worth writing about because he is "both so illuminatingly right and so illuminatingly wrong" about obligation (Gauthier 1969: vi). In one way or another, I think most philosophers today feel the same way.

The most important aspect of Gauthier's book was his claim that Hobbes's theory of obligation underwent an important change between De cive and Leviathan. In De cive, Hobbes's theory is a theory of alienation; in Leviathan, it is a theory of authorization. According to Gauthier, "authorization must involve some translation of right." Hobbes does not define this concept, and Gauthier struggles to identify it, initially by saying what it is not: "This [authorization with translation] is evidently not mere renunciation, nor is it transfer, in Hobbes's usual sense" (Gauthier 1969: 124). Unfortunately for Gauthier's interpretation, he eliminates the only two ways that Hobbes recognizes for laying down rights: renouncing and transferring. Gauthier's term "translation" is not Hobbes's, and it does not capture any concept of Hobbes.

From here until the end of this chapter, I will discuss only scholarship after 1975.

SCHOLARSHIP AFTER 1975
Political Philosophy

Jean Hampton explicates Gauthier's concept of "translation" as "loaning" (Hampton 1986: 116). But this does not work. When one person P_1 loans some object O to another person P_2, what P_2 does with O are his own actions, not the actions of P_1. If P_2 borrows money from P_1 and buys something with it, P_2 owns the object, not P_1. If P_2 borrows a gun from P_1 to go hunting and shoots a deer, the deer belongs to P_2. Or, if P_2 borrows a gun from P_1 and shoots someone, P_2 is liable for the shooting, not P_1. Of course, P_1 may have some liability if his loaning of the gun involves some recklessness, but this liability is logically independent of the concept of loaning.

One defect in Hampton's explanation of the difference between alienation and authorization is that she thinks that the latter is the same as a loan: to authorize x to do y is to loan something to x to do y. But that is not the correct understanding of authorization. When one person loans something O to another person, the first person loses the right and power to use O, as when a bank loans money to someone. The bank cannot use the money that it has loaned out for some other purpose. To loan something to someone for some period of time is to alienate one's right to that thing for that period of time. Authorization is not like that at all. If a client C authorizes a real-estate agent R to buy a house for C and R acts on that authorization, C is buying the house, not R. C has not alienated

C's right to buy a house. The mistake of thinking that authorization involves a loss of right has been made by other philosophers (Skinner 2002: 206).

Hampton's main thesis in her book does not depend on her analysis of authorization as loaning. According to her, Hobbes's theory does not properly contain a social contract, because social contracts are "trades of promises that introduce moral incentives that either supplement or replace each party's self-interested motivations" (Hampton 1986: 145, 147). What these moral incentives are depends on one's moral theory. For Hume, it is the sanction of not being believed in the future. For Kant, it is the authoritativeness of the moral law (Hampton 1986: 141). What Hobbes relies on in his theory are self-interested agreements; that is, each person acts in a way that serves his self-interest, as determined by rational calculation (Hampton 1986: 139). Such agreements are solutions to coordination problems in the sense introduced by Thomas Schelling in The Strategy of Conflict (1960) and elaborated by David Lewis in Convention (1969). Hampton follows Lewis's definition. Coordination problems are "situations of interdependent decision by two or more agents in which coincidence of interest predominates and in which there are two or more coordination equilibria" (Lewis 1969: 24). Coordination equilibria are "those situations in which the combination of players' actions is such that no one would be better off if any single player, either oneself or another, acted differently" (Hampton 1986: 138).

The important difference between self-interested agreements and contracts is that the former are motivated solely by the benefits that come to a person from keeping the agreement. No coercive power or moral consideration is needed (Hampton 1986: 142). The fact that neither coercion nor morality needs to play a role in achieving the ends of people faced with a coordination problem leads Hampton to say that Hobbes's theory does not involve a social contract, even though Hobbes uses the language of social contract.

A consequence of her position that Hobbes used self-interestedness rather than a social contract to found civil government is that Hobbes cannot use the concept of alienation (Hampton 1986: 257). Human beings retain their "ability to judge and act" from self-interest after the civil state is created, and it would be irrational for them to alienate these abilities (Hampton 1986: 257). Hampton's view fits with what Hobbes says in Chapter 21 of *Leviathan*, namely, that the words of authorization, "I authorize, or take upon me, all his actions," do not restrict the liberty one had before pronouncing those words (L 21.14). Obligations arise insofar as the end or goal of becoming a citizen requires a certain kind of action. Unfortunately for Hobbes, this kind of requirement is not obligation in the relevant sense, and his words of authorization are not the complete formula used in becoming a citizen. The prospective citizen also says that he "give[s] up" his right of governing himself (L 17.13). What Hampton in effect shows is that Hobbes's theory is inconsistent.

Published in the same year as Hampton's book was Gregory Kavka's *Hobbesian Moral and Political Theory*. As its title suggests, Kavka uses Hobbes's actual texts and ideas to develop a cogent moral and political theory. Interpreting Hobbes's philosophy is only a means to that end (Kavka 1986: xiv). This means that Kavka departs from Hobbes whenever it suits his philosophical purpose and is not overly concerned about getting Hobbes's view exactly right.

In his own theory, Kavka weakens three Hobbesian principles: (1) that "all human acts are motivated by self-interest;" (2) that "a sovereign's interests will coincide with those of his people" and (3) that "divisions of, or limitations on, sovereign power inevitably lead to civil war" (Kavka 1986: xii). Instead of (1), Kavka defends "Predominant Egoism," roughly, that most people, most of the time, act for their own self-interest (Kavka 1986: 64–5). Instead of (2) and (3), Kavka holds that the sovereign's interests sometimes do not coincide with that of his people and that limitations on a sovereign's power do not inevitably lead to civil war. With weaker, more plausible principles, including the "copper" rule, "Do unto others as they do unto you," Kavka develops a liberal theory of politics (Kavka 1986: xii, 4, 347).

Gauthier, Hampton, and Kavka all make use of the Prisoner's Dilemma to explicate Hobbes's idea of the state of nature as a war of all against all. In the Prisoner's Dilemma, criminals A and B are arrested for some crime. The police have evidence to convict A and B and, when convicted, each will get three years in jail. But the police suspect both of a worse crime. The police make the following deal with each of them, who cannot communicate with each other but know that the other is getting the same deal. If A gives evidence against B, then A will get one year in prison and B ten years, if B does not give evidence. If both A and B give evidence against the other, they will each get five years. Initially and without working out all the options, the sensible thing for A and B to do seems to be not to confess: If neither confesses, they do a total of six years in jail. However, a study of each possibility shows that the best alternative for each person is to confess, even though this means that each will spend more than three years in jail.

Let's look at this from B's point of view first. If A gives evidence and B does not, then B suffers greatly, because he will be sentenced to ten years in jail. So, if A gives evidence, B should. Now suppose that A does not give evidence. In this case, if B gives evidence he will get only one year in jail, and that is much better than the three he would get if he does not. So B does better by giving evidence whether A does so or not. A can go through with the same reasoning from his own point of view. So both decide to give evidence, and both do five years.

		B	
		Gives evidence	Doesn't give evidence
A	Gives evidence	5,5	1,10
	Doesn't give evidence	10,1	3,3

In the Prisoner's Dilemma, the choices made by A and B affect them on only one occasion. For at least this reason, it does not correctly capture the situation of people in the state of nature, because they are liable to be in situations in which their past behavior is known to the other person and very likely others. Even if two people A and B in the state of nature are never in a similar situation again, other people might well know how A and B acted when they were in the original situation. Their uncooperative behavior will put them at a disadvantage the next time they would benefit from cooperative behavior from another person. This problem with the single-occurrence Prisoner's Dilemma can be corrected by so-called iterated Prisoner's Dilemmas. Other problems could be raised (Martinich 1997); an objection that goes to the heart of the matter was first made, I believe, by Alan Ryan: "The twentieth-century obsession with the 'Prisoner's Dilemma' and with the temptation to be a 'free-rider' presupposes a theory of motivation that Hobbes did not believe in. What Hobbes's individuals maximize in the state of nature is *power*" (Ryan 1988: 92). And they maximize power because it is necessary for them to do so in order to preserve their lives, not to maximize utility.

Moral Philosophy

The power of Hobbes's thought leads philosophers to relate his views to contemporary disputes, sometimes in ways of which he himself did not conceive. Two of these will be considered in this section. The first is internalism, the view that if *x* is a moral precept for a person P, then P has a motive to follow *x* (cf. Darwall 1995: 9–10). According to Stephen Darwall, moral philosophy for Hobbes is the science of good and evil.

> Since he [Hobbes] insists that English language users invariably employ 'good' and 'evil' simply to refer to objects of their desires and aversions, respectively—there being no 'common rule of good and evil, to be taken from the nature of the objects themselves'—

Hobbes holds that ethics can equivalently be defined as the science whose subject is 'consequences from the passions of *men*' (Lev.vi.7, ix.4). Simplifying greatly, ethics is the subject that works out what people should do from premises about their desires and aversions, that is, from what they hold to be good and evil.

(Darwall 1995: 53)

This statement of Hobbes's moral philosophy is misleading because it does not make clear that Hobbes is not clear about whether "ethics" or moral philosophy is a normative science or not. In his famous diagram of the sciences, ethics is described as knowledge of the "[c]onsequences from the passions of men" (L 9.3), and it is separated from "the science of just and unjust." Perhaps, it is separated because justice and injustice are supposed to arise only in a civil state. But this does not seem to be correct for two reasons. First, Hobbes recognizes that various people make covenants in the state of nature (L 14.27). Second, whatever is not unjust is just (L 14.2); so, anyone in the state of nature who makes no covenants (and does not break any law of nature) is just.

Morality or obligation is certainly on the scene when Hobbes introduces life under law. Initially, this law is the law of nature, which includes "*justice, gratitude, modesty, equity, mercy,*" and so on (L 15.40). He calls these "moral virtues" and says "the science of virtue and vice is moral philosophy; and therefore the true doctrine of the laws of nature is the true moral philosophy" (L 15.40). We have already seen in Chapter 3 that the interpretation of "laws of nature" is hotly contested. Only one point needs to be made here. It is false or seriously misleading to say this: "Hobbes remarks that, strictly speaking, they [the laws of nature] are called laws 'but improperly'. What they really are, he says, are 'but conclusions, or theorems concerning what conduceth to the conservation and defense' of any person (*Lev*.xv.41)" (Darwall 1995: 54).

What Hobbes in fact says is this: "These *dictates of reason* men use to call by the name of law, but improperly" (L 14.41; my emphasis).

Hobbes is obviously drawing a distinction between dictates of reason and laws of nature, and he is not saying that the laws of nature are not properly called laws. Hobbes's use of the locution "men use to call" indicates that he is not including himself in the group that spoke improperly, and he never says "the laws of nature are not properly laws." He says that if we consider the dictates of reason "as delivered in the word of God that by right commandeth all things, then are they properly called *laws*" (L 15.41). It would be extremely odd if the philosopher who insisted on "apt" definitions and distinguished between right and wrong definitions would choose an improper phrase to denote one of the key concepts in his philosophy (L 4.13, 5.17). For Hobbes, obligation and normativity depend on the existence of laws.

One problem with Darwall's treatment of Hobbes's philosophy is that Hobbes never thought about the issue of internalism. So Darwall is mining Hobbes's text for answers to questions that Hobbes never asked.

For Darwall reason commands, and there is no justification for going further. He says:

> Reason dictates action just insofar as an agent already has ends, ends that do not derive from reason but that provide the background necessary to give right (theoretical) reasoning practical 'force'. It is in the transfer of motive force from end to means by right reasoning that reason's dictates consist. We may call this the *instrumental reason* view of normativity.
>
> (Darwall 1995: 59; see also 60)

The problem with this answer is that there is nothing normative in instrumental reason, and it does not give rise to obligation. For Hobbes, reason only calculates.

In my opinion, Darwall is falsely attributing to Hobbes the view that a necessary condition for being a normative or ethical precept is that it has to be motivating. Granted, Hobbes uses a premise that involves a motive for action – people desire to preserve their lives –

in order to deduce the content of the laws of nature. But what makes the laws of nature normative is that they are commands, the product of God's will. What Darwall says appears to be the case, namely, that Hobbes's concepts of "right, obligation, justice, and injury seem to move in their own normative space in *Leviathan*," is, I think, really the case (Darwall 1995: 60).

Internalism is intimately connected with moral psychology in that internalism requires morality to give people a motive for acting morally. Hobbes's ethics is "thoroughly egocentric" in the sense that all voluntary action springs from self-interest, which is equated with "well-being" (Deigh 1996: 33–4). Morality is derived from prudence: "The laws of nature, therefore, on the orthodox interpretation, are valid relative to this desire or the more general desire to promote one's good" (Deigh 1996: 34). John Deigh calls this the "orthodox" position among contemporary interpreters of Hobbes.

In contrast with the orthodox interpretation, the "dissenting" view maintains that, for Hobbes, natural law imposes obligations on humans. Deigh initiated an important debate by denying both the orthodox and dissenting positions. Although he does accept the negative thesis of the dissenters, that Hobbes's ethics is "logically independent of his moral psychology," he does not accept either of the two positive theses of the dissenting view, namely, that the natural law imposes obligations on humans "generally, not just in civil society" and that Hobbes held a divine command theory of morality (Deigh 1996: 34–5).

Deigh's view is that Hobbes derives the laws of nature from reason, construed as "reckoning (that is adding and subtracting) or consequences of general names" (Deigh 1996: 39–40, quoting L 5.2). This has the consequence that reason does not "by its very nature . . . determine the proper ends of action" (Deigh 1996: 39). Thus, he denies the orthodox claim that morality is deduced from prudence. On one interpretation of Hobbes's reply to the fool, the fool is maintaining that "when reason is exercised in the service of self-interest, that is, when its exercise consists in determining the fittest means to achieving the ends set by egoistic desires," reason dictates acting unjustly. Deigh rejects this interpretation because "it exemplifies strategic or means-to-ends thinking and not deduction" (Deigh 1996: 41). It is possible that one of the problems with the fool's reasoning, a problem that Hobbes himself did not explicitly point out, is that the fool, in order to support his view that injustice is sometimes not against reason, is thinking of prudence, of the knowledge gained by experience. His mistake is to make an inference from knowledge (gained by experience) to reason. Given his general view about prudence and reason, Hobbes ought to reject this inference. While, nonhuman animals have knowledge gained from experience (L 3.9), they do not have reason; that is, they do not have the knowledge that comes from knowing the consequences of the meanings of words. But, since ethics is a science, it cannot use prudence; it needs to reason from propositions that are either definitions of words or follow from propositions that follow from definitions.

Kinch Hoekstra rejects this solution on the grounds that if it were correct, Hobbes should have emphasized the distinction between prudence and reason in his reply to the fool (Hoekstra 1997: 652). However, there is no need for Hobbes to emphasize the distinction by rehearsing it. The reply to the fool comes in the context of proving the third law of nature, and this proof, like all the others, has to depend on reason alone; that is, it must come from definitions and what follows from them. Prudence can legitimately play no role in the proof. If Hobbes refers to prudence, it is inessential to the proof itself. (See also Hayes 1999 and Hoekstra 1999.)

Does the view that the laws of nature are deduced from the definition of the law of nature mean that reason does not play a part in means–end thinking? The answer depends upon what is meant by "means–end" thinking. Deigh and his principal critic, Mark Murphy, restrict its meaning to judgments about particular means to particular ends in particular circumstances. In this sense, means–

end thinking does not make use of reason, in Hobbes's technical sense of the addition and subtraction of words. If the meaning of "means–end thinking" is extended in a natural way to include "the best means to achieving" in general the ends of the agent, including those ends that "the agent is already inclined to pursue," then reason does play a role in means–end thinking (cf. Deigh 1996: 58). Surely a relation between means and ends is involved in the deduction of the laws of nature from the definition of a law of nature (Murphy 2000: 260–2; cf Deigh 2003: 99–100). The definition involves "the means of preserving" a person's life. And these means are specified by the laws of nature: make peace; lay down your right to all things; keep your covenants. The deduction of these means to achieve the end of preserving one's life does not appeal to empirical and contingent propositions of means–end reasoning, but only to the necessary relations that hold between propositions because of the meanings of their words.

It is possible that Deigh would reject this attempt to extend the concept of means–end thinking on the grounds that "means-to-end thinking . . . starts with an end, an object of desire, and proceeds from that end to the determination of those actions that are conductive to its realization" (Deigh 2003: 103). That is, means–end thinking does not involve propositions at all: the movement is from desires to actions. However, it is not clear to me why it is legitimate to restrict the concept in this way. Any thinking that goes from desires to actions can be represented as going by inferential steps from propositions about desires to propositions about actions that satisfy those desires. Given that, it seems legitimate to call the latter kind of reasoning means–end reasoning. (See also Deigh 2003 and Hoekstra 2003.)

A side issue in the debate between Deigh and Murphy is the logical form of the laws of nature. Are they indicatives or imperatives? Murphy thinks they are conditional indicatives. Deigh thinks they are imperatives; however, he concedes that Hobbes does not directly deduce imperative sentences. Rather, Hobbes deduces sentences of the form "X is a law of nature," where the values of "X" are imperatives, for example, " 'Make peace, etc' is a law of nature."[3] Hobbes's text is probably too indeterminate or contradictory to admit of a decisive interpretation.

There's a different issue concerning the logical form of the laws of nature. Kavka claims that the laws of nature always have, in addition to a main clause, an escape clause, by which an agent is "released from the requirement of the main clause if others are not satisfying that requirement" (Kavka 1986: 344). For example, Kavka claims that Hobbes's first law of nature is "That every man, ought to endeavor peace, as far as he has hope of obtaining it; and when he cannot obtain it, that he may seek, and use, all helps, and advantages of war" (L 14.4). There are two problems with this view. The first is that most of the laws of nature, as Hobbes stated them, do not contain the kind of qualifying clause that Kavka's interpretation requires. For example, the fourth is, "*that a man which receiveth benefit from another of mere grace endeavour that he which giveth it have no reasonable cause to repent him of his good will*," and the fifth is "*that every man strive to accommodate himself to the rest*" (L 15.16–17). Of course, these laws can be said to have an implicit qualifying clause. But the same thing can be said about most, non-Kantian, laws. "Do not exceed the speed limit [unless one needs to save a life or prevent a substantial evil]." So Kavka's theory says nothing specifically about the form of Hobbes's laws. The second problem with his interpretation is that the work of the supposed escape clause is done by something else in Hobbes's theory. The laws of nature always "oblige *in foro interno*, that is to say, they bind to a desire they should take place," but not always *in foro externo*, that is, "to the putting them in act" (L 15.36). That's one reason why Hobbes can express the first law of nature as "seek peace" *simpliciter* (L 15.16).[4]

Sovereign and Commonwealth

One of the most significant publications in Hobbes's scholarship in the past decade was the appearance of Volume III, *Hobbes and Civil*

Science, of Quentin Skinner's *Visions of Politics*. While the nature of the book and limitations of space prevent a complete discussion of his views, one topic is especially pertinent. Skinner thinks that there is an obvious problem in Hobbes's thought that scholars seem not to have noticed. On the one hand, Hobbes says that the sovereign or artificial man who is the commonwealth makes law through his reason and command, but on the other hand, the commonwealth does not have "the capacity to do anything" (L 26.5; see Skinner 2002: 177). How is this possible?

Skinner says that (i) "the state" (Skinner's phrase) is (ii) "but a word, without substance, and cannot stand." Concerning (ii), one might claim that Skinner has quoted out of context. Hobbes does not say that "a state" or "a commonwealth" *simpliciter* is but a word. He says that "a commonwealth *without sovereign power* is but a word without substance and cannot stand" (L 31.1, my emphasis). The restrictive prepositional phrase is crucial. Nothing that lacks sovereign power is a commonwealth. Skinner is taking "without sovereign power" to mean "without a sovereign" (Skinner 2002: 201). But it is doubtful that one can equate the power that a sovereign has with the sovereign himself. The sovereign legislates but the power does not.

Concerning (i), the phrase, "the state" is ambiguous between the commonwealth and the government of the commonwealth if there is a distinction between the two, as Skinner suggests there is. There is good textual evidence for thinking that Hobbes does not think that the commonwealth is different from its government or representative. In *Leviathan*, Chapter 26, paragraph 5, Hobbes says "The legislator in all commonwealths is only the sovereign." That is,

(A) The legislator = the sovereign.

He then says, "the commonwealth is the legislator," that is,

(B) The commonwealth = legislator.

From (A) and (B), this follows:

(C) The commonwealth = the legislator = the sovereign.

That is, the distinction that Skinner needs to generate his puzzle appears to be a distinction without a difference.

Of course things are never that simple with Hobbes. Sometimes he does seem to distinguish between the sovereign and the commonwealth, especially when he wants to argue that subjects must obey the commands of the government. For example, when he implies that the king is "the representant of the commonwealth" (L 42.130), he seems to be drawing a distinction between the king (or sovereign) and the commonwealth. An even better example is a passage in which Hobbes talks about the institution of the sovereign and the commonwealth:

> The only way to erect such a common power as may be able to . . . live contentedly, is to confer all their power and strength upon one man or upon one assembly of men, that may reduce all their wills by plurality of voices unto one will; which is as much as to say, to appoint one man or assembly of men to bear their person. . . . This is more than consent or concord; it is a real unity of them all in one and the same person . . .
>
> (L 17.13; see also 18.18)

In this passage, there seems to be only one artificial person, the sovereign, and the sovereign may be a monarch, group of aristocrats or the subjects as a whole. Since this sovereign, this artificial person, bears the person of the multitude and creates a "real unity of them all in one and the same person," it does not seem that there is need for another person. However, Hobbes does seem to introduce a second artificial person, the commonwealth, when he continues with this comment: "[T]he multitude so united in one person is called a COMMONWEALTH; in Latin, CIVITAS" (L 17.13). But then again he seems to take the distinction back when he immediately goes on to say, "This is the generation of that great

Leviathan, or rather . . . that mortal god to which we owe . . . our peace and defense" (L 13), because he is giving the impression that the commonwealth is the Leviathan, that is, the sovereign.

Skinner concedes that Hobbes's text is sometimes ambiguous or otherwise problematic but emphasizes that Hobbes sometimes distinguishes between the sovereign and the commonwealth. I concede that Hobbes sometimes distinguishes between the two, but emphasize that Hobbes's text is often ambiguous or otherwise problematic.

Skinner thinks that the distinction between sovereign and commonwealth explains "how the apparently insubstantial person of the state can nevertheless be the holder of sovereignty and the seat of power" (Skinner 2002: 199). Presumably, the commonwealth can act because the sovereign can act. But this is not really a solution. Why should the sovereign, who may consist of a small group of human beings or the entire population, taken as one, be in any better position to act than the entire population of subjects, taken severally? After all, a mob can act in virtue of the actions of its members even though no sovereign unites the members. The point is that given that both the sovereign and the commonwealth are artificial objects, the sovereign is just as "apparently insubstantial" as the commonwealth. If one cannot understand how the commonwealth can act, given that it is an artificial person, it is no help to be told that it can act because another artificial person, the sovereign, can act.

Distinguishing between the sovereign and the commonwealth seems to multiply entities with no gain in explanatory value in the case of democracies. In a democracy, there are the subjects individually and the subjects united in the person of the commonwealth. There is no third thing, no sovereign representative, not identical with the commonwealth itself. There may be a governmental organization, elected or appointed officials. But these officials are not the sovereign. My view is that Hobbes was confused about the nature of the sovereign and the commonwealth. Sometimes he distinguishes them, and sometimes he does not. In addition to *Leviathan* 26.5, discussed above, *Leviathan*'s famous illustrated title-page conflates the sovereign with the commonwealth. My guess is that what Skinner wants to get at is a distinction between a commonwealth and the government of the commonwealth. Subjects can criticize the actions of their own government, without thereby criticizing themselves, contrary to Hobbes's view.

The conflation or confusion of sovereign and commonwealth is a particular instance of Hobbes's confusion about artificial persons. In *Leviathan* 16.1, an artificial person is the person who represents someone or something else, for example, the manager of a bridge, the vicar of a Church, and the guardian of a minor. This view, which is often considered odd, is not so odd if one considers that the words "manager," "vicar," and "guardian" indicate the office that a natural person fills. The natural person does not act in his own right, but as something else, a representative of another object. However, later in *Leviathan* Hobbes says something different: He says a person is he "that is represented, as often as he is represented" (L 42.3). That is, the artificial person is not the representative but the thing represented. In *De homine* (1658), Hobbes again indicates that the artificial person is not the representative of something but the thing represented, for example, the manager, vicar, and guardian mentioned above. Skinner thinks that Hobbes finally settled on this latter view (Skinner 2002: 188–9). But that is not right. In "*An Answer to Bishop Bramhall's Book, 'The Catching of the Leviathan'*," Hobbes reverts to the view that the artificial person is the representative. He says that a person is "an intelligent substance that acteth anything in his own or another's name, or by his own or another's authority" (BB 310). This suggests that Hobbes remained undecided about whether the representative or the thing represented was an artificial person.

The explanation for the conflation of sovereign and commonwealth is related to his waffling about authorization and alienation. When he wants the actions of the sovereign to be free of criticism from the citizens (authorization), then he identifies the sovereign with the commonwealth. But when he wants the subjects to obey the sovereign (alienation), then he separates the sovereign from the commonwealth (cf. Skinner 2002: 207–8).

Skepticism and Toleration

Richard Tuck has been one of the most imaginative and learned interpreters of Hobbes. His argument that Hobbes's metaphysics was a response to Descartes's has won wide acceptance (Tuck 1988a). Tuck has also written powerfully about Hobbes's views about toleration and skepticism. Concerning the former of these, Tuck claims that Hobbes was greatly affected by the "Atheism and Prophanity [sic]" Bill, introduced in October 1666, and discussed at various times and in various forms into the 1680s. Especially troubling to Hobbes was the authorization of a committee of the Commons to collect information about *Leviathan* (Tuck 1990: 157–8). At least partly in reaction to these events, Hobbes wrote his *Dialogue of the Common Laws* and *An Historical Narration Concerning Heresy*. Tuck describes this reaction as "testimony to the terror into which he [Hobbes] was plunged by the events of 1666–8" (Tuck 1990: 159). Certainly Hobbes was worried about the possibility of being prosecuted, as any rational person would be. To say that he was terrified is to go beyond the evidence.

According to Tuck, Hobbes advocated religious toleration, because he thought that there should be no law against heresy (Tuck 1990: 160). But there is a big difference between advocating religious toleration and thinking that there should not be laws against heresy. Hobbes thought that persecuting heresy, a policy he associates with Roman Catholicism, was not a good idea. But the king had the right to enforce conformity to a state religion. It's quite possible for two religions to have the same dogma and be different religions, because of differences in ritual and Church government.

Tuck downplays Hobbes's position that an atheist "should be banished from the republic, not as a criminal, but as a danger to the public" (Tuck 1990: 161, quoting Hobbes). Tuck points out that

Hobbes never said that an atheist "would not keep his contracts" (Tuck 1990: 161). This, it seems to me, is splitting hairs. If Tuck were right that Hobbes thought that any atheist could keep contracts, then it would have been pointless for him to have said categorically that an atheist "should be banished from the republic . . . as a danger to the public" (Tuck 1990: 161, quoting Hobbes). Tuck also thinks that the fact that Hobbes denies that "oaths add anything to the force of contracts" implies that God has nothing to do with their force. I think this misses Hobbes's point: "It appears also that the oath adds nothing to the obligation. For a covenant, if lawful, binds in the sight of God, without the oath" (L 14.33). Why would a covenant bind in the sight of God, unless God necessarily backed up all contracts? And, if God necessarily backs up all contracts, then atheists, who do not acknowledge God, cannot be trusted to make contracts. That's why they need to be banished.

Tuck says that Hobbes's "most passionate defense of toleration" in *Leviathan* is the comment: "So we are reduced to the Independency of the primitive Christians to follow Paul, or Cephas, or Apollos, every man as he liketh best. Which, if it be without contention . . . is perhaps the best" (Tuck 1990: 163; L 47.20). But there is no passion here at all, only resignation: "[P]erhaps the best."

Toleration is conceptually linked to liberty of conscience in the ordinary sense. The former is a necessary condition for the latter. But Hobbes did not support liberty of conscience in that ordinary sense. He said that

> we are not every one to make our own private reason or conscience, but the public reason, that is, the reason of God's lieutenant, judge. . . . A private man has always the liberty (because thought is free) to believe or not believe in his heart . . . But when it comes to profession of that faith [in doctrines], the private reason must submit to the public.
>
> (L 37.13)

This guts the concept of liberty of conscience.[5] Hobbes was afraid of what the bishops might do to him, but he was not afraid of what the sovereign might require of him. So he had no need for a doctrine of toleration and did not press for one.

Concerning skepticism, Tuck thinks that Hobbes was greatly affected by it. Tuck proves many things, but not his thesis about Hobbes and skepticism. He shows that Mersenne was greatly affected by skepticism and used some of Hobbes's work on optics to overcome it (Tuck 1988b: 238–9). But Mersenne's use of Hobbes does not prove that Hobbes himself was greatly affected by skepticism.

Tuck also shows that Grotius intended his philosophy to refute ethical skepticism by building his theory on the universally accepted propositions that self-defense and "defense of the material objects necessary for one's existence" are justified (Tuck 1988b: 242–3, see also 258–9). However, it does not follow that Hobbes, who used very similar propositions, was motivated by a desire to refute skepticism. In developing a philosophical system, one wants to start with premises that will be accepted by as many (intelligent) people as possible; Grotius's premises look like they pass the test. No matter what Grotius's premises owe to skepticism in their origin, that origin is irrelevant to Hobbes's use of the premises. Similar remarks can be made about Hobbes's use of Gassendi's observation that the only knowledge people had was of their own sensations. Although Hobbes agreed with Gassendi on this point, this is little or no evidence that Hobbes's motivation for using it was the same as Gassendi's.

Tuck claims that Hobbes's skeptical motivation is revealed in his verse autobiography. But in the passage that he quotes, Hobbes says nothing about skeptical doubt. Rather, he says that he "thought continually about the nature of things" and that the only "true thing," which is the basis of "all those phenomena which we wrongly say are something," is "nothing but motion" (Tuck's translation, quoted in Tuck 1988b: 248). This is the project of a straightforward physicist or natural philosopher. To maintain that it must be the project of someone gripped by skepticism is to go beyond the evidence.

Tuck thinks that Hobbes "endorsed Descartes's hyperbolical doubt about dreaming" because Hobbes says, "nor is it impossible for a man to be so far deceived, as when his dream is past, to think it real" (EL 3.10). But possibility of doubt ("nor . . . impossible") is not the same as necessity of doubt (Tuck 1988b: 251; cf. Tuck 1992: 59 and Tuck 1993: 300–1). Although Hobbes expresses various doubts, they do not prove that Hobbes was a skeptic. Skeptics do not have a proprietary interest in all doubt, only universal doubt. (See Sorell 1993 for similar, more detailed criticisms.)

I have argued that Hobbes was not gripped by skepticism but thought he had a solution to it. He grounded his science on definitions, which are true by stipulation (see, for example, *Tractatus opticus*, Tuck's translation, in Tuck 1988b: 252). So long as science progresses by drawing inferences from definitions or what follows from definitions, no error can slip in. Inferences are not fallible as long as one concentrates on one's ideas. This is not to say that Hobbes's solution would convince any skeptic, but only that it satisfied Hobbes, rather easily.

Religion

S. A. Lloyd in *Ideals as Interests in Hobbes's* Leviathan (1992) presented a new perspective on the role of religion in Hobbes's political philosophy. Not discussing the relationship between God and the laws of nature, she argued that previous commentators had not taken seriously enough Hobbes's recognition that the behavior of ordinary people is to a great extent governed by "transcendent interests," that is, values grounded in beliefs in God and an afterlife. The stark evidence for this is the fact that people "go to war over their moral ideals and religious principles, and are capable not only of risking death in the service of their values but even of embracing death when they believe it will further their cause" (Lloyd 1992: 1). She thinks that the interpretation of Hobbes as a psychological egoist does not jibe with this fact. So, she argued, Hobbes wanted to prove to his readers that people have overwhelming reasons, either consistent with or grounded in their transcendent beliefs, to obey their sovereign. For this reason, Lloyd emphasizes the second half of *Leviathan*: Part III: Of a Christian Commonwealth, and Part IV: The Kingdom of Darkness.

As regards the religious principles of Christians, easy proofs that they should obey their sovereigns are such biblical texts as, "Servants, obey your masters" (Colossians 3:20) and "Render unto Caesar the Things that are Caesar's" (Matthew 22:21; see also Matthew 23:2–3, and DC 18.1, L 20.16, 43.2, and B 54). Most people do not act in accordance with the correct interpretation of these principles because of ignorance; consequently, what is needed is education. Lloyd emphasizes the role of education in Hobbes's theory perhaps more than any other commentator (Lloyd 1992: 45, 158–66; and Lloyd 1997; see also L 19.9, 27.11, 30.2, 30.4, 30.6, 30.14, 31.4, Review and Conclusion 4 and 16).

In addition to its intrinsic merits, Lloyd's interpretation is interesting because it is motivated to some extent by Ronald Dworkin's theory of interpretation. According to Dworkin, a good interpretation must fit "the particular claims, assertions, and arguments" of the text, must fit all or most of the text, and must account for its actual structure (quoted from Lloyd 1992: 15–16). Also the interpretation should show the text to be coherent, plausible, and in line with the author's stated purpose (Lloyd 1992: 15–16). By showing the importance of Parts III and IV of *Leviathan*, Lloyd's interpretation is prima facie better than the standard competitors. But one objection against Dworkin's principles of interpretation must be raised. The application of the first principle, that an interpretation should fit "the particular claims, assertions, and arguments" of the text, is problematic, for two reasons. First, if it means that what the words of the text appear to say is what the text actually says, then it will be challenged on the grounds that it does not take account of satiric and ironic texts. Second, if the first requirement does take account of satire and irony, it nonetheless does not give any help to one who wants to distinguish the satiric and ironic from the nonsatiric and nonironic. Another way of putting this objection is that "the particular claims, assertions, and arguments" are the result of an interpretation and do not preexist, waiting to be fitted together.

Another interpretation of Hobbes's philosophy, consonant with Lloyd's and published the same year, revived the divine-command interpretation of Hobbes's theory of the laws of nature but based its interpretation on both the text and broadly contextualist consider-ations (Martinich 1992). Great weight was given to two contextual facts: one was the challenge that modern science posed for tra-ditional Christian belief in the seventeenth century; the other was the political turmoil caused by religious beliefs. These two facts were emphasized because Hobbes and his friends seemed particularly concerned with them, as evidenced by Hobbes's own writings and the writings of other philosophers with whom he associated, not-ably, Pierre Gassendi and Thomas White. In 1992, I argued for two theses. First, that Hobbes tried to reconcile traditional Christian doctrine with modern science. This involved abandoning the Aristotelian theory subscribed to by scholastics, including English Protestant scholastics, like John Bramhall and, more broadly, reject-ing the influence that pagan Greek and Roman philosophy had had on Christian theology. In this regard, Hobbes was in line with the great Protestant reformers, Martin Luther and John Calvin.

Most scholars reject this interpretation because they think that it is obvious that Hobbes's reconciliation does not work and that Hobbes is left with no rational justification for belief in Christianity. Although I agree that Hobbes's reconciliation does not work, I am not convinced that this was recognized by the stubborn, arrogant, dogmatic and eccentric Hobbes, Hobbes the circle-squarer and champion of absolute sovereignty. There is as much reason to think that Hobbes was willing to accept his Christianity on faith, as any other philosopher. If Hobbes was not a Christian philosopher, then his clever division between the realms of faith and reason, his attempts to reconcile miracles with modern science, his attempt to present an intelligible and consistent theory of the Trinity, and his profession of Calvinist theology, were pointless. He could not sensibly be trying to cover up his atheism with these innovative theories and also be trying to convey that he is an atheist. My second thesis is that Hobbes tried to show that genuine Christianity, that is, Hobbes's reconstructed Christianity, dictates obedience to the sovereign. My views are very close to Lloyd's on this matter.

Many of the criticisms of my theory completely miss the mark. Some critics think that my claim that Hobbes was orthodox is obviously false because most establishment theologians of the day were outraged by his view and many thought he was an atheist. They ignore the explicit, technical definition of orthodoxy that I presented, namely, profession of the Thirty-Nine Articles, and I conceded that Hobbes's views were nonstandard (Martinich 1992: 1–10). But Thomas Aquinas's views were nonstandard in the thirteenth century and Luther's views were nonstandard for much of the sixteenth century, and both were sometimes condemned. (For criticism and replies relevant to Martinich 1992, see Curley 1996 and 2004, Wright 1999, and Martinich 2001a, 2001b, and 2004.)

Often no argument against my view is given at all. Some refuse to reconsider the old view that Hobbes is ironic or sarcastic when his words defend a certain type of Christianity. This old view was acceptable before strong contrary evidence was produced that indicated that Hobbes's view fit neatly within the seventeenth-century context, but no more.

CONCLUSION

Most scholarly work on Hobbes's philosophy over the past several decades has been on Hobbes's political philosophy. Two recent collections of essays on *Leviathan* indicate that that book remains his masterpiece (Foisneau and Wright 2004 and Sorell and Foisneau 2004).

Some of the work on his political philosophy has been a relatively straightforward attempt to derive a cogent political philosophy from it. Kavka (1986) is the single best example of this. Other philosophers have done the same thing with a more historically informed approach (Hampton 1986). The single most important issue in all of this work is the nature of the laws of nature. Are they genuine laws or not? Are they merely prudential or merely moral or both? What is the relationship between self-preservation and the laws, and how exactly does Hobbes deduce the latter? These remain open questions.

In addition to the philosophical project of constructing a cogent political philosophy, much Hobbesian scholarship has been grounded in extensive historical knowledge about the social, religious, and political conditions within which Hobbes worked. This information is considered crucial to accurately understanding exactly what Hobbes's arguments were (Skinner 1965, 1972, and 2002; and Martinich 1992), although, again, this information does not yield a unique answer to most of the important questions asked about his views. Historically oriented philosophers also disagree about whether a philosophical view is so context-bound that it is either not helpful or not legitimate to interpret it according to current philosophical concepts or to apply it to current problems in political theory. Some of these philosophers seem ambivalent about this general issue (Skinner 2002: 177–8).

Most of the important work recently done on Hobbes's religious views has been motivated to a greater or lesser extent by its relationship to his political views, and research in this area is likely to continue. Connected with it is a growing interest in Hobbes's history of the English Civil War in *Behemoth*, not to mention his translation of Thucydides' *Peloponnesian War*. A fine recent collection of essays on *Behemoth* may be difficult to get, but the fact that it was published in Slovenia indicates how broad the interest in Hobbes's philosophy is (Mastnak 2003). Space does not permit me to discuss other interesting areas of research, notably, his scientific and mathematical views, for example, by Shapin and Schaffer (1985) and Jesseph (1996 and 1999).

There is no sign of let-up in Hobbesian scholarship. Excellent work continues to be published and even an expert on the topic cannot read all of it.

FURTHER READING

Martinich, A. (1997) *Thomas Hobbes*, London: Macmillan. An explanation of Hobbes's philosophy and the major interpretations of the twentieth century.

Skinner, Q. (2002) *Visions of Politics*, Vol. III: *Hobbes and Civil Science*, Cambridge: Cambridge University Press. Influential essays that emphasize historical context for interpreting Hobbes, on a wide range of topics.

Sorell, T. (ed.) (1996) *Cambridge Companion to Hobbes*, Cambridge: Cambridge University Press. A good overview of Hobbes's philosophy, informed by recent scholarship.

Sorell, T. and L. Foisneau (eds) (2004) Leviathan *After 350 Years*, Oxford: Clarendon Press. A wide-ranging appraisal of *Leviathan* by many of the best Hobbes scholars.

Glossary

body any object that fills space, a material body. Human bodies are only one kind of body.

conatus the smallest motion; what counts as the smallest is relative to a system of measurement.

desire in a broad sense, desire is movement toward (appetite) or away from (aversion) an object; in a narrow sense, it is only appetite.

determinism the view that every event has a cause, and only events are causes.

egoism the view that each person acts for his or her own benefit.

free will a faculty that initiates actions. Hobbes thinks the concept is incoherent: will is the last desire before action; a person is free if his or her action is caused by a desire.

law of nature a precept discovered by reason about how to conduct oneself, for example, make peace, keep covenants, don't make a person regret being gracious to you. Laws of nature are not laws of physics.

materialism the view that only bodies exist.

mechanism the view that all causes operate in virtue of one body coming in contact with another body.

Nicene Creed a fourth-century statement of orthodox Christian beliefs. What is usually called "the Nicene Creed" is more precisely the Nicene-Constantinopolitan Creed, that is, the revision of the Nicene Creed approved by the Council of Constantinople (A.D. 381). It begins: "I believe in one God, the Father Almighty, maker of heaven and earth, . . . and in one Lord Jesus Christ, the only begotten Son of God."

nominalism   the view that only individuals, particular objects, exist, in contrast with universals. Hobbes is a nominalist. He held that the only thing that was universal was a word in the sense that a word can name many things.

reason   for Hobbes, reason is calculation, adding and subtracting.

state of nature   the condition of human beings when there is no law.

Thirty-Nine Articles   the official statement of orthodoxy by the English Church, first formulated during the reign of Elizabeth I and revised several times.

Notes

TWO METAPHYSICS AND MIND

1 I am told that John H. Randall, Jr. said something like this about Aristotle.
2 In fairness, it should be noted that Hobbes considered having a good reputation, friends, and wisdom as power. But I think his intention in Chapter 11 of *Leviathan* is to emphasize brute power and the problems it produces.
3 The chapter of *Leviathan* between 11 and 13 is "Of Religion." Why it should intervene would be a matter of speculation. I discuss Hobbes's views about religion in Chapter 5.

THREE MORAL PHILOSOPHY

1 Hobbes sometimes defines "ethics" more narrowly as "consequences from the *passions of men*" (L 9.3).
2 The objection is that in the diagram of the sciences, Hobbes defines "moral philosophy" as the science of the just and unjust; yet at the end of Chapter 13, he says that just and unjust do not exist in the state of nature. How can the just and unjust be the topic of moral philosophy, which is logically prior to civil philosophy, and justice and injustice exist only in a civil state?
3 The distinction between short- and long-term goods is often conflated with a different distinction, that between near-term and far-term goods. A near-term good is one that comes immediately; a far-term good is one that comes in the distant future. (Obviously, this distinction, like short- and long-term good, marks the extremes of continua.) The conflation occurs because people usually choose a short-term good that is near-term. Eating a cupcake is a short-term good; one is disinclined to put off the pleasure of eating it. The reason that short-term goods are usually chosen in the near term is that short-term goods that are chosen are those that give an intense enjoyment. The long-term goods that are chosen are usually not intense. But there is nothing logically odd about choosing a short-term good for the far term. The pleasurable taste of a

certain wine is so intense that a person saves money for a week to buy and taste the wine. And there is nothing logically odd about choosing a long-term good in the near term. A lottery winner who has a choice between receiving ten million dollars immediately and something else, say, a house worth twelve million dollars, beginning two years hence, may choose the ten million dollars, which gives him near-term satisfaction for the long term.

4 One might object that this is strictly false, because for Hobbes one's behavior is also restricted by abandoning a right. However, Hobbes has not yet introduced the idea of abandoning a right. In the current context I am assuming, as Hobbes does, a conceptual situation prior to the introduction of laying down of right or law. See below the discussion of the primary and secondary state of nature.

5 I think this is the general view, e.g. Skinner 2002: 121, n. 214.

6 Implicit in this argument is the premise: If someone may be dangerous, then you should fear him. I owe this point to Neil Sinhababu.

7 I am adopting a view espoused by "deconstructionists." I think the issue is much more complicated than I am representing it in this paragraph.

8 For being and nonbeing, this often generated a kind of sentence that infuriated Hobbes. Being is; nonbeing is not [being]. As an undergraduate, I was induced to believe that such a sentence was perfectly sensible. Concerning the practice of defining the favored term directly, Neil Sinhababu pointed out that this is not true for guilt and innocence. "Guilt" is often defined directly as "the condition resulting from breaking a law" and "innocence" is not guilt.

9 Since injustice is "not keeping . . ." it appears that injustice is a lack. But that is not important to my point.

10 The world is complicated. Since the United States is the largest consumer of foreign-produced goods and the largest importer of natural resources, economic reprisals could cause a collapse of the world economy. (I owe this point to Sharon Vaughan.) But, other countries may think that they could avoid catastrophe in some way. Alternatively, they could undermine the power of the United States in other ways. One idea is to make the euro the international monetary standard instead of the dollar.

11 If a person decides to kill himself, he is not acting from the right of nature, and, I suppose, not acting rightly. However, since there is no law against killing oneself, the person has also not acted unjustly.

12 It is sometimes reported that the autopsy of Charles Whitman, the notorious rifleman on the Tower of the University of Texas at Austin, revealed a brain tumor, but, oddly in my opinion, I don't recall anyone ever suggesting that this made him nonculpable.

13 Hobbes does not consider cases that straddle the line between a counsel and a command. Suppose that S has some position of authority over H with respect to actions of kind K, and S, thinking that doing the action A will benefit H but also S, says to H, "Do A," where A is of kind K. S's utterance would seem to be both a counsel and a command, even though one would like counsels and commands to be mutually exclusive.

14 This seems to be Hobbes's official view in Chapters 17 and 18. It is not perfectly clear how what Hobbes says in Chapter 18 is compatible with it.

15 Cf. my discussion in the section "Good and Evil", pp. 57–63, where I think Hobbes does use the similar phrase, "he for his part calleth *good*" to suggest that there is some problem with being good in this sense.

16 This is difficult to explain because it is not clear what kinds of ontological commitment properties involve. Existing is often held not to be a property because there is no such thing as existing in addition to the other properties of an object. A similar view is held about being true. But I'm not convinced that properties need a correlate in nature. Being bald is a property, not because being bald adds something to a human being, but because the human being does not have the property of having hair. Similarly, being pale is a property, not in virtue of adding something to a person's skin. It's a consequence of not having what is necessary for a tan.

17 Again notice that like the pair, war and peace, Hobbes in effect takes the term with a negative connotation, "injustice" as the primary one, and defines "justice" as "not injustice."

18 I owe this point to Ben Ryder.

19 One might think that using the word "laws" undermines my claim that they are "dictates," but incorrectly. The belief or thought expressed by "I believe or think it is raining" is the proposition "it is raining" not what is expressed by "believe or think."

20 Oddly, the propositions of the laws of nature benefit the addressee. This suggests that they are counsels. But counsels can be taken or ignored without complaint.

21 Complaisance could easily lead to the creation of a government. Suppose that one or more people defer to person S on a regular basis. This could be the beginning of a tacit covenant that makes S the sovereign.

22 Scholars who think that Hobbes is often ironic should be tempted to interpret Hobbes as holding that "the fool" is not the fool, but any person who thinks that justice exists.

23 I think that Hobbes is criticizing Oliver Cromwell and the jurist Edward Coke when he says, "From such reasoning as this, successful wickedness hath

obtained the name of virtue; and some that in all other things have disallowed the violation of faith, yet have allowed it when it is for the getting of a kingdom" (L 15.4). Cromwell and his followers violated their faith in Charles I when they overthrew him, and once they succeeded, Cromwell was praised as a savior. Coke argued that if an heir to the throne acquired it through a treasonous act, the offense was "void" if the heir succeeded (L 15.4). Hobbes's view is that the action does not change its character, even though it is true that the successful heir becomes the legitimate sovereign.

24 I fear that some scholars will say that Hobbes's misrepresentation of the golden rule was intentional and that he was being sarcastic and that he did not accept the gospels at all. If this is true, then Hobbes was truly bizarre and acting at cross-purposes with himself. A seventeenth-century reader who recognized that Hobbes did not represent the gospel correctly, would not infer that the gospel is false or bunk; he would infer that Hobbes is stupid or perverse, and in either case, not credible.

FOUR POLITICAL PHILOSOPHY

1 Some want political philosophy, in contrast with political science, to include a normative component, such that political philosophy aims at discovering what good government is.

2 The sovereign is the government. In a monarchy, the sovereign consists of a single human being; in an aristocracy, it consists of a small group of people; in a democracy, it consists of all the people. This view is problematic. See Chapter 7 and Skinner 2002: 177–208.

3 The chapter on persons, "Of Persons, Authors, and Things Personated," is the last chapter of Part I and clearly transitional. Hobbes thinks he needs it in order to get cogently from the laws of nature to the generation of the commonwealth.

4 "[P]ersona est, cui verba et actiones hominum attribuuntur vel suae vel alienae: si suae, persona naturalis est; si alienae, fictitia est (DH 15.1).

5 Of course some actors, for example, Marlon Brando, can change dialogue, but they can do this because they are considered not mere actors, but artistes. Or they have a lot of clout at the box office.

6 The greatness of the nobility is not an intrinsic trait of theirs; it results from decisions of the sovereign to attribute greatness to them: "[A]nd the violences, oppressions, and injuries they do are not extenuated, but aggravated by the greatness of their persons" (L 30.16). Hobbes's sympathy for the poor and denigration of the nobility was probably deepened by the fact that the nobility had been abolished by Parliament.

7 I can't take seriously the objection that "x is needed" means "x is desired" and

that what is desired is good, and hence that any law that is desired is a good law. The context of Hobbes's discussion makes such an interpretation impossible.

8 Another reason it is odd for Hobbes to have a political theory of pure authorization is that the second law of nature, people lay down their right to all things, is logically prior to the third law, people keep their covenants. That is, sovereignty depends on covenants and covenants depend on rights having been laid down.

9 One might think that the theory of authorization fits sovereignty by institution neatly and the theory of alienation fits sovereignty by acquisition neatly. But that is not the case. First, since authorization and alienation are significantly different, assigning one to each "kind" of sovereignty would result in sovereignties with two different essences, a result Hobbes would seriously object to. Also, authorization does not neatly fit the idea that each person who participates in making a sovereign by institution fears every other person who participates.

10 Hobbes's distinction leaves out the case in which a person or persons are threatened by an overwhelming force, and they commit themselves to some other currently nonthreatening sovereign.

11 Because the parent (virtually) always has irresistible power over the children, this should fall under the rubric of natural obligation, the same type that God has over his humans. But Hobbes does not apply that concept here, probably because it would complicate his account.

12 I don't think Hobbes is justified in holding that a child "ought to obey him by whom it is preserved," because the child belongs to the same category as fools and the mad and hence is not a person that can have obligations. However, if the mother is a sovereign, then she may be the artificial person who represents the child and may therefore act for the child, in particular to make the child subject to herself.

13 Some scholars think that Hobbes does not require consent for sovereignty by acquisition, because some of his contemporaries seemed to think that mere victory gave de facto sovereignty. I think the passage just quoted makes that thesis highly dubious.

14 This is clearer in Latin: "*Neque ob submissionem ejus, obligatur victor vitam ei condonare, nisi ante id promiserit*" (LL 20.12).

15 This issue leads into all sorts of problems that can't be discussed here. If a false proposition is considered as true, how should its entailments be treated? Some of them will be inconsistent with other propositions that are and are treated as true. So the system of propositions will be inconsistent.

FIVE   LANGUAGE, LOGIC, AND SCIENCE

1 See <http://www.georgetown.edu/faculty/ballc/animals>.

2 Hobbes's use of name, "nomen," is much broader than the current usage; it includes proper names, common nouns, adjectives, infinitives, and even verbs (see, for example, DCo 5.2).

3 Since Hobbes does or should think that names are bodies as much as anything else, he should have changed "bodies" to "bodies that are not names" in order to make his view more precise.

4 The distinction between sense and reference also applied to sentences. But we do not need to explain the distinction as applied to sentences.

5 A friend of Paul Grice once asked him whether he was influenced by Hobbes's theory of meaning and whether J. L. Austin was influenced by Hobbes's comments about uses of language, because she perceived a similarity among the views of these philosophers. She said that Grice smiled impishly but did not reply.

6 What Hobbes calls "a proposition" might be better called a statement or assertion. For simplicity, I will follow Hobbes's usage.

7 Francis Bacon had said that knowledge is power. Hobbes had been Bacon's secretary. Whether Hobbes or Bacon deserves the credit for holding that sentiment explicitly is not known.

8 Angels are also not objects of science (DCo 1.8).

9 For the first six chapters, I quote from my published translation of the Latin version (Hobbes 1655a). For the remainder, I give my own translation, staying as close to the English version of 1656 as feasible.

10 The example given above about what makes subject-predicate sentences true or false is not an example of a scientific sentence in Hobbes's view.

11 Since the passing away of something is always the coming to be of something else, I will not use the phrase "the passing away" any more. I think this fits Hobbes's own way of talking.

12 If we had used the deductive part of the propositional calculus, we would have seen that often what is proved, the "effects," are apparently structurally different than the causes.

13 Hobbes calls these rules "postulates" and denies that they are part of scientific knowledge (DCo 6.13).

14 I note in passing that "the truth of general propositions" is not obviously the same as "truth by consequences." Even if we restrict "general proposi-tions" to "universal scientific propositions," it is not the case that all truths of consequences are truths of general propositions. For example, the particular sentence, "If Fido is a dog, then Fido is a mammal," is a truth of consequence,

as is, "If some things are dogs, then some things are mammals." Hobbes is conflating the idea of universality with the idea of semantic consequence, that is, the semantic connection between the subject and predicate.

15 The true, conditional proposition for the third hypothesis is this: (3) If this figure is not a circle, then it is not the case that each point on the perimeter is equidistant from some fixed point inside of it.

16 To proceed synthetically is to begin with definitions (or simple things) and prove theorems (or construct complex things).

17 To proceed synthetically is to begin with what is psychologically simple – and these may be concepts or definitions – and discover what is complex.

SIX RELIGION

1 Hobbes's insightful views about biblical interpretation will not be discussed here because they are not strictly philosophical. See Martinich 1992: 311–32 and Malcolm 2003a: 383–431.

2 I have shown that if the same reasoning is applied to his mathematical and political theories then one would have to conclude that Hobbes was an amathematician and an anarchist. To apply one standard to religion and another to mathematics and politics is to commit the fallacy of special pleading. Some scholars have claimed that the cases are different, without explaining how they are different.

3 The criteria I have applied for understanding Hobbes's religious views are reasonable ones to apply to a seventeenth-century Englishman because they are criteria that a seventeenth-century Englishman could have understood. It is important not to confuse my technical use of "orthodox" with informal uses.

4 Notice that this helps to show that Christianity is not politically destabilizing. This is another major project of *Leviathan*. See Martinich 1992.

5 A seventeenth-century intellectual may accept that because the first rainbow was a miracle for Noah it is a miracle indirectly for all Christians, not to mention Jews and Muslims.

6 It is worth mentioning a possible counterexample: in Episode #44: "Amends" of *Buffy the Vampire Slayer*, Buffy is telling her Watcher Giles that she was in Angel's dream the previous night. Giles tries to make her description more precise, "You had a dream about Angel." Buffy corrects, "I was in Angel's dream. . . . [S]omehow I got sucked in." One must remember that the physics of the world of Buffy the Vampire Slayer is quite different from ours. For example, our world does not have a Hellmouth.

7 However, as modern science progressed, the realm of science grew and the realm of faith shrunk to nothing.

8 Hobbes writes this before his discussion of immediate and mediate revelation.
9 The same point can be made with respect to "democracy" and "anarchy," and "aristocracy" and "oligarchy" (DC 7.2; L 19.2).
10 While Hobbes seems to talk about the desire to identify causes of past events in 12.3, he seems to project the desire into the future in 12.5.
11 He also talks in the singular about "the natural seed of religion" (L 11.26–7), which seems to comprise the four (L 12.11). I will follow Hobbes and not be strict about using "seed" or "seeds."
12 Hobbes's preferred proof is a hybrid of the proof from motion and the proof from efficient causality, as we saw above.
13 Any jackass can kick down a barn, but it takes a carpenter to build one.

SEVEN   HOBBES TODAY

1 It is ironic that the press named after one of Hobbes's enemies, Lord Clarendon, is publishing Hobbes's complete works.
2 Warrender himself may be guilty of the same fallacy (see Warrender 1957: 275).
3 My view that the content of the law of nature is a "that"-clause, for example, "that one lays down the right to all things" and that the imperativeness of the law comes from the illocutionary force-indicating phrase, "God commands," is a third alternative. It explains how the laws of nature have an imperative force and can also be propositions that are deduced.
4 A highly sophisticated treatment of the laws of nature, too complex to be explained here, can be found in Braybrooke 2001: 114–20.
5 Tuck also relied on Quentin Skinner's interpretation of a manuscript that Hobbes wrote about the Exclusion Crisis. But it has been argued that Skinner's interpretation is mistaken (Martinich 1999: 347–8).

Bibliography

The year I use for references is usually the year of original publication of the work. When a later edition is used, that information is also included.

Aubrey, J. (1680) *Brief Lives*, Vol. I, Andrew Clark (ed.) (1898) Oxford: Clarendon Press.

Bacon, F. (1996) *Francis Bacon: A Critical Edition of the Major Works*, Brian Vickers (ed.) Oxford: Oxford University Press.

Bramhall, J. (1658) *The Catching of Leviathan, or the Great Whale*, in T. Hobbes (1651) *Leviathan*, A. P. Martinich (ed.) (2002) Peterborough, Ontario: Broadview Press, pp. 562–79.

Braybrooke, D. (2001) *Natural Law Modernized*, Toronto: University of Toronto Press.

Brown, K. C. (ed.) (1965) *Hobbes Studies*, Cambridge, Mass.: Harvard University Press.

Burton, T. (1828) *Diary of Thomas Burton, esq. Member in the Parliaments of Oliver and Richard Cromwell, from 1656 to 1659*, John Towill Rutt (ed.) London: Henry Colburn.

Calvin, J. (1559) *Institutes of the Christian Religion*, trans. John T. McNeil (1960) Philadelphia, Pa.: Westminster. References are to book, chapter and section.

Curley, E. (1996) "Calvin or Hobbes, or, Hobbes as an Orthodox Christian," *Journal of the History of Philosophy* 34: 257–71.

—— (2004) "The Covenant with God in Hobbes's *Leviathan*," in T. Sorell and L. Foisneau (eds) *Leviathan after 350 Years*, Oxford: Clarendon Press, pp. 199–216.

Darwall, S. (1995) *The British Moralists and the Internal 'Ought' 1640–1740*, Cambridge: Cambridge University Press.

—— (2000) "Normativity and Projection in Hobbes's *Leviathan*," *The Philosophical Review* 109: 313–47.

Deigh, J. (1996) "Reason and Ethics in Hobbes's *Leviathan*," *Journal of the History of Philosophy* 34: 33–60.

—— (1999) "Motivational Internalism," in R. Audi (ed.) *The Cambridge Dictionary of Philosophy* 2nd edn, Cambridge: Cambridge University Press, pp. 592–3.

—— (2003) "Reply to Mark Murphy," *Journal of the History of Philosophy* 41: 97–109.

Descartes, R. (1641) "Objections and Replies," in *The Philosophical Writings of Descartes*, Vol. II, trans. J. Cottingham, R. Stoothoff, and D. Murdoch (1984) Cambridge: Cambridge University Press, pp. 63–383.

Eire, C. (1986) *War Against the Idols: The Reformation of Worship from Erasmus to Calvin*, Cambridge: Cambridge University Press.

Foisneau, L. and G. Wright (eds) (2004) *New Critical Perspectives on Hobbes's* Leviathan *upon the 350th Anniversary of its Publication*, Milan: FrancoAngeli.

Gauthier, D. (1969) *The Logic of Leviathan*, Oxford: Clarendon Press.

Goldsmith, H. (1991) "The Hobbes Industry," *Political Science* 39: 135–47.

Hampton, Jean (1986) *Hobbes and the Social Contract Tradition*, Cambridge: Cambridge University Press.

Hanson, D. W. (1990) "The Meaning of 'Demonstration' in Hobbes's Philosophy of Science," *History of Political Thought* 11: 639–74.

Hayes, P. (1999) "Hobbes's Silent Fool," *Political Theory* 27: 225–9.

Hobbes, T. (1629) *Thucydides: The Peloponnesian War*, trans. Davide Grene (1989) Chicago, Ill.: Chicago University Press.

—— (c.1630) "The Short Tract on First Principles," in *Court Traité des premiers: Le Short Tract on First Principles de 1630–1*, ed. and trans. Jean Bernhardt (1988) Paris.

—— (1640) *The Elements of Law, Natural and Politic*, ed. J. C. A. Gaskin (1994) Oxford: Oxford University Press.

—— (1641) "Third Set of Objections," in *The Philosophical Writings of Descartes*, Vol. II, trans. J. Cottingham, R. Stoothoff, and D. Murdoch (1984) Cambridge: Cambridge University Press, pp. 121–37.

—— (1643) [*Anti-White*], *Thomas White's* De Mundo Examined, trans. H. Jones (1976) London: Bradford University Press.

—— (1647) *De cive* in *Man and Citizen*, B. Gert (ed.) (1991) Indianapolis, Ind.: Hackett Publishing Co., pp. 87–386.

—— (1651) *Leviathan*, A. P. Martinich (ed.) (2002) Peterborough, Ontario: Broadview Press.

—— (1654) "Of Liberty and Necessity," in *English Works*, W. Molesworth (ed.) Vol. IV, pp. 229–78.

—— (1655a) *De corpore*, in *English Works*, W. Molesworth (ed.) Vol. 1.

—— (1655b) *Logica: Part I of De corpore*, trans. A. P. Martinich (1981) New York: Abaris Books.

—— (1656) *The Questions Concerning Liberty, Necessity, and Chance*, in *English Works*, W. Molesworth (ed.) Vol. V.

—— (1658) *De homine*, in *Man and Citizen*, B. Gert (ed.) (1991) Indianapolis, Ind.: Hackett Publishing Company, pp. 33–85.

—— (1668) *An Answer to Bishop Bramhall's Book, 'The Catching of the Leviathan'*, in English *Works*, W. Molesworth (ed.) Vol. 4.

—— (1679) *Behemoth or The Long Parliament*, F. Tonnies (ed.) (1990) Chicago, Ill.: University of Chicago Press.

—— (1839–45) *The English Works*, W. Molesworth (ed.) 11 volumes. London.

—— (1845) *Opera latina*, William Molesworth (ed.) 5 volumes. London.

—— (1994) *Correspondence of Thomas Hobbes*, N. Malcolm (ed.) Oxford: Clarendon Press.

Hoekstra, K. (1997) "Hobbes and the Foole," *Political Theory* 25: 620–54.

—— (1999) "Nothing to Declare? Hobbes and the Advocate of Injustice," *Political Theory* 27: 230–5.

—— (2003) "Hobbes on Law, Nature, and Reason," *Journal of the History of Philosophy* 41: 111–20.

—— (2004) "The *de facto* Turn in Hobbes's Political Philosophy," T. Sorell and L. Foisneau (eds) *Leviathan after 350 Years*, Oxford: Clarendon Press, pp. 33–73.

Hooke, R. (1663) "Letter to Robert Boyle," Sloane Ms. 1039, Add 6193, British Library.

Jesseph, D. (1996) "Hobbes and the Method of Natural Science," in T. Sorell (ed.) *The Cambridge Companion to Hobbes*, Cambridge: Cambridge University Press, pp. 86–107.

—— (1999) *Squaring the Circle*, Chicago, Ill.: University of Chicago Press.

Joy, L. (1987) *Gassendi, the Atomist*, Cambridge: Cambridge University Press.

Kavka, G. (1986) *Hobbesian Moral and Political Theory*, Princeton, NJ: Princeton University Press.

Kenyon, J. P. (1986) *The Stuart Constitution*, 2nd edn, Cambridge: Cambridge University Press.

Lewis, D. (1969) *Convention*, Cambridge, Mass.: Harvard University Press.

Lloyd, S. A. (1992) *Ideals as Interests in Hobbes's* Leviathan, Cambridge: Cambridge University Press.

—— (1997) "Coercion, Ideology, and Education in Hobbes's Leviathan," in *Reclaiming the History of Ethics*, A. Reath, B. Herman, and C. Korsgaard (eds) Cambridge: Cambridge University Press, pp. 36–65.

Lloyd, S. A. (ed.) (2001) *Special Issue on Recent Work on the Moral and Political Philosophy of Thomas Hobbes, Pacific Philosophical Quarterly* 82.

Macpherson, C. B. (1945) "Hobbes's Bourgeois Man" (original title, "Hobbes Today"), *Canadian Journal of Economics and Political Science* 11; reprinted in K. C. Brown (ed.) (1965) *Hobbes Studies*, Cambridge, Mass.: Harvard University Press, pp. 169–83.

—— (1962) *The Political Theory of Possessive Individualism*, Oxford: Clarendon Press.

Malcolm, N. (1988) "Hobbes and the Royal Society," in G. A. J. Rogers and A. Ryan (eds) *Perspectives on Thomas Hobbes*, Oxford: Clarendon Press, pp. 43–66.

—— (2003a) *Aspects of Hobbes*, Oxford: Clarendon Press.

—— (2003b) "*Behemoth Latinus*: Adam Ebert, Tacitism, and Hobbes," *Filoszfski Vestnik* 24: 85–120.

Marshall, J. (1985) "The Ecclesiology of the Latitude-Men 1660–1689: Stillingfleet, Tillotson and 'Hobbism'," *Journal of Ecclesiastical History* 36: 407–27.

Martinich, A. P. (1992) *The Two Gods of Leviathan*, Cambridge: Cambridge University Press.

—— (1996) *A Hobbes Dictionary*, London: Blackwell.

—— (1997) *Thomas Hobbes*, London: Macmillan.

—— (1998a) "Thomas Hobbes in Ben Jonson's *The King's Entertainment at Welbeck*," *Notes and Queries* 243, new series 45: 370–1.

—— (1998b) "Francis Andrewes Account of Thomas Hobbes's Trip to the Peak," *Notes and Queries* 243, new series 45: 436–40.

—— (1999) *Hobbes: A Biography*, Cambridge: Cambridge University Press.

—— (2001a) "Interpretation and Hobbes's Political Philosophy," *Pacific Philosophical Quarterly* 82: 309–31.

—— (2001b) "Hobbes's Translations of Homer and Anticlericalism," *The Seventeenth Century* 16: 147–57.

—— (2004) "The Interpretation of Covenants in *Leviathan*," in T. Sorell and L. Foisneau (eds) *Leviathan after 350 Years*, Oxford: Clarendon Press, pp. 217–40.

Mastnak, T. (2003) "Behemoth," *Filozofski Vestnik* 2: 1–320.

Murphy, M. (2000) "Desire and Ethics in Hobbes's *Leviathan*," *Journal of the History of Philosophy* 38: 259–68.

Oakeshott, M. (1957) "Introduction," in Thomas Hobbes *Leviathan*, Oxford: Basil Blackwell, pp. vii–lxvi.

Pasquino, P. (2001) "Hobbes, Religion, and Rational Choice: Hobbes's Two Leviathans and the Fool," *Pacific Philosophical Quarterly* 82: 406–19.

Peters, R. (1967) *Hobbes*, 2nd edn, Harmondsworth: Penguin.

Pope, W. (1697) *The Life of the Right Reverent Father in God Seth Ward etc.*, London.

Raylor, T. (2001) "Hobbes, Payne, and *A Short Tract on First Principles*," *The Historical Journal* 44: 29–58.

Ryan, A. (1988) "Hobbes and Individualism," in G. A. J. Rogers and Alan Ryan (eds) *Perspectives on Thomas Hobbes*, Oxford: Clarendon Press, pp. 81–105.

Schelling, T. (1960) *The Strategy of Conflict*, New York: Oxford University Press.

Schuhmann, K. (2004) "*Leviathan and De cive*," in T. Sorell and L. Foisneau (eds) *Leviathan after 350 Years*, Oxford: Clarendon Press, pp. 13–32.

Shapin, S. and S. Schaffer (1985) *Leviathan and the Air-Pump*, Princeton, N.J.: Princeton University Press.

Skinner, Q. (1965) "History and Ideology in the English Revolution," *Historical Journal* 8: 151–78.

—— (1972) "The Context of Hobbes's Theory of Political Obligation," in Maurice Cranston and Richard S. Peters (eds) *Hobbes and Rousseau*, Garden City, N.Y.: Anchor Books, pp. 109–42.

—— (2002) *Visions of Politics*, Vol. III, *Hobbes and Civil Science*, Cambridge: Cambridge University Press.

Sommers, F. (1970) "The Calculus of Terms," *Mind* 79: 1–39.

Sorell, T. (1986) *Hobbes*, London: Routledge.

—— (1993) "Hobbes without Doubt," *History of Philosophy Quarterly* 10: 121–35.

—— (2004) "The Burdonsome Freedom of Sovereigns," in T. Sorell and L. Foisneau (eds) *Leviathan after 350 Years*, Oxford: Clarendon Press, pp. 183–96.

Sorell, T. (ed.) (1996) *Cambridge Companion to Hobbes*, Cambridge: Cambridge University Press.

Sorell, T. and L. Foisneau (eds) (2004) *Leviathan after 350 Years*, Oxford: Clarendon Press.

Springborg, P. (1975) "Leviathan and the Problem of Ecclesiastical Authority," *Political Theory* 3: 289–303.

—— (1995) "Thomas Hobbes and Cardinal Bellarmine: *Leviathan* and the Ghost of the Roman Empire," *History of Political Thought* 16: 503–31.

Strauss, L. (1952) *The Political Philosophy of Thomas Hobbes Its Basis and Its Genesis*, Chicago, Ill.: University of Chicago Press.

Taylor, A. E. (1965) "The Ethical Doctrine of Hobbes," in K. C. Brown (ed.) *Hobbes Studies*, Cambridge, Mass.: Harvard University Press, pp. 35–55.

Thomas, K. (1965) "The Social Origins of Hobbes's Political Thought," in K. C. Brown (ed.) *Hobbes Studies*, Cambridge, Mass.: Harvard University Press, pp. 185–236.

Tuck, R. (1983) "Grotius, Carneades, and Hobbes," *Grotiana* 4; reprinted in V. Chappell (ed.) (1992) *Grotius to Gassendi*, New York: Garland, pp. 51–91.

—— (1988a) "Hobbes and Descartes," in G. A. J. Rogers and A. Ryan (eds) *Perspectives on Thomas Hobbes*, Oxford: Clarendon Press, pp. 11–41.

—— (1988b) "Optics and Skeptics," in E. Leites (ed.) *Conscience and Casuistry in Early Modern Europe*, Cambridge: Cambridge University Press, pp. 235–63.

—— (1989) *Hobbes*, Oxford: Oxford University Press.

—— (1990) "Hobbes and Locke on Toleration," in M. Dietz (ed.) *Thomas Hobbes and Political Theory*, Lawrence, Kan.: University of Kansas Press, pp. 153–71.

—— (1992) "The Christian Atheism of Thomas Hobbes," in M. Hunter and D. Wootton (eds) *Atheism from the Reformation to the Enlightenment*, Oxford: Clarendon Press, pp. 111–30.

—— (1993) *Philosophy and Government, 1572–1651*, Cambridge: Cambridge University Press.

—— (1999) *The Rights of War and Peace*, Oxford: Oxford University Press.

Warrender, H. (1957) *The Political Philosophy of Hobbes*, Oxford: Clarendon Press.

—— (1965) "A Reply to Mr. Plamenatz," in K. C. Brown (ed.) *Hobbes Studies*, Cambridge, Mass.: Harvard University Press, pp. 89–100.

Watkins, J. W. N. (1973) *Hobbes's System of Ideas*, 2nd edn, London: Hutchinson University Library.

Woodhouse, A. S. P. (1992) *Puritanism and Liberty*, 3rd edn with new preface, Rutland, Vermont: Charles E. Tuttle.

Wright, G. (1991) "Hobbes's 1668 Latin Appendix to *Leviathan*," *Interpretation* 35: 323–413.

—— (1999) "Hobbes and the Economic Trinity," *British Journal for the History of Philosophy* 7: 397–428.

—— (2002) "Curley and Martinich in Dubious Battle," *Journal of the History of Philosophy* 40: 461–76.

Classical Modern Philosophy
A Contemporary Introduction

Jeffrey Tlumak, Vanderbilt University, USA

Classical Modern Philosophy introduces students to the famous philosophers of the seventeenth and eighteenth centuries and explores their most important works. Jeffrey Tlumak takes the reader on a chronological journey from Descartes to Kant, tracing the themes that run through the period and their interrelations.

234x156: 256pp
Hb: 0-415-27592-X
Pb: 0-415-27593-8

Understanding the Political Philosophers

Alan Howarth, London Metropolitan University, UK

'I would certainly recommend this as a first political philosophy book to any student and, indeed, as a refreshingly unpretentious read for a wider audience.'
– *Tim Hayward, Times Higher Educational Supplement*

234x156: 320pp
Hb: 0-415-27590-3
Pb: 0-415-27591-1

Routledge Philosophy GuideBook to Descartes and the *Meditations*

Gary Hatfield, University of Pennsylvania, USA

Gary Hatfield guides the reader through the text of the *Meditations*, providing commentary and analysis throughout. He assesses Descartes' importance in the history of philosophy and his continuing relevance to contemporary thought.

198x129: 384pp
Hb: 0-415-11192-7
Pb: 0-415-11193-5

Routledge Philosophy GuideBook to Locke on *Government*

Lloyd Thomas

'Lloyd Thomas provides an exemplary model of how students should go about this sort of work with a text to hand. He shows how to read a text both scrupulously and open-mindedly.' – *Mind*

198x129: 152pp
Hb: 0-415-09533-6
Pb: 0-415-09534-4